ABILENE STORIES

Edited by

Glenn Dromgoole,
Jay Moore &
Joe W. Specht

ABILENE STORIES
From Then to Now

Copyright 2013 by Glenn Dromgoole, Jay Moore, and Joe W. Specht

ISBN 978-0-89112-368-2
LCCN 2012043643

Printed in the United States of America

Library of Congress Cataloging-in-Publication Data
Abilene stories : from then to now / edited by Glenn Dromgoole, Jay Moore, Joe W. Specht.
     pages cm
  ISBN 978-0-89112-368-2
 1. Abilene (Tex.)--History--Anecdotes. 2. Abilene (Tex.)--Social life and customs--Anecdotes.
3. Abilene (Tex.)--Biography--Anecdotes. I. Dromgoole, Glenn. II. Moore, Jay, 1960- III. Specht,
Joe W., 1945-
  F394.A15A245 2013
  976.4'727--dc23
                                                                               2012043643

Cover photo: Jennifer Raney Collection
Caption for cover photo: Parade along Pine Street, 1920s.

Cover design by Greg Golden
Interior text design by Sandy Armstrong

For information contact:
Abilene Christian University Press
1626 Campus Court
Abilene, Texas 79601

1-877-816-4455 toll free
www.abilenechristianuniversitypress.com

13 14 15 16 17 18 / 7 6 5 4 3 2

TABLE OF CONTENTS

Introduction

Abilene Is Hometown 9

Prologue: The Spirit of Abilene

Village of My Heart—A. C. GREENE 15
Abilene's Special Secret—GLENN DROMGOOLE 18
Train Whistle—JAY MOORE 20

Buffalo Days: Before Abilene

A Perfect Arrowhead—BOB GREEN...................................... 25
Site of the Indian Fights of 1871, Abilene—NAOMI SHIHAB NYE 27
Letter from Fort Phantom Hill—CLINTON LEAR...................... 28
Fort Phantom Hill—JOHN H. KNOX 30
The Butterfield Stage—A. C. GREENE 31
Buffalo Days—JAMES HALEY 34
Paso por Aqui—WILLIAM STAFFORD 37
Let Them Eat Cactus—MARY HAMPTON CLACK 38
Frontier Failures—ROBERT F. PACE AND DONALD S. FRAZIER............. 41

Here Comes the Train: Early Years

Here Comes the Train!—TOMMIE CLACK 45
Let the Sale Begin—FRANK GRIMES 47
Early Ordinances on Morals and Decency
    —ABILENE CITY COMMISSION 49
Moving the County Seat—KATHARYN DUFF 52
The San Jacinto Day Shootout—ROBERT W. SLEDGE................ 55
Chinese Laundry—TOMMIE CLACK 57
Cock Fighting—TOMMIE CLACK.. 59
A Hanging in Abilene—ABILENE REPORTER 61
Police Chief Clinton—LARRY ZELISKO 64
The First Dry Hole—KATHARYN DUFF 66
Bankhead Highway—JOE W. SPECHT 68
Lindbergh Refused the Throne—ABILENE DAILY REPORTER 72
When Amelia Earhart Crashed in Abilene—BILL WHITAKER................74
The First Lady Visits Abilene—ELEANOR ROOSEVELT................ 78

Camp Barkeley & Beyond: Military Town

How Camp Barkeley Shaped Abilene—Jay Moore 83
The Barkley in Camp Barkeley—Jay Moore 88
Making Out at the Paramount—Wally Akin 90
German Prisoners Escape—Ruth Ann Shirley 92
Bataan Death March—William E. Dyess 95
Thanka You Verra Much—Sam Pendergrast 98
Abilene's First Woman Doctor—Loretta Fulton 101
A Tremendous Bargain—Frank Grimes 104
The Day the B-1B Came to Town—Jared Fields 106
Abilene and Dyess—Doug Williamson 109

Growing Pains: Coming of Age

When TV Came to Abilene—James Hallmark 113
Dealing with Racism—Jane McHan 118
Discrimination Policy Challenged—Letter to *The Optimist*
    from ACU Students 122
A Letter to the Superintendent—John P. Rice 125
Hispanic Student Boycott—*Abilene Reporter-News* 127
Abilene Goes Wet—David Coffey 131
Jorge Solis: A Man of Firsts—*Abilene Reporter-News* 133
Razing the Guitar Mansion—Ray Hollis
    as told to Sam Pendergrast 135
The Woman Who Saved Downtown—Glenn Dromgoole 139
However You Spell It—*Abilene Reporter-News* 142
The Abilene Paradox—Robert W. Sledge 144
Circlin' Mack's—Jay Moore 146
All-America Fun—April Nixon 149
The Last Day at Harold's—Greg Jaklewicz 151

Setting the Tone: Church & School

Parson's Gift—Jay Moore 157
The Original Tonight Show—Jim Wilson 163
Stop This Collection Now (and Other Church Stories)—Rupert N.
    Richardson, Ruth Gay, David Ramsey, Charlie Shedd 164
Recollections of Simmons College—R. L. Paschal 167
A Tip of the Hat to ACU—Don Morris and Max Leach 171
The First Day at McMurry College—Paul D. Lack 173
Too Much Jazz and Not Enough Jesus—Gerald McDaniel 175
Dam-it the Dog—Rupert N. Richardson 177
The First High School Band—Bill Whitaker 179
Howitzer on The Hill—John C. Stevens 182

A Tipi Tradition—LORETTA FULTON 185
A Prayer for Abilene—GLENN DROMGOOLE 188

Prairie Renaissance: Arts & Culture

A Better Place to Live—KATHARYN DUFF 193
'Prettiest Town I've Ever Seen'—JOE W. SPECHT 196
Piano Lessons—KATHARYN DUFF 201
Old Musician—MAUDE COLE 202
Wedding of the Century—GERALDINE SATTERWHITE 203
When Lawrence Welk Lived in Abilene—LINDA HONEA 205
Bob Wills and the Butane Boys—ARCHIE JEFFRIES
    WITH BETTYE PEARCE 208
Leltie Faucett & MizCheevus—ROY HELEN ACKERS 211
'Don't Let the Stars Get in Your Eyes'—JOE W. SPECHT 214
Fifth Row for Elvis—GREG JAKLEWICZ...218
Prairie Renaissance—MARY HELEN SPECHT 221
Done with Distinction—GARY MCCALEB 227

Open Minds: Literature & Letters

The Prophet from Abilene—CHARLIE MARLER 231
Young Minds of Abilene—PATRICK BENNETT 234
The Disappearance of Gertrude Beasley—MARY HELEN SPECHT 238
From Pony to Publisher—ED N. WISHCAMPER 243
Getting a Job by Riding the Railroad—A. C. GREENE 245
Thinking About Cows at Ten O'Clock in the Morning,
    Abilene—NAOMI SHIHAB NYE 247
What a Darlin' Ballpeen Hammer—JACK BOYD 248
Called to Poetry, Abilene—ROBERT A. FINK....................................251
My Last Christmas????—LAWRENCE CLAYTON................................. 255

The Old Mesquites: Weather & Nature

Captain Jeff's Prairie Dogs—K.O. LONG 259
Water, Water, Water—NEWSPAPER ACCOUNTS 261
The Old Mesquites Ain't Out Yet—FRANK GRIMES 265
The Time It Never Rained—ELMER KELTON 266
Drought: Sure Signs in Abilene, Texas—ROBERT A. FINK 267
Now *That's* Praying for Rain!—KATHARYN DUFF 269
The Crape Myrtle Sex Scandal—BILL WHITAKER 272
Alligator on the Loose—MIKE ROARK...274
Why Abilene Creeks Flow North—BRENT MCCLELLAN.....................276
Haunting Echoes—SHERILYN HANKS 278
Catclaw Creek—GREG YOUNG 281

Reunion of Champions: Sports & Leisure

Louis Kelley Excelled On, Off the Field—Eddie Soriano 285
The West Texas Speedway—Jay Moore 289
Summer of '46 with the Abilene Blue Sox—Bob Lapham 292
Poker at the Abilene Club—Elbert E. Hall 296
Three Olympic Gold Medals—Garner Roberts 298
Chuck Moser's Eligibility Slips—Al Pickett 301
Three in a Row—Michael Grant 304
Reunion of Champions—Carlton Stowers 307
McMurry Football Team Survives Plane Crash
 —*Abilene Reporter-News* 310
The Catch—Phil Ashby 313
It's Our Time—Al Pickett and Chad Mitchell 315
Peyton Little Leads Wylie One Last Time—Daniel Youngblood 318

Parting Tribute: Pass the Word

52 (pretty much) True Facts About Abilene—Glenn Dromgoole 323

Contributors 327
Credits 335
Suggested Reading 343
Index 345

Introduction

ABILENE IS HOMETOWN

Abilene (the one in Texas near the old Butterfield Trail and not at the end of the Chisholm) is the focus of this anthology. This collection of stories should feel quite comfortable if Abilene is your Hometown, even if it is not your present address. For Hometown is not always the place you live; it is that place where you feel completely comfortable. In your Hometown, you know the streets and the shortcuts and the best places to get a steak. Hometown is where you know the teams and the troublemakers, the victors and the vanquished. You know who has the money and whom to see if the ox is in the ditch. Proper dress and proper decorum are not a mystery in one's Hometown. Childhood memories play in your Hometown and defining moments lie scattered all about. In your Hometown, you state opinions with conviction because you have a stake in the place. It is where you know the routine and breathe easy. It is where the sunset is a familiar hue. Hometown is more than place. It is a mindset that stamps who you are.

As for us, Hometown is Abilene.

Perhaps you are holding this book as a gift given with you in mind, or maybe you borrowed it from the local library; you may have plopped down hard-earned cash to purchase it and have it rest on your shelf. However it is that you came to be reading these pages, it is a near certainty that your Hometown is Abilene, too. You are reading these pages because these pages record a little of you.

Abilene native—and our most acclaimed writer—A. C. Greene aptly described his Abilene Hometown as "A Personal Country." And although Abilene is a personal place, it largely feels comfortable from the common experiences which mold us into a civic congregation—experiences which have ripened into a shared harmony. It is the sights and sounds which we know in concert—a roaring C-130 soaring overhead, a rumbling train passing through, "The Eyes of Texas" from the horns of the Cowboy Band—that create a familiar, pleasing sound. Our Abilene Home is where our common vernacular always conveys much, much more—wind farms, cross-town rivalry, Impact, Woodson High—and where the odd words are not odd at all—Catclaw, Shotwell, Phantom, Dinosaur Bob—and where you know that the Winters Freeway doesn't go to Winters.

Together we proudly claim joint citizenship with local boys made good such as Slim Willet, Jack Mildren, and Jorge Solis. We jointly rue the passings—Harold's BBQ, the Guitar Mansion, Mack Eplen's—and we take our lumps and laurels en masse. We understand the same things—why "Rain" is always on the church prayer list, the honor due our neighbors as a string of daytime headlights come our way. Hometown—where we jointly raise triumphant arms—winning Camp Barkeley, gaining Dyess Air Force Base, being named All-America City, damming up a creek! And where we nod and smile in agreement over the inside jokes and collectively pity those stuck in Dallas traffic. To millions (thank you, Bob Gibson and Lester Brown) Abilene is simply the prettiest town they've *never* seen. But if it is Hometown to you, then you know the beauty which comes from the complexity and shared sensibilities of our mutual Abilene life.

Although Abilene has long been in the shadows of literary limelight, it has not been for a lack of good writing, good writers, or interesting stories. *Abilene Stories, From Then to Now* is a community scrapbook, offering just a bit of spotlight to those who put pen to paper and wrote about our neck of the woods. This anthology is like a gathering of more than a hundred friends who have stopped by for a visit. They fill every room; the laughter is heavy and the smiles broad as stories are told and memories are jogged.

Some of the stories are along the lines of *"I remember when . . ."* (although you may remember it a bit differently) while others offer, *"Here's what I think of that . . . ."* Still others are Abilene stories that we hope leave you saying, *"Well, I never knew that"* or, perhaps, *"Oh, yes, I had forgotten that."* All in all, it has been our aim to better acquaint you with your Hometown through the people and events which have shaped it.

If you have been around these parts for a while, you will recognize the names of many of the writers. Chances are you know a few personally. Some have played a past role on the Abilene stage, leaving their mark in the words they wrote. So, pull up a chair next to Katharyn Duff as she relates a few historical chestnuts. Give your attention to Miss Tommie Clack for a ringside seat to the past. Step into the poetry of those who know this place well and a few who just observed it in passing. Appreciate the sharp insight and the peerless pen of Pulitzer-nominated Frank Grimes. Listen for the personal element which A. C. Greene wove into nearly all of his writings. And when you finish this book, pick up and read his evocative *A Personal Country* and be reminded that home is your fortune.

You will find Greene's works listed along with many others in a Suggested Reading list at the back of this book. It is a treasure-trove for anyone with an interest in Abilene.

Leaf through the tales and pick one that suits you or read it cover to cover. However you choose to take in these *Abilene Stories*, we trust you will enjoy the passages and pieces excerpted from our Hometown—from our Abilene.

"We are convinced that no finer people live on earth than those who call Abilene and West Central Texas home. We have seen them in adversity and prosperity, in victory and defeat, in gladness and sadness, and we've never known them to bug out, quit, absquatulate or run for cover."—Frank Grimes, *Abilene Reporter-News*

Prologue

THE SPIRIT OF
ABILENE

The Grace Hotel along Cypress Street in the 1920s

Frank Grimes, editor of the *Abilene Reporter-News* from 1919 to 1960, considered Abilene "the world's number one dwellingplace." Native Abilenian A. C. Greene, who became one of Texas' best-known man of letters, knew it as "the village of my heart." Longtime

Reporter-News columnist Katharyn Duff for years chronicled the efforts of Abilene leaders to make the city a better place in which to live, raise a family, and conduct business. As a newcomer to Abilene in the 1980s, not steeped in its history or culture, *Reporter-News* editor Glenn Dromgoole quickly discerned that Abilene had a special secret having to do with optimistic people working together for the common good. Hearing a train whistle one evening, historian Jay Moore reflected on the city's rich heritage and how he should pass it along to the next generation.

How did Abilene, with little in the way of natural advantages, grow into the Key City of West Texas while other towns along the same railroad tracks struggled to survive? "Like many other successful cities," wrote McMurry history professor Paul Lack in 1991, "it did not just happen; it generated much of its own growth. The means for this was, in general terms, civic cooperation. Historically the word is boosterism."

As a prologue to this collection of Abilene stories, we begin with three pieces—actually more essays than stories—focusing on the civic spirit that has been the rock, the foundation, upon which successive generations of Abilenians would build not just a town or a city, but a sense of community.

Perhaps the city's best known writer, A. C. Greene grew up in Abilene and started his writing career with the Abilene Reporter-News *before going on to literary fame in Dallas. In his book,* A Personal Country, *Greene paid homage to his roots.*

VILLAGE OF MY HEART

A. C. GREENE

Every man has a village in his heart, whether he comes from abounding Manhattan or the prairies of West Texas. It may be a crossroads town where every face was a daily familiarity, it may be one certain block within a metropolis, but there is a village he has kept. The village is what he refers to when he is making his life decisions. When he cannot go back to the village and display his prizes, in pride or in scorn, he finds less satisfaction in achievement. He does not always love the village but he can never destroy it, for it is himself in it that makes it his village.

Abilene is my village. It is the place I know best, the spot I have kept against change, although the town that made my village is very different, and so am I.

What does it mean to say you know a place? Must you remember the streetcars running through a cotton patch to get to McMurry College, or the big sign shaped like a tube of toothpaste that stood in front of Sloan's Drug? Or what about Raymond Choate, the plumber, driving a Dodge truck painted and decorated to look like a fire engine, or knowing that Old Mrs. Gorsuch's Detroit sedan was the last electric in town?

Does knowing a place have anything to do with being evacuated during the night in a rowboat named Miss Christine when Catclaw

Creek flooded in 1932, or remembering the black porters sitting in cane-bottom chairs on the sidewalks in front of the south side hotels but not understanding what a whorehouse was when your uncle said that was what those places were?

Is having a village being there the night Al Shapiro brought a team down from Stamford and introduced the windmill pitch to Abilene softball, and the umpire stopping play for thirty minutes while the rule book was being searched to see if it was legal? Or, at age five, recalling Dixie Blanton, the professional flagpole sitter, who stayed on top of the new Hilton Hotel for two weeks?

And can there be understanding of the things a town says unless you are able to hear the voices that go with the lost names, the ones whose flame was bright but whose candle was short: Freeman Holly, with me at that interrupted ball game; Arnold Pruitt, who lived on Sunset just across South Seventh from us; Parramore Sellers, born the same time I was; and Earl Proctor, the roughest, meanest boy I ever knew, but my friend.

And Jack Perry, whose dad ran a little grocery store on Grape Street, the father always answering the phone in a weary kind of voice, drawing out, "Perry Foood . . ." and we would wait a second, on the other end of the line, suppressing our laughter, and say with exaggerated concern, "He did?"

That list is long with them: Alfo Baker, R. L. Berry, Guy Kemper, Billy Pennington, R. V. Rucker. Kept forever young by being offered in a war that consumed them before they were twenty-five. How much of your remembering is not what they were but what you think they would have been? Those who seemed gifted toward some pre-scribed use? William Smith, of dour loyalty; Chuck Francis, the fairness in him already recognized by us as unusual; Delmon Rice, with a watchmaker's scrutiny of things.

Are our villages but the extension and expansion of human ego, or the last possible Eden where reality can retreat to innocence? I would rather think not. To me a village is where, for the last time, everything around you seemed made for your use and measurement. The beauty or the drama of the locality may be as unimportant as whether or not the clock face, across which the time was measured, was beautiful.

Never again, after we leave this village, do we have such reliable references with which to frame our judgments and measure our importance. All we knew, in that brief time, was ourself. Thus, if we try to go back, our yardsticks look unfamiliar, their scales and markings wiped smooth. We can't remember what we were measuring against the deep-scored, beveled-edged bricks of the Elks Hall, or the significance of the steepness of the steps going up to the old City Hall's east doors, the length of the no-longer-used passenger platform at the T&P station. The only place where they can still tell you something about yourself is in the village of your heart.

Glenn Dromgoole had been editor of the Abilene Reporter-News *for about a year and a half when he wrote this piece in 1987 about Abilene's civic spirit.*

ABILENE'S SPECIAL SECRET

GLENN DROMGOOLE

One of the things most impressive to a newcomer about Abilene is the sense of community here. I have lived in towns and cities small and large and I've never felt a civic spirit like Abilene's.

Before I moved here, I can recall seeing Dick Tarpley at editors meetings and hearing him talk about Abilene being such a great city. I discounted that as provincial civic pride. Now I know it wasn't.

It was apparent almost from the first day I moved here that this was truly a special place.

It's certainly no garden spot. A visitor here wouldn't see much at first glance that seemed special. The entrances to town from almost any direction are not impressive. I've lived in more scenic places but not in friendlier places. Given the choice, I'll take friendly.

And it's not just a hail-fellow-well-met friendliness. Rather it's a spirit of optimism, of satisfaction, of being in control. People like living here, it seems, because they like themselves and they like having control over their lives.

That is contagious. Put a few folks together in a room who feel good about themselves and about life in general, and pretty soon most people in the room feel good. Put a lot of people like that together in a town, and pretty soon most people in town feel good.

We have our share of soreheads, to be sure—people who are suspicious and negative and mean-spirited—but they aren't the ones who have made Abilene what it is, and they aren't the ones who will determine what kind of city we will be.

The ones who make Abilene a great city today and will make it a great city tomorrow are those who believe in the possibilities of the city, who sense that there is a special spirit here that must be nurtured, who look forward rather than backward.

Without people like that, a city stagnates. With people like that, a city thrives. We have people like that. We may have economic setbacks from time to time like we've been going through for the past year, but in the long run Abilene will thrive.

Abilene will thrive because Abilene knows a secret. The secret is that life is more fun when people are involved and care, when people work together for the common good.

It is that spirit, that secret ingredient, that makes Abilene special.

In an essay written in 1998, native Abilenian Jay Moore reflected on what he hoped to pass along to the next generation about the city's heritage.

TRAIN WHISTLE

JAY MOORE

From my house, I can hear the whistle blow. Late at night, I can hear the whistle and low rumble of the passing trains. Our home is six blocks from the tracks, and in the quiet night air I hear the trains announce their Abilene arrival.

Tucking my three-year old daughter into bed, I ask if she hears the train. She nods and asks, "Why does the train go by?" I tell her that the very reason Abilene exists is because the train goes by. Listening in the dark, I think about our hometown and of the people who built it and of the stories I will tell my daughter.

Some days we go to the park and, as she grows, I want her to understand that before the names Scarborough, Kirby, and Will Hair became parks, they were men who helped build this city, each serving as mayor. I will tell her how restaurant owner Clover Johnson became mayor and pushed and prodded his fellow citizens—at the height of the Great Depression—to build a lake near Fort Phantom and how his foresight won us an Army training base vaulting us out of those dark economic days.

I want her to know that the generosity of a wealthy couple from Burkburnett and a preacher from New York—strangers to one another—are the reason the names Hardin and Simmons are now linked. I hope she will understand that McMurry and Abilene Christian universities are here due to the generosity and initiative of early Abilenians. I would like to tell her of the accomplishments of Jim Radford and Jesse Sewell so both will be more than just an auditorium or a college theater. I want her to know the one-time president of Baylor University, the former state superintendent of schools, and the namesake of a high school are all the same person—Oscar Henry Cooper. I will tell her about Coach Chuck Moser and the mighty Abilene Eagles of the 1950s and I will explain why her grandparents still see a high school along South First. We will drive past Carter G. Woodson High School and I will explain how things once were and how glad I am that she was born after those prejudicial days.

I will tell how my grandparents watched newly-arrived Camp Barkeley soldiers march down Pine Street in 1941 bringing an unprecedented economic boost to this small West Texas town. And how I stood decades later and watched as the first B-1 swooped low on its way to Dyess Air Force Base. I will explain who Lt. Col. Edwin Dyess was and the heroism he lived out to the very end of his short life. I will tell of the day Senator Lyndon Johnson came to Abilene to announce an air base would be located here. I want her to appreciate its presence and understand it is due to the tenacity and foresight of civic-minded men named Wright, McMahon, Meek, Campbell, and others who raised more than $800,000 to buy land for the base.

Perhaps such stories will instill in my daughter some measure of the same pride that today compels fellow Abilenians to cultivate Pentagon relationships, to revitalize downtown, to set aside tax funds for enticing industry and jobs, to look to the future.

While listening to the church bells chime near our house, I will tell her the story of a woman in Brookline, Massachusetts, willing to donate $1,500 to a local congregation's building efforts in the early 1880s with the stipulation that the church be named Heavenly Rest. I want my daughter to know that the architect of Washington's National Cathedral, Phillip Frohman, was also the architect of that beautiful Abilene landmark. Hearing the bells peal from the tower of First Baptist Church, I will tell her of the love and devotion that caused George Anderson to remember his wife in such a beautiful way. I will tell her of Reyes Flores and how his name came to be etched on the Vietnam Veterans Memorial.

Driving down streets named Sayles and Legett, I want her to know that first they were people. Henry Sayles, son of a Civil War general who came here to practice law and whose home still stands at Sayles and South 7th, was a Presbyterian who joined with K. K. Legett, a Baptist, to donate land for a Methodist college. I will tell her that Kirvin Kade Legett was one of the founders of Hardin-Simmons University, served as board chairman of Texas A&M, and that the street named in his honor is misspelled. I will tell her who E. T. Ambler and Judge Tom Willis and Shelby Treadaway were and how the street signs came to bear their names.

I will tell her about young Horace Wooten and Mary Clack and W. J. Bryan and how each walked over this Taylor County prairie dog town before Abilene was even auctioned into existence.

Gazing up at the stars of the Paramount Theater, I will point out the quiet philanthropy that helped keep them lit, the same generosity that lined the railroad right-of-way with grass and trees. I will tell my daughter that the hospital in which she was born was only still in existence due to an Odessa couple who were nearly broke when oil was discovered beneath their land and how they came to live in Abilene and saved a struggling Baptist hospital in 1935. My daughter and I will sit in Everman Park and listen to the fountain, and I will tell her about the land auction just across from it held on a cold March day in 1881 that set our hometown on her path.

Tucking my daughter into bed tonight, I will ask if she hears the train go by. As that steady, low rumble recedes in the dark, I hear the past go by. From our house, we can hear the whistle blow.

BUFFALO DAYS
BEFORE ABILENE

Buffalo hunt in Taylor County, 1874

Prior to the coming of the railroad, the ground of the yet uncharted Taylor County was simply a place to pass over, not a spot for setting down roots.

For hundreds of years prior to laying that fateful ribbon of steel, the area had been sporadically inhabited by nomadic Comanche hunting the roaming buffalo and, by the 1850s, U.S. Army troops had a short stint hunting the roaming Comanche. John Butterfield's Overland Stage was a periodic visitor before the Civil War and, once the fighting was done, Eastern buffalo hunters ventured into the area for hides and meats to cart back to market. Land promoters goaded immigrants to locate here with little long-term success.

But, beginning in the 1870s, hearty-souled early settlers began to crest the eastern rise and settle at Buffalo Gap, along Lytle Creek and over in Mulberry Canyon. As 1881 got under way, a temporary tent city could be seen flapping in the Taylor County breeze alongside freshly laid rails and ties. No sooner had the auctioneer set down his hammer on March 15 than charter Abilenians took up theirs and nailed imported East Texas lumber into a town with an uncertain future.

Albany rancher and historian Robert "Bob" Green was born, raised, and lived his entire life (except for World War II) on the Shackelford County ranch land where his father first settled in 1881. A gifted writer and storyteller, his observations and musings and unpretentious, down-to-earth style struck familiar chords with West Texas readers, connecting the past with the present.

A PERFECT ARROWHEAD

BOB GREEN

I found a perfect arrowhead today. I could tell even before picking it up that it was an extraordinarily fine one. Rushing water from the recent rain had stripped away the dirt that had hidden it away for—how long? Surely hundreds of years, possibly even a thousand. I stood looking at it for a moment before reaching down.

As usual, the wild, gypsy part of my mind started roaming. Had it been shot in anger at an enemy, or had it whickered by a bounding deer in a near miss? It could have been lost out of a rawhide quiver or even just discarded as obsolete. The only sure thing is—there it lies, where it has waited all this time for me to come along and pick it up.

I have picked up many in my life, but I still enjoy that mystical moment when my fingers close around it, and I visualize that the last hand that touched this object was a person from another age, almost another world.

In that moment, the link with the vanished past seems very real, the continuity of life very apparent, even though the person who so carefully fashioned this artifact will, of course, remain forever unknown and faceless. Still, I don't feel that the Arrow Maker is a complete stranger to me. We really share a lot in common. He was probably born near this spot, as I was. He thought of his particular part of this world as belonging to him, as I do. He spent his waking hours wresting a living from what the land affords, as I do.

He very likely fought, even killed, other men in the belief that it was his primary duty to keep the land safe from invaders. That is the way I rationalized about those I killed in warfare too.

He surely wanted his sons and grandsons to call this land theirs, as I do. He has sadly buried his dead nearby, as I have. He himself has moldered away and added his dust to the land, as I shall do, but while alive we both have watched the sun come up over the same eastern hills and go down behind those same western ones, sidling across the horizon and back again as the solstice laws of the seasons directed.

And he looked up at night into the very same stupendous sky, the most spectacular thing either of us will ever behold, and I think he probably instinctively knew, as I do, that somewhere out there lies the answers to who and where and why.

So—I salute you, old arrow maker friend, wherever you are now. In your time, you were just as much a part of creation and life as I am today. I'm glad you left me your arrowhead. I'll appreciate it for what it is—a simple useful thing of true lasting beauty you made yourself and left behind to show you were once here.

I hope we modern men can do as well.

San Antonio poet Naomi Shihab Nye penned these lines during a visit to Abilene in 1973.

SITE OF THE INDIAN FIGHTS OF 1871, ABILENE

NAOMI SHIHAB NYE

little purple flowers under our feet

it's hard to imagine
the Indians finding one another
in this huge space
and having something to fight about

Lt. Col. John Joseph Abercrombie, along with 231 men comprising five companies of the U.S. Fifth Infantry, established Fort Phantom Hill—officially known as the Post on the Clear Fork of the Brazos—in November of 1851. To be assigned to Fort Phantom was to know hardship, perhaps the greatest being isolation. Among those who accompanied Abercrombie was a young lieutenant named Clinton W. Lear, who included this description in a letter to his young wife, Mary, on November 20, 1851.

LETTER FROM FORT PHANTOM HILL

CLINTON W. LEAR

Dear Mary,

When I say to you that we have a beautiful valley to look upon I have said everything favorable that could be said of this place. I have ridden for 5 or 6 miles in every direction from the post & nothing but barren hills meet the eye on every side.

Our camp is pitched in a small grove of "black jack," of about five acres extant, within 200 or 300 yards of a creek the water of which is salt, or brackish & bitter. A spring has been discovered 10 miles off and which affords very little water. There is not timber of the proper kind to build a log hut 18 feet square. Everybody disgusted, it is thought, however, that after the Col. makes his report that we will seek a better resting place for our weary limbs.

We are like the dove after the deluge, not one green sprig can we find to indicate that this was ever intended for man to inhabit. Indeed I cannot imagine that God ever intended white man to occupy such a barren waste.

The ladies will have to live in tents all winter; how much they will suffer is sad to contemplate. The Col. & I get along better than you can possibly imagine—he asks me to dinner & sends the orderly for me alone to drink whiskey punch with him at night, and indeed the most amicable relations exist between us. I gave Mrs. Abercrombie nearly all my plank, sent a [tar]paulin to the Col. to cover his tents, & all such little polite courtesies. I am now only waiting to have the result of my application; in the event of its failing I shall instantly renew it, & the Col's approval, as comd. officer of the Regt. will insure my success.

My health is as good as ever in my life. I have gained from 8 to 10 pounds since I left Washita, and the exercise I take gives me a healthy appetite & our table is never set without wild turkey. I believe there are now three large fat fellows hanging in the tree before my tent.

Again my sweet wife I beg God to bless & protect you. A sweet good night to my own angel wife.

Although abandoned long ago, the stone chimneys and other remnants of the U.S. Army post located on the Clear Fork of the Brazos have continued to inspire poets, painters, and songwriters.

FORT PHANTOM HILL

JOHN H. KNOX

They tell us that gray shades assemble here
At dusk, upon this hill where long ago
The redman and the shaggy buffalo
Fell back before the warrior pioneer.
Nothing is left between these peaceful fields
To say who won or lost, who fought or fell,
Nothing save ruined chimneys and a well,
These, and the shadows that the twilight yields.

Now there is rustic peace upon the place,
A calmer wildness than was here of old;
Lee and his men have vanished, and the foe
Are dust upon the brown earth's wrinkled face.
But some say when the norther bleak and cold
Whines round the hill, pale ghostfires leap and glow.

A. C. Greene touched on Fort Phantom Hill in his 1994 book, 900 Miles on the Butterfield Trail. *The abandoned fort was a stop on the stage line from 1857 to 1861.*

THE BUTTERFIELD STAGE

A. C. GREENE

It is too bad that lack of roads means you can't approach Fort Phantom Hill from the east or northeast, as the Butterfield stage did, because coming from those directions you are able to see why the ghostly name was attached to this unspectral elevation. The Butterfield station, which used the old guardhouse, is in fair condition. The fireplace and hearth where meals were prepared for Butterfield passengers could today be used for the same thing. The little rock magazine which the agent used for storage has been nicely repaired, although the copper lining the building once had to protect the munitions from the flash-fire is long since gone. The commissary, unfinished at the time the post was abandoned and used by Butterfield agents as a stable, may remain in about the same shape as it was when the stage came through.

And yet, visiting the remains of Fort Phantom Hill today in broad daylight—the chimneys, fireplaces and foundations, the few standing walls and silent parade grounds—brings on a moment of historical apparitions, visions and sounds associated with neither the bright sun nor the moving wind. It is the name Phantom Hill that starts the visioning process, or does it depend on knowing the history of the spot, seemingly cursed from its creation? Because it had so short a military life, did the unrecorded tragedies remain stuck to those lonely stone chimneys, unerased by later, bolder events?

My apologies for lingering over what was a relatively unimportant U.S. Army outpost. But if I must point to one spot, one place, and say this is where I found history or where history found me, then it must be Fort Phantom Hill. Being a native of Abilene and born less than fifteen miles from the old fort, I knew, from my earliest recollection, it was where something "historic" had happened near my relatively unhistoric hometown. Visiting Fort Phantom Hill, as I often did, clambering over the stone magazine, searching among the chimneys, letting my young mind embrace whatever imaginative adventures it was creating, I felt the past take on immediate importance for the first time. That grip has never loosened. It only tightens as I approach this little hill that disappears—phantom-like—while the boy reappears, phantom-like, when I come to it.

Tracing the trail westward, you go down a slight bluff on a neglected little road that you find just a few yards south of the fort. Go an additional hundred feet and find the old fort's cemetery which, despite a popular legend, does not contain the grave of Robert E. Lee's child. Incidentally, the grave of the cowboy who requested, "Bury me not on the lone prairie," won't be found locally, either, despite persistent West Texas legend. The legend of the Lee child has a slightly better basis. Colonel Robert E. Lee camped among the remains of Fort Phantom Hill at least twice in 1857-58 while in command of Camp Cooper.

The gravel road follows closely the Butterfield Trail, skirting the bluff above the Clear Fork valley, although the stage line never crossed this frequently powerful river. Near where the old trail crossed U.S. 83 is a modern, but ironic, tribute to the mail company, the "Butterfield Trail airport" for private planes. The old road went across this deceptively flat country in fairly straight fashion, but surely, in those days, they must have had real problems getting through the sudden freshets when there was rain. Today in wet weather, the researching traveler may well be faced with a washed out culvert or a dangerously slippery section of county road (as did this traveler).

But eventually you emerge and go south to the edge of the town of Tye. Originally Tebo, it was whimsically called, in my youth, "Tebo Tye, Taylor County, Texas." At Tye you join I-20 west and come to the marker for the Butterfield crossing which the Taylor County surveyor located and the Daughters of the American Revolution's Abilene chapter erected in 1929. Pause a while here and you will again be given an ironic composite shot: a B-1 bomber or some other faster-than-sound military jet will descend right over the monument to the Butterfield stage, Tye being home of Dyess Air Force Base.

This article by James L. Haley drew much of its content from an interview with buffalo hunter Emil Oberwetter by historian Walter Prescott Webb concerning a buffalo hunt in the Buffalo Gap area in January 1874.

BUFFALO DAYS

JAMES L. HALEY

For the daily hunts, most of the men were armed with Sharps .44 caliber rifles, with which they shot buffalo at 150 yards or so. Some owned the heavier "Big Fifty," a more effective weapon for "taking a stand," the technique of working downwind from a herd, shooting the leader, and then dropping the others one by one as they milled in confusion. An expert hunter might kill a hundred buffalo before the herd finally bolted or wandered out of range. Frank Collinson of Kansas once got 121.

"We aimed to hit the buffalo just behind the shoulder," recalled Emil Oberwetter, "so that the bullet would pass through the lungs and the bottom of the heart. When fatally wounded in this way, the buffalo would stop, switch his tail and walk off by himself. If he lowered his head and began to cough up blood we knew it was useless to bother with him anymore. He would go down on one forefoot, then on the other, then would drop on his hind feet and roll over on his side to die."

Professional hunters came to prefer their own custom-made bullets, some repacking the bottlenecked, three-inch Big Fifty cartridges with an extra twenty grains of powder. Old hands got to where they could identify other hunters sight unseen just by the peculiar reports of their buffalo rifles. "In those days," said Oberwetter, "I have heard the guns booming like an artillery battle."

With a day's hunt completed, teams of skinners would go out. According to one old hider, killing more than could be skinned in a day "would waste buff, which wasn't important; it would also waste ammunition, which was."

"There was an art in skinning a buffalo," said Oberwetter. "First, you cut the hide around the neck until a rope could be tied on it. Then the animal was snubbed to a tree or peg, the rope hitched to the wagon and the hide stripped off by driving up the team. Men stood ready with knives to keep the flesh cut away from the hide in case it began to tear. The cow hides were more valuable in the market than the bull hides, and as a result we killed as many cows as possible."

As well as hides, the teams would also collect meat. Bulls were too tough to use anything but the tongues, but from the cows they would also take backstrip, hump, tenderloin, and hindquarters. Back in camp the meat was salted and placed in a hide-lined pit for five or six days before being taken out and hung up on a wooden scaffold.

Then, said Oberwetter, "The next thing was to build a slow smoke fire under the scaffold. This fire had to be kept up day and night for two weeks. We made it of green mesquite, or willow with enough brush and dried wood or buffalo chips to keep it going. In time a crust would form on the outside of the chunks of meat, and the longer the meat smoked the thicker the crust would get. The right method was to stop as soon as a good crust formed, leaving the meat inside fresh and sweet. After being treated in this fashion, the meat would be handled like stove wood.

"The green hide of a buffalo might weigh anywhere from seventy-five to 150 pounds. The bull hides—especially the old ones—were likely to be thick and scabby and of less value than the cow hides which were darker, glossier and easier to handle. They made beautiful robes, then becoming popular as winter lap robes for buggies and carriages and northern sleighs. The hides were brought into camp and pegged down to dry. When the sun hit them they would contract, pull the stakes, and curl up. Then it was a job for two or three men to get them down again. When dry, they were tied together and were ready for market."

When Oberwetter's expedition finally broke up camp, they packed the cured meat into the wagon beds, stacked the hides atop them, and set out southeast to the nearest settlement, some two hundred miles away. They had stacked the hides with the tails hanging outside, and when they regained civilization, a number of city folks asked for buffalo tails to send as souvenirs to relatives back East.

Members of this outfit profited about a hundred dollars apiece for their trip. The hides brought $1.55 apiece, considerably less than what was being paid in Kansas, and the meat they sold for thirteen cents per pound. Buffalo tongues were in heavy demand for the hotel and restaurant trade, and these brought $9.00 a dozen.

This hunt, having been made in dead of winter, led to no clash with hostile Indians, who seldom strayed from their snug, sheltered strongholds until spring. Standard issue for a buffalo hunter, however, was his "bite," a Big Fifty cartridge emptied of powder and filled with cyanide. Then, if he found himself surrounded by Indians and out of ammunition, he could at least commit suicide and spare himself the maniacal tortures of the Comanches.

A couple of months after Oberwetter's group left the area, two other buffalo hunters, Dave Dudley and Tommy Wallace, were found scalped, staked, gutted, castrated, and their genitals stuffed into their mouths. How much was done before they died couldn't be determined, but their heads had been propped up so they could watch.

Almost every hunter on the plains could tell of someone who had "bit the bite."

Acclaimed poet and essayist William Stafford visited Abilene Christian University in 1977 and again in 1984. A visit to the Buffalo Gap cemetery helped connect him with the past.

PASO POR AQUI

WILLIAM STAFFORD

Comanches tell how the buffalo
wore down their own pass through these hills,
herds pouring over for years, not finding
a way but making it by going there.
Comanche myself, I bow my head
in the graveyard at Buffalo Gap and begin
to know the world as a world invented
by breath, its hills and plains guided
and anchored in place by thought, by feet.

Tombstones lean all around—marble, and pitiful
limestone agonies, recording in worn-out words
the travailed, the loved bodies that rest here.
No one comes quietly enough to surprise them;
the earth brims with whatever they gave. It spills
long horizons ahead of us, and we part its grass
from above, staring hard enough to begin

to see a world, long like Texas,
deep as history goes after it happens,
and ahead of us, pawed by our impatience.

We came over the plains. Where are we going?

Mary Clack chronicled an early Taylor County buffalo hunt by a band of men which included her husband, J.B. Clack.

LET THEM EAT CACTUS

MARY HAMPTON CLACK

"This is where we camped when we were out here hunting buffalo," remarked my husband one day soon after our arrival. We were passing up a dim road leading from the present site of Colony Hill to Buffalo Gap. "Our wagon stood over there by that bank under that oak tree," he added, referring to a small elevation near the road which had served as a slight protection from the severe norther and snowstorm that overtook them.

I listened with renewed interest to the story which was not new by any means, but having viewed the spot with my own eyes gave the adventure a realistic flavor that I had not felt until now. They were Tarrant County boys who spent the winter of 1873-74 in Taylor County hunting buffalo. The enthusiasm exhibited in the recital of the story told of the amount of pleasure derived from their adventures. Even misfortunes and hardships which befell them were considered a sort of "rough fun" it seemed.

The hunting party was composed of J. B. Clack, John Allen, Billy Adams, Rufe Allen and Mr. Stroud along with others whose names I am unable to recall.

In case the Indians attacked one of the party, it had been agreed at the outset that a few discharges from his gun would suffice to bring the whole company to his relief at once. On a certain occasion one of the boys rambled off alone. In a short time the camp was aroused by the firing of several shots in the direction he had gone. Not only that, but the shots were accompanied with yelling to better attract attention.

Feeling sure that the man was menaced by a band of Red Skins, the rest of the boys hastened to his rescue. They were rather disappointed to find him hovering about the carcass of a huge buffalo which he had killed. He had adopted this plan to secure help to convey the beast to camp. While dressing and preparing the meat for use, the boys made what they considered a wonderful discovery—namely, that it was beyond the power of one man to lift a large buffalo hide off the ground and place it on the wagon. Many trials were made by different members of the party before they were willing to give it up as an impossibility.

They also found wild turkeys here in great numbers, which seems rather queer, as the country was overrun with coyotes, bobcats and other species of animals which inhabited the country, with nothing save their own efforts to protect them from the ravages of their numerous enemies. In a grove of pecan trees near Buffalo Gap the boys captured four birds which netted them ninety-six pounds. This meat was especially prized when they ran short of bread stuffs during the cold spell and were forced to subsist on meat alone until the weather moderated enough to make traveling over the earth possible. Turkey was a welcome change from the buffalo meat which they had been compelled to eat for some time.

Their teams, which consisted mainly of oxen, were fed on roasted prickly pears. In preparing the pears for the cattle someone had tasted a bit of "the roast" and decided that it would be a good substitute for bread. It was soon arranged that part of the crowd would roast pear leaves for both man and beast while the remainder were to go on a chase and bring the meat.

After a tiresome trudge through heavy snow, more buffalo meat was secured and the boys returned to camp tired, hungry and anxious to sample the roasted pears which they did not think to doubt awaited them. But there were no pears in sight.

An investigation revealed that those in charge of this part of the work had become impatient and, after a few nice, juicy leaves had been prepared, they had "fallen to" and feasted to their hearts' content and eaten all of them with the intention of roasting more for the meat committee when they should return. But by the time the last leaf was disposed of, they had begun to feel the nauseating effects of the food and had gone to bed, where the hunting party found them when they returned.

"Where are the pears you were to roast while we were gone?" inquired one member of the party.

"We ate them," came the answer from among a disordered roll of bed-clothing accompanied by an unmistakable note of pain.

"You ate them!" shouted another indignantly.

"Yes," came with a grunt, "but you didn't want any of the abominable stuff."

"How do you know we didn't want any?" This question was hurled at the sufferer's head by more than one disgusted boy.

"Why, the things are poisonous," he said.

"Yes," corroborated another who was recovering from a spasm of vomiting. "We are all sick from eating them!"

The Eagle Colony was situated where Abilene's Lytle Shores Addition is located on the east side of Lytle Lake. For many years, stones marking the colony land could still be seen.

FRONTIER FAILURES

ROBERT F. PACE and DONALD S. FRAZIER

By the late 1870s, with the threat of Indian attacks gone, many land promoters went to work trying to bring more settlers to West Texas. In the days before the railroad, few of these ventures met with much success. One such effort involved the Texas-Franco Land Company, which had bought several tracts of land in West Texas. In 1878, the company tried to entice two hundred Russian Mennonites to the center of Taylor County. The Russians sent an advance guard to inspect the site, and they determined that these immigrants could probably do better in Arkansas.

The Eagle Colony would have a more disastrous outcome. In the spring of 1878, a land promoter calling himself Coldwater convinced a group of German immigrants that West Texas was the promised land. These Germans, recently arrived in America, were working at the Studebaker Wagon Factory in South Bend, Indiana. Coldwater told them that for $250 per family, he would furnish wagons and mules, oversee the move from Indiana, and set them up in their new location.

Sixteen families handed over their life savings to Coldwater and began the long journey to West Texas. They traveled by train to Fort Worth, then by wagon through Weatherford, Breckenridge, and Fort Griffin to their final destination—Lytle Creek in Taylor County. At first, the immigrants were convinced that West Texas was a paradise.

The creek provided good water and abundant fish, deer and other game crowded the area, and even their small gardens grew quickly in the first few weeks after their arrival. Delighted, the Eagle colonists started to lay out streets for a huge town and build picket houses and rock fences.

Then everything fell apart. Coldwater, who had been holding their life savings for safe keeping, disappeared with the money. The colonists believed they could push on, because at least they had new teams and wagons. They would be able to build up their community. But Coldwater had not even paid for their wagons—he had taken out a note, due in November 1878.

The Taylor County sheriff traveled from Buffalo Gap to the colony to foreclose the wagons and repossess them. A few colonists heard that the sheriff was on his way and hid their wagons in the creek bed and covered them with brush. But most of them lost everything.

Without wagons or teams, crops failed. Then the winter arrived early. In the bitter cold, the colonists ran out of food; some of the children died of malnutrition. The Eagle colonists probably would not have survived the winter had it not been for several cattle outfits taking pity and providing them with food. Most of the Eagles left the area and moved back East. A few, however, remained, and would become some of the earliest families of Abilene when it was founded two years later.

HERE COMES THE TRAIN
EARLY YEARS

Texas & Pacific steam locomotive, 1882

The hometown newspaper exuberantly hailed our crowning as "Best County in Texas" at the 1889 State Fair, proudly promoting the lure of Abilene.

Still in our youthful years, the city was beginning to shape an Abilene identity as we swept aside a salacious reputation solidly earned along the plank sidewalks—complete with street shootouts, cock fights, red light hotels, a hanging spectacle and even the predictable Chinese laundries of the Wild West.

By the time Abilene reached the age of forty, this Home City of West Texas began to take off with huge gains in population and a coveted spot along the Bankhead Highway. By the time we entered our fifties, we were feeling the mature confidence to invite a couple of the biggest names of the day—Lindbergh and Earhart—to stop by, as well as First Lady Eleanor Roosevelt.

The Texas and Pacific Railway set aside land for Abilene-to-be at mile marker 407, specifying the distance from the railroad beginning point in Marshall, Texas. In time, the Texas and Pacific would fade into oblivion with the rails and ties becoming part of Union Pacific whose familiar yellow and black engines continue to daily "come over the rise."

HERE COMES THE TRAIN!

TOMMIE CLACK

Abilene was "opened" late in the evening of February 27, 1881, when the first official train arrived.

That must have been quite a day. In the morning, Abilene's first church was formed when W. A. Minter gathered his family and friends together alongside the newly-laid tracks and organized the First Presbyterian Church. That evening Abilene had its first celebration, a party saluting the arrival of the first train.

Cowboys and early homesteaders joined tent-dwellers already come to await the sale of town lots on March 15. All these gathered near the tracks, eyes straining to see the first glimmer of the headlight as the train came over the rise from Baird. My Aunt Mollie was in the group.

It was a huge and noisy celebration. An anvil was "fired," or "struck." An anvil is a massive iron or steel block on which metal pieces—horseshoes, for example—are hammered into shape. Firing an anvil is accomplished by pouring gunpowder into the indentation on the top of the block, setting another large piece of iron or steel atop that, then putting a torch to the gunpowder. The resulting noise will frighten horses and cattle three miles away.

This terrific boom sounded out that evening as Abilene's first official train arrived, its brakes screeching, whistle blaring, clangor filling the air.

Rail service, provided in this region by the Texas and Pacific, broadened the economic base of what had been a frontier. Immigrants came to try the new land which, with transportation available, could now be put to farming. Land values began to rise. Retail and wholesale marketing enterprises began to develop. This I now know because I have seen it happen, but as a child this meant nothing to me.

These things I remember clearly: the gatherings at the small railway station when the train was expected to come in with new settlers or with friends who had been away for visits to folks back east; the stock pens, which were reserved for men only in early years; the piles of buffalo bones alongside the tracks waiting to be shipped; and the small shops of the Chinese laundrymen.

Nobody missed the arrival of the afternoon train in early Abilene unless the snow was too deep or a tornado hovered in the sky. A rail car served as the first railway station. Then a two-story building was erected with bedrooms and a café to serve passengers.

Early hotels, the old Palace and, later, the Grace Hotel, sent porters to meet each train. The porters would cry out the advantages of their inn to incoming passengers and would be ready to help with luggage.

Snuggled as close as possible to the depot, along North and South First, were Abilene saloons: Ackerman's, Delmonico, the Arcade, the Cattle Exchange, the White Elephant, etc. Naturally, the White Elephant had mounted above its entry an elephant—painted white.

March 15th—the Ides of March—boded well for the charter citizens of Abilene as they placed their bids on a new life in a brand new town in 1881. Editor Frank Grimes, fifty-five years later, noted the appreciation in land value, citing a 1929 lot sale which closed at $100,000. That lot—the corner of North 4th and Cypress—had been sold by Jim Radford to Horace Wooten, who built a hotel on it.

LET THE SALE BEGIN

FRANK GRIMES

Nobody knows how many people were here March 15, 1881, when the town lot sale took place. Some say eight hundred to a thousand; others are just as positive there were eight to ten thousand. They had come from far distances, some of them; and the surrounding country drained itself of humanity to swell the throng.

Many were here from Buffalo Gap—as a matter of fact, many Buffalo Gap people had come as soon as the location was definitely made, and some of them opened businesses here. Several hundred came on the special train from the east, hundreds more in wagons, hacks and on horseback.

The day, most old-timers agree, was ideal. The sun shone brightly and warmly.

The auctioneer—nobody remembers his name now but all agree he knew his business—stood in front of a small warehouse located on the right of way at the point where Chestnut street strikes the railroad tracks. At his back was a large plat of the town, showing streets and subdivisions and the location of lots.

Hundreds were packed around the auctioneer as he began "selling the town of Abilene." On the outer fringes were cowboys, astride restive ponies.

The auctioneer had the crowd with him from the start by making some humorous preliminary remarks. It was about the time the world's largest steamship, the *Great Eastern*, had been floated; and the auctioneer predicted that it was only a matter of time when Cedar Creek would be widened and the ship would dock at Abilene to discharge its "costly bales" from the world.

The buyers were given their choice of lots, and Colonel J. T. Berry bid in the first lot for W. T. Berry & Company—his son. Recollections of the price vary from $150 upward, but contemporary newspaper accounts say $360. The lot was the one now occupied by the old Central State Bank building, corner of North Second and Pine.

Cameron Phillips bought the second lot, the one now occupied by Woolworth's, southwest corner of Second and Pine. The next, across the street due east from the bank, now occupied by Linton Drug Company, went to William Cameron. Henry Montgomery bought the fourth, now occupied by part of the seven-story Alexander Building, First and Pine.

Lots went like hot cakes, but there was a hang-over session on the 16th to wind up the business. Contemporary newspaper accounts said the two-day sale totaled 178 lots, which brought an aggregate of $27,550. Since then, one of those lots has sold for $100,000.

Two years after Abilene's birth, citizens voted to legally incorporate into a municipality and in the same election selected attorney Dan B. Corley as the first mayor. Corley and the City Commissioners quickly set out to codify proper bounds for Abilene behavior.

EARLY ORDINANCES ON PUBLIC MORALS AND DECENCY

Approved by the Abilene City Commission, March 9, 1883

Section 1

Be it ordained by the town council of the town of Abilene. That it shall be unlawful for any male person to voluntarily walk or ride in the streets of the town of Abilene with any commonly reputed prostitute or lewd woman.

Section 2

It shall be unlawful for any one to appear in the streets or public places of the town in a nude state, in a dress not belonging to him or herself or in an indecent or lewd dress or to expose his or her person or be guilty of an indecent or lewd act where persons passing might ordinarily see the same.

Section 3

It shall be unlawful for any person in the town of Abilene to exhibit, sell or offer for sale any indecent or lewd picture or other thing or to exhibit or perform or to permit to be exhibited or performed upon premises under his or her control or management any immoral or lewd play or other representation.

Section 4

It shall be unlawful for any one to bathe, wash or swim in Lytle or Cedar creeks within the corporation of this town between sunrise and sunset.

Section 5

It shall be unlawful for any one to stick, paint, brand or stamp or put upon any house or fence, wall, pavement or any public or private place in this town any written, printed, or painted advertisement bill, note or picture without the consent of owner or proper party.

Section 6

It shall be unlawful for any one to deface any building, fence, tree, lamppost or other property public or private in the town of Abilene or to hitch any horse or other animal to any awning, post or building or ride, drive or hitch any horse on or across any sidewalk. Provided an animal may be hitched to a ring driven in curbing.

Section 7

It shall be unlawful for any male person to visit any generally reputed house of prostitution in the town for the purpose of associating, boarding with or otherwise living with prostitutes.

Section 8

Any one who violates any of the foregoing sections shall be deemed guilty of a misdemeanor and upon conviction in the mayor's court shall be fined in any sum not less than five nor more than one hundred dollars.

Section 9

It shall be unlawful for the proprietor of any saloon or other place of public resort in the town to allow any disorderly conduct in his place of business or to employ therein as beer carrier, bartender or waiter or in any other capacity any generally reputed lewd woman. Any one violating this section shall be guilty of a misdemeanor and upon conviction fined not less than ten nor more than fifty dollars.

Section 10

That this ordinance take effect from and after its passage and publication.

The snug setting of Taylor County's first county seat—nestled in the Buffalo Gap of the Callahan Divide—would cost that picturesque village the courthouse. The Texas and Pacific Railroad opted to lay her tracks along the flatlands north of the Gap in order to avoid the changes in elevation, thus setting in motion the loss of the county seat for the good people of Buffalo Gap.

MOVING THE COUNTY SEAT

KATHARYN DUFF

Buffalo Gap was a flourishing community when Abilene came into being in the spring of 1881, a promotion of the Texas and Pacific Railroad. But the older town found itself with a challenger, this brash and ambitious newcomer over in the corner of the county.

Abilene became an incorporated town before it was two years old. The first municipal election was on January 2, 1883. And right away the newly organized village set out to get the seat of county government moved from Buffalo Gap. It was not an easy undertaking

The county seat should be on the railroad, in what was already the largest town in the county, Abilene argued. No, it should be near the center of the county where it already was, Buffalo Gap retorted.

Abilenians started a petition for a county seat election and by September 1883 had the needed signatures, one hundred freeholders. The election was set for October 23. There was a month of intensive campaigning. Abilene orators, accompanied by a newly-formed town band and a barrel of whiskey to serve voters, toured the county. Gap residents had their campaigners at work, too.

Election day proved, as one old-timer put it, "county folks listened to the Abilene music and speeches and drank the whiskey but voted for Buffalo Gap." Every box outside Abilene went to the Gap. But Abilene rolled up a whopping majority, more than the two-thirds margin needed to win. The Abilene vote was 864 to 11. County total was 905 to 269.

Gap residents protested the results. They said Abilene did not have 864 voters. They charged outsiders had ridden the T&P in that day, gone to the polls, then by a lumberyard where free whiskey was being served.

Abilenians had counter charges about some Buffalo Gap tricks. Evidently there were shenanigans on both sides, but this was before modern election laws so there may have been few if any illegalities.

Gap folk declared, however, they would not give up county records without a fight. Abilenians said they would be glad to accommodate their neighbors.

The vote was to be canvassed at Buffalo Gap on October 30. A delegation of Abilenians, armed with Winchesters and six-shooters, rode down for that happening. And down at the Gap a delegation armed themselves and waited. A bloody confrontation seemed in the making.

As the Abilene posse approached Buffalo Gap they met a courier with news of the armed guards already in place. There was a pause and a conference. Wiser minds prevailed. Clabe Merchant, an Abilene founder, was delegated to ride on into town to arrange a truce. He talked both sides into stacking arms.

With crowds watching through windows of the frame house, the commissioners canvassed the vote and decided by split decision that Abilene had won.

Buffalo Gap businessmen still refused to allow county records to be moved. They held firm for several weeks until District Judge T. B. Wheeler threatened to call in the Texas Rangers. Then the Gap gave up. Records were moved to a rented house in Abilene. Work began almost immediately on the first formal courthouse.

The T&P donated the site, the third block of Oak Street. The first building was a stone and brick beauty, two stories plus impressive cupola.

Taylor Countians tangled in another courthouse ruckus in 1913. Buffalo Gap, which had got a railroad, tried to get the county seat again but failed. The next year a new courthouse was built in Abilene on the site of the first one.

Two of Abilene's more upstanding citizens took sights on one another and rang out their differences in the middle of Pine Street. Both men were arrested.

THE SAN JACINTO DAY SHOOTOUT

ROBERT W. SLEDGE

Drunken cowboys and angry saloonkeepers were not the only early-day gunfighters. In 1885, the editors of two of Abilene's three newspapers faced each other and shot it out on San Jacinto Day, April 21. The duel occurred on a downtown street in front of the First National Bank, much to the delight of the editor of the third paper, who said, "They try to prove the sword is mightier than the pen."

The two men had been at odds for some time, taking opposite positions on nearly every controversial issue confronting the town. In the exchange of bullets, C. E. Gilbert of the *Abilene Reporter* was grazed by a shot across the forehead while W. E. Gibbs of the *Magnetic Quill* was bruised on the arm by a blow from a "loaded whip."

"It is an affair which all good citizens cannot fail to regret," the editor of the *Taylor County News* said piously. "Since the trouble occurred, friends of both parties have interfered to bring about peace between them and they have agreed to engage in no further hostilities. An amazing part of the affair is that each party thinks the other beat a hasty retreat."

In fact, both did retreat afterward. Within a couple of months, Gibbs closed the *Quill* and moved on to start a new career as a Church of Christ preacher. The embarrassed Gilbert resigned as Sunday school superintendent of the local Methodist church. Gilbert later moved to Dallas and founded the *Dallas Times-Herald* and then to

Austin, where he was prominent in church affairs. Presumably he had put his Abilene past well behind him.

Abilene insurance maps from the 1880s indicate that Chinese laundries could be found fronting on North 1st and South 1st Streets.

CHINESE LAUNDRY

TOMMIE CLACK

The path beside the railroad tracks leading from Pine Street to the stock pens was not the most desirable path in early days, but it was attractive and scenic to little girls; and it was reasonably safe. The path went by the homes of the Chinese laundrymen.

When we were living in town, I went exploring with some other children and saw the "Chinamen" sprinkle clothes for the next day's work. It was a Wednesday afternoon. Our mothers were cleaning the lamp globes and filling lanterns with coal oil for the walk to prayer meeting. Maude Tarpley, a fourteen-year-old friend, came by to tell (sister) Bobbie and me to be ready a half-hour earlier and we would walk down the railroad path.

"Don't let your ma know about it," she cautioned.

Just before early candle light, the small girls in the neighborhood started off. Buffalo bone piles were dwindling by now, but still a few remained. We did not stop to investigate them. We were on our way to see the Chinese, the foreigners in our midst.

These were mystery people. We wanted to know about them. Perhaps they had come to Abilene as workers on the railroad and had stayed to make their living washing shirts for the cowboys and the young dudes about town—washing them and starching them until they were ever so stiff, then ironing the garments.

We had heard from other children rumors about the way the shirts were sprinkled and rolled up before they were ironed. Now we would know for ourselves.

It was an unforgettable sight that we saw as we peered through the tiny windows. There were the men with their long queues hanging down their backs, moving to and fro in the crowded room. On a long ironing board lay the stiffly starched shirts and from a tin cup "Ching" would take a big mouthful of water and spurt it all over the garments to be ironed! Imagine spitting on laundry to get it ready to iron!

Next Sunday men would wear their shirts with fronts and cuffs stiff as a board and shiny as a well-honed razor. How did we small girls who had followed Maude's advice feel? Well, we had learned that all that glamour in those shirts had come from a Chinese mouth. It was a sobering discovery.

I never knew what happened to the Chinese laundrymen. I looked around for them one time and found that they had left Abilene.

An acceptable sport in the time period, gamecock fighting was made illegal in Texas in 1907.

★ ————————————————————————————— ★

COCK FIGHTING

TOMMIE CLACK

On Saturday the horses would be hitched to the wagon and Papa and Mamma and the children, dressed in their best jeans or gingham, were all ready to go to town. Once arrived at the courthouse grounds, Papa and the boys would water the horses at the public water trough and Mamma and the girls would go "trading."

We never "shopped." We "traded," often in the literal sense, swapping eggs, butter, vegetables, anything marketable—for goods needed at home. We walked from store to store on the narrow board sidewalks or on the dusty, sometimes muddy, streets, seeing friends or stopping to visit.

While the women were "trading," Papa and the other boys headed east to the stock pens for the cock fights. It was a sport as old as the nation and as vital to men as "trading" was to the women. Anyone could participate, if he owned a chicken big enough to wear a gaff and with pride enough to defend himself. The fee for admission was the ability to climb the stock pen fence. The sport was thrilling and colorful; it gave a man the opportunity to indulge in the exercise of gambling a dollar or two on a rooster that recommended himself highly.

One particular Saturday morning the stock pen was scene of an event which caused merriment in the town. The crowd was gathered, among them Col. Walter Bowen, a sportsman who enjoyed wagering on cocks.

This day there were many chickens—and two of them were already in the pit. One was an Irish gray, yellow-legged, rather bedraggled chicken; the other a big black cock whose glossy feathers and exultant crowing captured the fancy of onlookers.

Just as the fight was about to start, a late-comer came galloping up. The onlookers knew who he was and that he liked cock-fighting and would wager on anything, no matter the odds. The late-comer hopped off his pony, tied the bridle reins to the nearest dusty mesquite bush and called out, "I'll bet you $10 and give you your choice of birds." Ten dollars was indeed an unheard of bet when $2.50 was big money, but the bet was immediately covered by Col. Bowen, "Glad to accommodate you, sir! I'll take Big Black."

By this time the newcomer had looked down from the top of the fence and had discovered the ridiculous specimen he was betting on; but he was game and was backing that Irish gray he had taken, sight unseen, all the way. "Bet you $10 more that mine makes yours run first."

Col. Bowen took that bet also. The crowd yelled, and the fight began. It seems like a fairy tale. That yellow-legged rooster was an expert when it came to using gaffs. His footwork was elegant and his timing perfect. Round and round the stock pens the birds raced with Big Black squawking and screaming as the Irish Gray's gaffs drew blood.

For weeks after, the cowboys laughed hilariously as they told how John Merchant took Col. Bowen's easy money.

*After being granted a new trial and a change of venue from Comanche
to Abilene, a jury convicted W. H. Frizzell a second time for the murder
of his wife, Annie Bowers, and assessed the death penalty. With a crowd
estimated at 1,500, Frizzell was hanged on November 20, 1891, the only
legal execution ever performed in Taylor County.*

A HANGING IN ABILENE

ABILENE REPORTER

At the opening of the fall term of court, Judge Conner had Frizzell brought into court and passed sentence on him fixing today as the date of execution.

Frizzell's conduct since sentence was passed on him indicates that he has suffered very little annoyance while awaiting his doom. He seems to have been anything but penitent, though he has been frequently visited by the members of this city who have implored him to prepare for death. He has been the most jovial prisoner in the jail and has amused himself by drawing vulgar pictures, acting as judge on the jail kangaroo court, fining visitors for not bringing cigars, etc.

He was always glad to see the press boys and would talk as long as they would stay and listen. When asked to sit for his picture [for the newspaper], he only made one request before consenting, and that was the picture would be just as it appears in the *Reporter*.

The condemned man rested well last night and ate a hearty breakfast this morning. Jailer Jack Haley had a fine breakfast prepared at Kemp's restaurant, which consisted of broiled chicken, broiled bass, oysters, potatoes, etc. Frizzell was in good spirits this morning and received all visitors with a smile. His spiritual adviser, Dr. J. C. Wingo, pastor of First Baptist Church, was with him a great deal yesterday and nearly all of the forenoon. He ate a light dinner and showed less concern than any of his attendants. He said he had been kindly treated by the jailer and guards and would quit this life with malice toward no man.

The Reporter called on Frizzell yesterday afternoon. He was in better spirits than at any time since his confinement. When asked if it was true that he had sold his body to local undertakers, he said: "No sir, they can't pile money enough in this house to get it. I have agreed that Flint & Knapp could have my remains to embalm, they agreeing to furnish a metallic coffin and to send my body to my father at the end of thirty to sixty days."

"Is it true that you have asked that the band be present to play a certain piece of music?"

"Yes sir."

"May I ask what that piece was?"

"Yes sir, 'Dixie.'"

"Has the band consented to play for you?"

"Dr. Wingo said he would let me know this evening whether they could or not."

Promptly at 2:20, Sheriff Cunningham and guards left the jail with the condemned man. Frizzell's step was firm, and, with the exception of an occasional twitching of the muscles of his face, he showed no sign of fear. At his request, Sheriff Cunningham permitted him to walk up to the scaffold unaided and without the hands of any of the officers resting on him. Reaching the floor of the scaffold, Frizzell took a seat, and Sheriff Cunningham then read the death warrant, after saying: "Ladies and gentlemen, it becomes my painful duty to execute one of my fellow men."

Closing the reading of the death warrant, Dr. Wingo arose and asked all present to join in a short religious service. During the service, Frizzell sat looking over the crowd and smoking a cigar. At the closing of the service, Frizzell said: "Well people, I haven't much to say," and [he] talked for forty-five minutes advising young men and all present to lead a Christian life.

[He concluded]: "It was reported I would commit suicide, and as I was satisfied it was a sin, I would not commit it. I want to show what I had in my pocket for over nine months." And reaching in his pocket, he pulled out a small four-bladed pocket knife, which he said was a present from his wife and that he wanted to die with it in his pocket. Sheriff Cunningham said his request should be granted.

After thanking the officers for their uniform kindness, he announced ready at 3:15. The sheriff adjusted the ropes, tied his arms and legs, and placed the black cap over his head.

At this juncture, Frizzell asked the crowd to sing, this done he said: "That's good." Turning to the sheriff, "That's all," and the sheriff sprung the trap at 3:21. At 3:36, County Physician Dr. M. B. Crawford of Buffalo Gap pronounced Frizzell dead, and the body was cut down and put in a coffin.

When the Abilene Reporter-News *picked a slate of Abilenians of the Millenium at the end of 1999, John J. Clinton was selected as top lawman.*

✯ ———————————————————————— ✯

POLICE CHIEF CLINTON

LARRY ZELISKO

John J. Clinton was the type of tall Texan that legends are made of. And like many legendary figures, some tales of his past may have been made up. But whether he was really marshal of Dodge City or fought Indians at the Battle of Adobe Walls doesn't matter. It's Clinton's thirty-six years as Abilene police chief that he is remembered for.

"He won the love and respect of everyone; even his prisoners admired him," Robert Bassetti wrote in his master's thesis on Chief Clinton in 1941. "It is said that he gave more to charity in proportion to his means than any other man in Abilene. He befriended the downtrodden and unfortunate. At the home of the distressed could be seen his old horse Charlie waiting for his master to return."

Abilene was three years old in 1884 when Clinton happened to pass through the county driving a herd of cattle. He stayed when he was offered the job of deputy marshal. In 1886 he ran for town marshal but lost to W. A. George. Several months later, however, George resigned and Clinton was appointed to the top job. Clinton never lost another election. His title was later changed to police chief, a position he held until his death May 31, 1922. He also headed the volunteer fire department.

Another unique trait about John J. Clinton was that he never failed to attend a funeral in town. At times he and the undertaker were the only people present.

Chief Clinton, however, is best known for a tradition he started in 1885. Warned that a group of cowboys planned to shoot up the town on New Year's Eve, Clinton declared that all saloons should close at midnight. As a signal to the saloons, Clinton stood at the corner of South First and Chestnut streets and emptied his ivory-handled revolver into the air. There was no trouble, and the firing of the revolver became an Abilene tradition on New Year's Eve—even after Abilene voted itself dry.

After Clinton's death, the tradition was carried on until 1951 by his friend Jinks McGee. A state historical marker now commemorates Clinton at the site.

[Clinton's pistol, an ivory-handled single-action Colt .45, is displayed at the Abilene Police Department Museum.]

Although the first oil well drilled in Taylor County was an economic failure, it spurred interest for subsequent exploration resulting in the development decades later of Abilene as a hub for independent oil operators.

THE FIRST DRY HOLE

KATHARYN DUFF with
BETTY KAY SEIBT

Frank P. Fox, an Indiana oil man, came to Abilene early in 1916 to drill a "deep" well about six miles south of Abilene near Cedar Gap. Dr. Vernon Spence tells about the episode in his book, *Judge Legett of Abilene*. The drilling site became a favorite picnic area for Abilenians. Spectators who swarmed the area caused Fox to complain.

When he had drilled to 2,700 feet without success, Fox announced he was abandoning the well. A group of Abilene businessmen, in a called meeting at Citizens National Bank, said they would pay Fox $2,000 if he would continue drilling to 3,000 feet. So it was agreed. Fox kept going past the mark and at 3,230 got a very slight show.

Chamber of Commerce manager Wood brought two quarts of crude to town and excited Abilenians knew they were in for a boom. But it was merely a show of oil, not enough to be profitable, so Fox announced he was moving on. The Indianapolis driller sent the following telegram to his associates in Indianapolis: "Quit at 3,340. Dry. So Am I. Frank Fox."

To coax him to stay, the businessmen organized the Hunch Oil & Gas Co. of Abilene. Hunch? That, the locals felt, was as good a way as any to locate a particular spot on the globe to drill for oil. George Paxton, Citizens Bank president, headed Hunch Oil. Stockholders were the leading businessmen of the town. "Their investment was less an expression of confidence in the Fox enterprise than in Abilene's future oil industry," Dr. Spence said.

Fox continued drilling. His second well struck oil at 1,890 feet, and he drilled forty feet deeper but got no gusher. He was about to drill even deeper, when a wind storm toppled his eighty-two-foot derrick. The delay intensified local interest so there was a mild boom for mineral rights.

Fox rebuilt his rig, and on August 19, 1916, the stockholders of Hunch Oil gathered at the site to see the first pumping of commercial oil in the county. The well was good for a disappointing twenty-five barrels daily. Fox drilled another unsuccessful well in 1917, and the Hunch Oil Co. called it quits.

Hunch sold its equipment to Reese Allen, an oil operator at the oil town of Electra. The sale was dated September 9, 1917—about six weeks before a major oil strike at the Eastland County town of Ranger. Taylor County might have no oil worth the cost of recovery, but its neighbors did.

Abilene leaders considered it a major achievement when the nation's first all-weather transcontinental highway—the Bankhead—was routed through Abilene in 1920. In 2009 the Texas Legislature established the Historic Roads and Highways Program and designated the Texas portion of the Bankhead as the first Texas Historic Highway.

BANKHEAD HIGHWAY

JOE W. SPECHT

Over the years, my wife Alice, a collector of Abilene-related post-cards, and I have had numerous adventures sleuthing for the roadbed of the Bankhead Highway. We've ranged as far east as Weatherford and west to Big Spring. The quest began in 2000 when Alice showed me a photo card of Abilene Courts, now slowly decaying on South 11th. The caption for the card read: "Abilene Courts, Abilene, Texas, on Highway No. 80 and No. 1." Of course, we were familiar with U.S. Highway 80, but what was Highway No. 1?

In 1916, U.S. Senator John Hollis Bankhead of Alabama, who became known as "the father of good roads" as well as the grand-father of actress Tallulah Bankhead, served as an important catalyst in the passage of the first Federal Aid Road Act, which provided matching funds to states for improving the country's road system. The next year the Texas Legislature created the Texas Highway Department in response to the federal legislation, and by 1919 the department had finalized plans for locating the state's primary high-ways. The roads were assigned numbers: Texas Highway No. 1 ran from Texarkana to Dallas, through Abilene, with a terminus in El Paso (approximately 845 miles).

With the enactment of the Federal Aid Road Act, the Bankhead Highway Association—named in honor of Senator Bankhead—organized in Birmingham, Alabama, to lobby for and promote the establishment of the nation's first *all-weather* transcontinental highway. In April 1919 at the annual convention of the Bankhead Highway Association, delegations from Texas and surrounding states met in Mineral Wells with the intention of defining the path of the Bankhead from Memphis to El Paso. The Board of Directors designated the all-Texas route—Texas Highway 1—as the official artery crossing the state from Arkansas to New Mexico. B. F. Bennett, secretary of the Abilene Chamber of Commerce, was in attendance, and he sent a telegram to the *Abilene Reporter*, which the newspaper reprinted the next morning: "Texas and Abilene have just won the Bankhead Highway. Great enthusiasm!"

While the Texas and Pacific Railway put Abilene on the map, the Bankhead Highway ensured the city's presence on another east-west transportation corridor, one that became as economically important for the city as the railroad.

As the first all-weather transcontinental highway, the Bankhead took on an additional sobriquet, "Broadway of America." And to emphasize the year-round accessibility, a U.S. Army convoy, consisting of twenty officers and 160 enlisted men along with forty-four trucks, seven cars, and four motorcycles, traversed the route in 1920. The convoy stopped in Abilene on August 20 to a most receptive crowd. Mayor Dallas Scarborough, addressing the assemblage, made it clear that Abilenians were active supporters looking to the future: "I am glad to welcome such a party as this and feel that it marks the beginning of a new era in road development. I hope that the United States government will be induced to take hold of the Bankhead Highway and complete it from coast to coast. I think the next generation will be great advocates of good roads."

In 1921, Congress amended the Federal Aid Road Act to shift more of the financial responsibility for road construction and design to the states. The Texas Legislature, in turn, passed some of the financial obligation on to the counties. As a result, the highway upgrade in Taylor County did not reach completion until 1929. The January 28, 1929, edition of the *Abilene Reporter* announced "the last 3,000 feet of concrete for Highway 1, also known as the Bankhead Highway, through Taylor County will be poured within the next few days . . . . the stretch between Catclaw and Big Elm creeks will be given twenty days to harden and should be ready for traffic on February 20."

From the east, the Bankhead Highway entered Taylor County from Clyde on what is now FM 18. It cut through the northern edge of land presently occupied by Abilene Regional Airport, running east and west behind the Taylor County Expo Center, before turning north to South 11th. The thoroughfare turned north again on Oak and then west on South 1st, paralleling the railroad to the Old U.S. 80 West underpass (across from the current location of Abilene Speedway). It continued to Tye, Merkel and Trent on the north side of the T&P tracks before exiting the county.

Abilene was unique because there was also a northern, alternative route of the Bankhead, Texas Highway 1A. At Metcalf Gap in Palo Pinto County, the road divided: Texas 1 turned south to Strawn and west to Ranger, Eastland, Cisco, Putnam, Baird, Clyde and Abilene, while Texas 1A headed to Breckenridge, Albany, and Abilene. The highway entered town on what is now Ambler, then south on Pine, west on North 5th, south on Cedar and over the T&P tracks (the Cedar Street underpass was built in 1936) to reconnect with Texas 1 on South 1st. A Federal Aid Project marker is still in place at the corner of Cedar and North 1st.

Other reminders along the original route include the Ponca Motel on South 1st and Abilene Courts on South 11th, both of which provided accommodations for travelers. Remnants of the concrete roadway within the city limits still exist, too: a stretch of pavement is on the northern end of airport property, another can be found behind the Expo Center, and still another on Old U.S. Highway 80 West.

But the best preserved section of the 18 foot-wide highway in Taylor County is just west of Trent. Here, bordered by cactus and mesquite, one can get a sense of what travel was like in the 1920s, an era when the goal of good road proponents was to "be able to drive out of any county seat in the United States at thirty-five miles an hour and drive into any other county seat—and never crack a spring."

Just four months following his solo conquest of the Atlantic, Charles Lindbergh piloted the Spirit of St. Louis *to Abilene's Kinsolving Field on September 26, 1927. From touchdown to takeoff, the famed "Lone Eagle" was in the city for just ninety-six minutes but the effect was a stimulated interest in aviation resulting in the establishment of a city airport.*

LINDBERGH REFUSED THE THRONE

ABILENE DAILY REPORTER

Charles A. Lindbergh, the man who has walked with kings, refused to sit on a throne during his visit to Abilene. It happened like this.

Lindy stepped out of the *Spirit of St. Louis* at 9:36 a.m., one minute after the slim gray trans-Atlantic plane came to its berth in a wired-off enclosure of Kinsolving Field. He walked between a lane of soldiers, standing at attention and flanked by a cheering crowd, and came to a stop before a waiting Nash car.

The back seat of the car contained a velvet and flag-draped chair—for Lindy to sit in. It was, for all the world, a throne. Lindy looked at it, and the points of his high cheekbones turned red. He was painfully embarrassed as he leaned down to speak to Mrs. Moody, wife of the governor [and Abilene native].

"Please," he said—and the rest was lost amid the blare of band music and a tumult of shouting.

"I beg your pardon, Colonel?" inquired Mrs. Moody.

"Please," he repeated, "I would much rather not ride up there. I would appreciate it if you would let me ride on the back seat with you."

Willing but rough hands took hold of the velvet-draped chair. When it resisted, crowbars were used. It was jerked out of the tonneau and pitched out on the ground. The flag, however, was carefully retrieved and draped over the back of the car.

Mrs. Moody started to enter the front seat beside the driver, L. E. Derryberry, but Lindy touched her on the arm.

"If you don't mind, I would rather have you ride back there with me," he suggested. Mrs. Moody entered the car, Lindy following and taking the left side. The front seat was occupied by Derryberry, Abilene Mayor Thomas E. Hayden, Jr., and C. W. Bacon, president of the Chamber of Commerce. As the car bearing the flying Colonel started west on the highway for town, followed by two press cars, Lindy seated himself on the top of the left side, so that the crowd might get a better view of him.

Coming into the city, he said to Mrs. Moody, "I am willing to do almost anything—I don't mind sitting where they can see me—they have come a long way and are entitled to see me if they want to—but I can't go these thrones."

Aviatrix Amelia Earhart made a 1931 stopover in Abilene as a part of a nationwide promotional tour of Beech-Nut chewing gum. Piloting an autogiro, Earhart crashed while taking off from the Abilene airport on June 12. She was uninjured but the aircraft was totaled and the plucky "Lady Lindy" was reprimanded by the Department of Commerce's aeronautics branch for "carelessness and poor judgment."

WHEN AMELIA EARHART CRASHED IN ABILENE

BILL WHITAKER

Pioneer aviator Amelia Earhart crashed at Abilene's airport on June 12, 1931, in what was then called an "autogiro." The crash happened only moments after a nervously slow takeoff saw her autogiro graze three cars in the parking area.

An estimated 1,500 spectators watched the crash, including a Mr. W. C. Crosby, who shot moving pictures of the takeoff and subsequent calamity. He was quickly besieged with offers for the film.

"Immediately after the crash," the *Abilene Reporter-News* said in the next day's edition, "Miss Earhart, calm, stood up in the cockpit and reassured the crowd no one was hurt. Workmen immediately began dismantling the damaged aircraft, and all evidence of the wreck was cleared before noon."

If Miss Earhart had second thoughts, they might have been about the autogiro. Although this cross between a plane and a helicopter was touted as being so easy to fly that a ten-year-old could pilot it, veteran pilots gravely doubted the aircraft's worth. The aircraft was later dubbed "the Edsel of aviation."

Nevertheless, Miss Earhart, thirty-two, was determined to become the first person to fly one of these bizarre contraptions from coast to coast. Beech-Nut Packing Company agreed to sponsor the attempt. Soon the aviator found herself with a shiny red $15,000 autogiro.

While Miss Earhart expected little in the way of competition for this dubious feat, she no sooner landed in Los Angeles from the East Coast than she discovered another pilot had captured the world record just days before. She promptly turned the autogiro around and resolved to make the first round trip, coast to coast, in an autogiro. Because the craft only held two hours or so of fuel, she again made lots of stops.

One of those stops was Abilene. On June 11, Miss Earhart flew into Abilene, visibly tired and thoroughly sunburned from her trip. She had made refueling stops at an oil-field camp near Guadalupe station, again in Wink, then again in Big Spring, before making the day's final leg to Abilene. From Big Spring to Abilene, the flight took her an hour and thirty minutes.

If the crowd welcoming her to Abilene wasn't larger, it was because no one knew for sure her arrival time. Nevertheless, she was welcomed with open arms and spent the night with Abilene's prominent Oldham family at their country home west of Lytle Lake.

The *Reporter-News* marveled at the strange-looking aircraft at the municipal air terminal that summer day in 1931. "More than anything else, it resembled a winged windmill," the hometown paper reported. "Miss Earhart put it down to earth almost vertically, as if a bird had been shot dead in mid-air. The plane has a humpish appearance and is not so much to look at, but it contains superlatively superior qualities over the fast-flying and fast-landing biplanes and monoplanes. The deadly spin, death to so many pilots, is not possible in the autogiro."

The problem came the next morning, when Miss Earhart returned to the airport to fly on. Flying into the south, she quickly realized her takeoff was too slow to clear a line of parked cars and so decided to put down in an open area. Before she crash-landed the autogiro, though, the aircraft grazed three parked cars (fortunately, no one was inside any of the vehicles) and caught a fence enclosing a landing field light, causing the autogiro to swing around violently.

When Miss Earhart and her mechanic, Eddie DeVaugh, climbed out, they found the landing gear and wings had been torn off and the rotor blades were badly damaged. A replacement autogiro was immediately shipped to Oklahoma City by the manufacturer.

Meanwhile, all traces of the wreckage were picked clean. "I was just ten or so, but I remember that thing going down and then everyone getting excited and grabbing pieces off it," Mack Eastus said. "The one she crashed in was a red one and they got her a white one. I used to have some of the red canvas from that thing, and now I can't find it to save my life."

For her part, Amelia Earhart was doing damage control. "I underestimated my distance," the affable aviator said. "Possibly I did not take a long enough run. The distance, however, was ample for the giro under ordinary conditions. I saw the ship lacked altitude to clear the second line of cars and I picked the only place available to drop the ship. I didn't care what happened as long as we struck no one on the ground."

Although Miss Earhart dismissed the incident as "one of those breaks" and refused to even dub it a crash, the Department of Commerce's aeronautics branch figured otherwise and reprimanded the aviator for "carelessness and poor judgment." She in turn insisted they were fine ones to talk, that their inspector in Abilene, R. W. Delaney, had never seen an autogiro in flight, let alone flown in one. In any case, area pilot Dick Young flew Miss Earhart to Oklahoma City in his monocoupe to get another giro.

Within a few days Miss Earhart returned to Abilene in her replacement giro, just to prove it could fly, then she continued on her way. In a few years, though, the autogiro, for all the talk of its changing the aviation world, was as dead as the dodo.

As for Amelia Earhart, she winged her way to other feats and, in time, into stature as a bona fide aviation legend. And while she momentarily flopped in Abilene, folks here were no less impressed by her sense of high-flying adventure.

First Lady Eleanor Roosevelt first came to Abilene in 1933. On March 10, 1939, she made a second stopover to speak to an audience of more than 1,800 assembled at the HSU auditorium. Mrs. Roosevelt was back in town the next year for a return visit.

THE FIRST LADY VISITS ABILENE

ELEANOR ROOSEVELT

We were late in arriving at Abilene, Texas, on Friday night, but even the crowd at the station was kind and considerate. We were whisked quickly to the [Hilton] hotel and had ample time to dress and dine before going to the lecture, which was in the auditorium of Hardin-Simmons University.

For travelers like myself, I would like to say a word about the comfort and good service of the Texas hotels. Almost everywhere that we have been, we have had good food, good accommodations and kindly interested service.

After the lecture Friday night, we went to the Chamber of Commerce Building where they have an exhibition showing West Texas products, developed and undeveloped natural resources, and the possibilities for industrial expansion. It is interesting to see the accomplishments, but, to me, it is far more interesting to see the many developments which wait for future enterprise. It seems a pity one cannot bring together the money and the people who need employment throughout the country to develop some of these resources.

This is a cowboy country. Even in the cities they are conscious of the picturesqueness of this part of their population. Bellboys in the hotels are dressed as cowboys and the Texas [Hardin-Simmons University] Cowboy Band, which has travelled widely in this country and Europe, played in a truly inspiring way before the lecture. This band is going to the San Francisco Fair in May and will be in New York City at the Fair in June, and I am sure they will draw big crowds in both places.

Saturday morning, before leaving, we paid our respects to the 71-year old president of the university, Mr. Jefferson Davis Sandefer, who was too ill to attend my lecture Friday night. Thirty years of his life have been given to the development of this university and it must be a satisfaction to him to realize in what high esteem his fellow townsmen hold him.

CAMP BARKELEY & BEYOND
MILITARY TOWN

Lt. Woodrow Aten and wife Leoda at camp entrance

12th Armored Division Museum Collection

Few factors have played a greater role in shaping the look and feel of Abilene as has the military. From the overwhelming influx of Camp Barkeley soldiers in early 1941 to the ongoing arrival of Dyess personnel, the culture of Abilene has been enlivened, boosted and forever improved by those in uniform.

Both installations came into reality because Abilene generously and wisely emptied her piggy banks to purchase land to accommodate Uncle Sam. The recipe of Abilene's friendly spirit, lively civic initiative and our deep sense of patriotism have combined into the ideal model of military support.

Abilene and Dyess enjoy a next-door neighbor friendliness well recognized in military circles and, since 1998, it has been a point of civic pride for the Air Force's Air Mobility Community Support Award to be named the "Abilene Trophy," recognizing the stellar camaraderie.

Fittingly, two Texans—a young man from San Antonio, David Barkley, and another from nearby Albany, William Edwin Dyess—have become a part of our Abilene vocabulary and whose daring and bravery in France and Bataan we should not forget.

Although the Army left here in 1945, for six decades now the sounds of Taylor County have included the roar of Air Force B-47s and B-52s, the hearty hum of C-130s and the low rumble of B-1 bombers headed into the wild blue yonder of Abilene skies.

Although Camp Barkeley was a part of the local scene for just four years during World War II, the impact which it created continues to shape the culture of Abilene.

HOW CAMP BARKELEY SHAPED ABILENE

JAY MOORE

Throughout the difficult days of the 1930s, at least one small Abilene business managed to survive and thrive despite effects of the Great Depression. A sandwich and soda stand located at South 14th and Butternut made its owners a good enough living that in 1941, ten years after they opened, Charles and Charity Langford replaced their original Dixie Pig with a larger building that still claims the southeast corner at the end of Abilene's Friendly Mile.

One reason for the Dixie Pig's growth was due to its location at the intersection of two highways—South 14th, then numbered as Texas Highway 158, and U.S. Highway 83/84 that became Butternut Street once inside the city limits. That busy highway intersection made the Dixie Pig one of the first restaurants travelers from the west and south would come to as they entered Abilene in the '40s and '50s. But the real catalyst for growth was that in 1941, just barely nine miles down South 14th was, what was at one time, the twelfth largest "city" in Texas—a city that grew to a population of around 60,000 with nearly all of the residents young men with hearty appetites.

That city was, in fact, a U.S. Army training base named Camp Barkeley. At the same time, Abilene would be home to just 26,000. For those people—as well as for us—Abilene would never be the same.

Abilene's love affair with the men and women of the U.S. military began on February 28, 1941. On that highly-anticipated day, the young men of the U.S. Army's 45th Infantry came marching into the heart of Abilene and the hearts of Abilenians. As the thousands of Barkeley troops and trucks passed into town, they were met by an equal number of cheering citizens, waving out a rousing welcome.

Once settled at the camp, many of the boys of the 45th made the short return trip into town. Some shot pool for a dime a game. Others went to see a movie at the Queen or the Texas. They stopped in at Abilene restaurants, went to nightclubs, such as Charlie Blanks, and had their fill of flirting with the Abilene girls. Stores remained open late as the boys ambled along Pine, Cypress and Chestnut—stopping for nickel shoe-shines, to send a telegram, or to stock up on candy bars and cigarettes. By 11 p.m. the khaki-clad boys paid the twenty-cent bus fare or splurged on a one dollar taxi ride back to the camp in order to meet the military curfew.

Just a week after troops first arrived, an Army truck would back up to the side door of the Citizens National Bank at North 1st and Pine while, both inside and out, soldiers manning machine guns warily watched as seven 100-pound safes stuffed with cash and coins were loaded aboard and trundled off to the camp for payday. It would only be a matter of hours before many of those greenbacks would find their way back into town where they would snugly come to rest in Abilene cash registers. Abilene was on the verge of being yanked out of the Great Depression.

In just the first month following the soldier's arrival, the *Abilene Reporter-News* added 3,000 subscribers and boasted 12,000 new readers. The classified ads listing rooms to rent soared as any available Abilene contractor got busy converting garages into rentable space. For the first time since opening eleven years earlier, the Wooten Hotel experienced days, weeks and even months of one hundred percent occupancy. Diners began staying open all night and nightclubs had more business than they could handle. Hendrick Hospital would expand to accommodate the rise in population and increased number of births.

Simply transporting soldiers to and from the base quickly became a lucrative business—so much so that Chamber of Commerce Manager Merle Gruver retired to manage a bus line which he started to meet the need. Buses left every half hour around the clock. And with the Barkeley buses turning the corner at Butternut and 14th, soldiers frequently filled every booth and sat at every counter stool of the Dixie Pig waiting for a lift back to the base.

In promoting hospitality and entertainment, the moral orthodoxy of Abilene was severely tested when city commissioners approved the showing of movies on sacrosanct Sunday night. And many felt ethical ruin was imminent when street dances and a Sunday opening of the fair were also permitted.

Camp Barkeley changed Abilene's religious scene, too. The influx of Jewish families and servicemen prompted the small Jewish population to organize and form Congregation Mizpah. A synagogue on Chestnut was completed in 1942. And, with many of the troops being Catholic, those local congregations also experienced increased attendance and a need to expand as they helped serve soldiers far from home.

By some estimates Camp Barkeley exposed close to one million soldiers to the spirit of Abilene and to the good people of nearby towns. It would be the positive experience of West Texas which drew many soldiers back here after the war. A fair number returned to an Abilene wife or to pursue a local sweetheart. The year before Camp Barkeley—in 1940—the Taylor County Clerk's office issued just over 500 marriage licenses. By 1944, with the camp in full swing, the number had grown to three times that many. Many of those couples went on to raise their children and invest their lives here.

Evidence of the once-bustling camp remains all around Abilene. You can still drive down Pershing Boulevard although the buildings have long since been removed. In 1946 and 1947, the War Assets Administration held over fifteen auctions to dispose of the 3,400 buildings and anything else that had been left behind. Barkeley's largest building was moved to Hardin-Simmons where it was re-assembled and re-christened as Rose Field House. A Camp Barkeley building was brought to Eagle Field (Rose Park) to serve as the locker room for the Abilene High Eagles of the 1950s and where it still stands. The Camp's colonial-inspired Red Cross building was given to the Abilene Chapter and remains in use. Out along Grape Street, another camp structure now serves the VFW and Disabled Vets. Camp Barkeley lumber would be salvaged and used in the construction of scores of Abilene homes and businesses.

Barkeley chapels were moved as far away as Kermit, Ennis and Waco, but at least six were brought to Abilene. Fair Park Methodist bought one and moved it to South 6th and Larkin where it was refaced in brick and where it still serves as a church today. The First Nazarene Church relocated a chapel to South 14th and Jeanette where it too was bricked. First Baptist Church expanded its mission church, Friendship Baptist, and located one of the chapels at South 8th and Pecan—the least altered of any former Barkeley church.

But the most lasting and the preeminent effect of Camp Barkeley has been the blossoming of a civic-minded can-do spirit. The loss of the camp was thought to mark Abilene's demise. In fact, it was the catalyst for a renewed entrepreneurial civic-mindedness. Municipal pride was quickly evident as a group of Abilene backers organized a precursor to today's Development Corporation—known as Abilene Industrial—and quickly raised $50,000 to fund efforts for attracting new industry. It would be that seed money along with our cultivated Washington connections and Abilene's military friendliness that would pay off on a grand scale just a few years after the Camp's closing when the U.S. Air Force chose to locate a Strategic Air Command base on land just north of the shuttered Barkeley.

To look in Abilene's western skies in 2012 and see a soaring B-1 Bomber or hear a C-130 roar past is to know the greatest echo of Camp Barkeley—the cultural, economic and social enrichment we mutually enjoy hosting our Dyess neighbors.

Abilene's Camp Barkeley was named for a World War I hero from Texas, even if it was misspelled.

THE BARKLEY IN CAMP BARKELEY

JAY MOORE

One name deeply woven into the fabric of Abilene's past is that of "Barkeley." The U.S. War Department's selection of acreage near Abilene in 1940 as the site of an army training base not only served to shape the life of Abilene but also provided an economic stimulus for the desperate financial straits of many Abilenians.

In January of 1941, the base was officially designated as "Camp Barkeley" in honor of an American infantryman who fought and died in World War I—David Barkley. When a government typist mistakenly entered Private Barkley's name with an extra "e," the Abilene camp was forever misspelled "Barkeley" but, nonetheless, honored the sacrifice of a Texas hero and Medal of Honor recipient.

David Bennes Barkley was born in Laredo in 1899. When David was just five years old his father, Josef Bennes Barkley, abandoned the family and David's devoted mother reclaimed her maiden name of Cantu. Antonia Cantu, a Mexican-American native of South Texas, chose to move her family to San Antonio in 1904 seeking a better life. In order to help support his struggling mother, David Barkley dropped out of school at age seventeen and ultimately enlisted in the U.S. Army. With America's entry into World War I, Barkley soon headed overseas with the American Expeditionary Force to fight in France in 1918.

Despite his Hispanic heritage, David chose to use his Anglo father's surname to avoid being segregated into a non-combat unit.

Barkley even instructed his mother not to include "Cantu," when writing letters fearing it would result in his removal from the front-line action.

On November 8, 1918, Barkley's Company A of the 89th Division was surveying the Meuse River in northern France in order to locate enemy positions. An officer called for volunteers willing to swim across the river near Pouilly-sur-Meuse and explore German-held territory; Private Barkley and Sergeant M. Waldo Hatler stepped forward. Successfully swimming the river despite incoming enemy fire, Barkley then crawled 400 yards to scout German gun emplacements before entering the frigid river for the return swim. Seized with cramps from the cold water, the nineteen-year-old Barkley was unable to reach the opposite bank and drowned—losing his life just three days before the end of the war. Sergeant Hatler survived to bring news of Barkley's death to their unit.

Commended by General John Pershing, Barkley was posthumously awarded the Medal of Honor for his actions, one of three Texans to be so recognized during World War I. The French government awarded the young Texan the Croix de Guerre, and Italy bestowed the Croce al Merito di Guerra. David Barkley's body was returned to his mother in San Antonio as the city chose to honor his sacrifice with his body lying in state inside the Alamo.

In 1941, Antonia Cantu came to Abilene, paying scant attention to the extra "e" as her cherished son was honored in the naming of Camp Barkeley. Proudly wearing David's Medal of Honor, she watched as a military parade of 4,000 soldiers marched down Pine Street in homage to her son's heroic sacrifice.

In 1989, after his hidden heritage was brought to light, David Cantu Barkley was officially recognized by the United States Army as the nation's first Hispanic Medal of Honor recipient.

Paramount Theatre Manager Wally Akin was not only a first-class showman, but he knew just when to extend Abilene hospitality to those needing a little privacy.

★———————————————————————————★

MAKING OUT AT THE PARAMOUNT

WALLY AKIN as told to JAMIE O'TOOLE

This happened to be on a weekend on Saturday afternoon [in 1942] when most men were on the loose, and the town was just flooded with them. At that time we only had about two good motels and two good hotels. That was about all the places they had to go. So, they just . . . a lot of them just had to walk the streets. And then they were just packed and jammed into the theater.

I was walking down the aisle, and I saw one of the enlisted men making love to his lady friend down in the middle of the audience. I went down there, tapped him on his shoulder, and said, "I'd like to see you in the lobby."

He got up and came back to the lobby. I said, "Uh, I am just awfully sorry, but we just don't allow that in the theater." They were really doing some heavy courting.

He grabbed me by the necktie and pulled it tight, and my tongue flew out. He said, "I want you to know that was my wife down there."

"Well," I said, "I'm very sorry. I can't just get up on the stage and tell two thousand people that's you and your wife sitting down there making love, and it's all right. That just wouldn't work."

Then I thought of something. I said, "But I'll tell you what I'll do. My company keeps a room permanently in the Wooten Hotel, paid for by the month, so that the folks from the main office will have a place to stay when they come to town. Here's the key to that room.

It's just right here next door. I want you to take this key and take your wife up to the room in the hotel and stay as long as you like. Stay two or three hours if you like, and then bring the key back to me."

So he took the key and took his wife and went up to the room in the hotel. He came back in about three hours. He put his arms around me and kissed me on the cheek and said, "You're the finest guy I have ever met in my life. My wife comes to Abilene to see me on weekends, and we have no place to go. The hotels are full, and we walk the streets. I go out and march all week long. This is one of the greatest things that has happened to me."

Captured German soldiers found a temporary home at Camp Barkeley in October 1943 where they were warmly greeted by County Farm Agent Elmo Cook, glad to have the extra labor to pick an estimated 10,000 bales of Taylor County cotton still in the fields. POWs were paid eighty cents per day for their efforts. Their labors apparently continued after hours as they dug a tunnel.

GERMAN PRISONERS ESCAPE

RUTH ANN SHIRLEY

Camp Barkeley also served as a prisoner of war camp from 1943 to 1946. It held German prisoners, most of whom were from an elite corps of tank operators called the Afrika Korps. On March 28, 1944, twelve of the prisoners escaped from the camp.

The prisoners worked on their premeditated escape for three months. Every evening the men dug underneath their hutment. Every night they removed a small amount of dirt, inching to their goal. The tunnel went from one side of the camp and ended under a hutment outside the POW part of the base. The tunnel stretched sixty feet long and lay eight feet underground. The tunnelers wired the shaft with electric lights to work during the night. To keep the tunnel from collapsing, the prisoners placed timbers inside to secure their safety during the escape. The Germans placed the dirt they removed into their pockets, and then scattered the dirt throughout the camp at night in places such as flower gardens and work areas. The men worked slowly so they would not be detected by the guards.

The escape plan also involved careful consideration of how the men might survive the great expanse of West Texas. The prisoners collected plenty of food and survival items. According to the *Abilene*

Reporter-News, the escapees took "at least ten days' worth of food including candy, chewing gum, and incidentals . . . and a pup tent." Each one of them traced on tissue paper precise copies of a map of the Abilene area they acquired in the camp. They drew "highways, railroads, towns, and even names of principal ranches." The men strategically planned every move.

Although the twelve escapees used intelligent tactics for their escape, the next steps were a little less strategic. When guards discovered the escape the next day, a manhunt occurred throughout the countryside around Abilene. Four of the men stole a car in Tuscola, seventeen miles south of Abilene. The prisoners spoke little English. The police captured them only a few miles south of Ballinger. The arresting officer explained that the men were driving "crazy-like," which made him suspicious. Henry Kemp, a night watchman in Ballinger, chased the escapees and forced them to run off the highway. One of the prisoners jumped out of the car and ran into the nearby woods. The others chose not to put up a fight, and they were returned to Camp Barkeley.

Officials captured two more prisoners in Winters, forty miles south of Abilene. The two prisoners broke away from the others after the group had traveled through the Abilene State Park. The two men made their way to Winters, but when they hid in a ditch to avoid detection by police, a man on horseback discovered them. More precisely, the horse became skittish when it neared the lurking refugees. The Germans did not fight with the cowboy, deciding their lives superseded their freedom.

Three more of the escapees left the group and followed the ranch routes they had drawn on their homemade maps. These three men chose to rest in an abandoned ranch house twenty-two miles south of Abilene. Once morning arrived, the rancher discovered the three strange men sleeping in his ranch house. The local constable arrived shortly, and the authorities returned the men to Camp Barkeley.

Two other Germans made it ninety-two miles to San Angelo before the dragnet caught them. The men decided to take a stroll through town at midnight. Finally realizing that walking out in the open was a bad idea, they turned down a side-street thinking they would be out of sight. Only one block later a night watchman spotted the escaped prisoners. The night watchman said he saw the two dressed in trench coats. When they ignored his orders to halt, the watchman pulled his gun on them. The two men immediately gave up. One of the men was the same prisoner who had escaped from the stolen car in Tuscola.

The final two escapees made it all the way to the Texas and Mexican border. In full German uniform, the men slept during the day and traveled at night, jumping from field to field with "the aid of maps." Once in Sweetwater, forty-one miles west of Abilene, they hopped onto a freight train that led them west to the Odessa area. Then from Odessa, they traveled all the way to El Paso. A special agent of the Southern Pacific Railroad found the men walking along the railroad tracks in El Paso.

The men captured in El Paso wore their German uniforms even though they needed to blend in. The escapees, once captured, explained that they were headed towards Mexico to get a boat and head back to their Fatherland. The men's mentality inspired them to fight to get home and "take up arms."

In this excerpt from The Dyess Story, *Colonel (then Captain) Ed Dyess describes one episode from the brutal Bataan Death March. After surviving the march and escaping from a Japanese prison, Dyess returned to the U.S. and told his story. It was published a month after he died in a training plane crash in December 1943.*

BATAAN DEATH MARCH

WILLIAM EDWIN DYESS

At 3 a.m. of April 12, 1942—the second day after our surrender—we arrived half dead at Orani, in northeastern Bataan, after a twenty-one-hour march from Cabcaben near the peninsula's southern tip. That thirty-mile hike over rough and congested roads had lasted almost from dawn to dawn.

It would have been an ordeal for well men. Added to the strength-sapping heat and blinding dust were the cruelties devised by the Jap guards. Considering our condition, I often wonder how we made it. We had had no food in days. Chronic exhaustion seemed to have possessed us. Many were sick. I know men who never could remember arriving at Orani. They were like zombies—the walking dead.

Near the center of the town the Japs ordered us off the road to a barbed wire compound a block away. It had been intended for five hundred men. Our party numbered more than six hundred. Already in it, however, were more than 1,500 Americans and Filipinos.

The stench of the place reached us long before we entered it. Hundreds of the prisoners were suffering from dysentery. Human waste covered the ground. The shanty that had served as a latrine no longer was usable as such.

Maggots were in sight everywhere. There was no room to lie down. We tried to sleep sitting up, but the aches of exhaustion seemed to have penetrated even into our bones.

Jap soldiers told us there would be rice during the morning. We paid no attention. We not only didn't believe them, we were too miserable to care. The sun came up like a blazing ball in a copper sky. With the first shafts of yellow light the temperature started up and, it seemed to me, the vile stench of the compound grew in intensity. Breathing the heavy heated air was physically painful.

I remember pondering that even if we had firearms none of us would be capable of using them. We were succumbing to the oriental tortures that subdue men, break their spirits, and reduce them below the level of animals.

As the sun climbed higher, Americans and Filipinos alike grew delirious. Their wild shouts and thrashings about dissipated their ebbing energy. They began lapsing into coma. For some it was the end. Starvation, exhaustion, and abuse had been too much for their weakened bodies. Brief coma was followed by merciful death. I had a blinding headache from the heat, glare, and stench. Several times I thought my senses were slipping.

When it was observed that men were dying, Japanese non-commissioned officers entered the compound and ordered the Americans to drag out the bodies and bury them. We were told to put the delirious ones into a thatched shed a few hundred feet away. When this had been done the grave digging began.

We thought we had seen every atrocity the Japs could offer, but we were wrong. The shallow trenches had been completed. The dead were being rolled into them. Just then an American soldier and two Filipinos were carried out of the compound. They had been delirious. Now they were in a coma. A Jap noncom stopped the bearers and tipped the unconscious men into the trench.

The Japs then ordered the burial detail to fill it up. The Filipinos lay lifelessly in the hole. As the earth began falling about the American, he revived and tried to climb out. His fingers gripped the edge of the grave. He hoisted himself to a standing position.

Two Jap guards placed bayonets at the throat of a Filipino on the burial detail. They gave him an order. When he hesitated they pressed the bayonet points hard against his neck. The Filipino raised a stricken face to the sky. Then he brought his shovel down upon the head of his American comrade, who fell backward to the bottom of the grave. The burial detail filled it up.

For many of those who had been taken into the shade of the thatched shed the respite came too late. One by one their babblings ceased and their bodies twisted into the grotesque postures that mark a corpse as far as it can be seen.

When Charlie Blanks died, Reporter-News *editor Frank Grimes wrote,* "Practically everyone who knew Charlie Blanks liked him. It was mutual. Charlie liked practically everybody."

THANKA YOU VERRA MUCH

SAM PENDERGRAST

Abilene has been widely known, for most of its first century, as a church and college town, a good place to raise a family, and "the Buckle on the Bible Belt." But when the definitive book on [Abilene] comes to be written it must include—along with the churches, the schools, the doctors, the ranchers, and the transportation pioneers—some reference to a chunky, "foreign-looking" guy who never learned to read or write, who at best skirted religious and social convention, and who never owned much but a home site and a small piece of floodplain property with a few fanciful buildings he mostly built himself with the help of an extended family and a few friends.

He didn't even have a "real name" in the usual sense, but spent some forty years making the most of an arbitrary name he said was given to him by a judge at a citizenship hearing in Davenport, Iowa. He recalled—probably "for the record" just before his death in 1956—being born near Rome, Italy, in 1895 under the name Kitalo Balango. When the Davenport judge couldn't pronounce the Italian name and arbitrarily picked the name "Charlie Blanks," Charlie added the middle name of "Henry," told the judge "Thanka you verra much . . ." and set out to do his own thing in this great country that accepted him as a boy of thirteen.

Charlie worked hard. In fact, he probably went to an early grave—at sixty-one—in part because of a lifetime of exploitation of his body as a youthful wrestler-strongman and, in the magnum opus of his life, the painstaking hand construction of his rangy "nite club" and half a dozen out-buildings along Cedar Creek at the corner of South 14th and Old Colony Road.

In some forty years in and around Abilene, he got to know everybody with a "fun streak" (he never met a stranger) and was known to most people in town as a colorful, friendly, and marginally scandalous character. To many of Abilene's church-oriented people the negative image predominated for two simple and (in Abilene) unarguable facts: drinking and dancing went on in his club. That was all that mattered to many Abilenians most of the years in which he was building his then-huge club.

The "better people" of Abilene reportedly didn't set foot in Charlie Blanks' in those days, and those that did didn't talk about it. The place was strictly off-limits to students of the three church colleges—subject to dismissal and policed on occasion by at least one college president.

During the "Big War" from 1941 to 1945, when tens of thousands of mostly very young and heavily "Yankee" men were trained at Camp Barkeley out past the other end of South 14th, Charlie's place achieved a kind of functional "King's X" simply because of the perceived necessity of broadening local tastes and mores to accommodate the massive influx of people to whom West Texas must have seemed almost as foreign as the Nazis and Fascists and Orientals they were preparing to combat for the basic existence of the American way.

The European-looking complex with good food—savory Italian dishes as well as huge "gorgeous" steaks hard to find elsewhere under wartime food controls—plus a big, fine dance floor with a hit-filled Wurlitzer and frequent live (often "name") bands was an immediate and abiding hit with the relative handful of lonely soldiers who could find a way to get ten miles off the base with enough money for food and—yes—drink (it didn't hurt that Commanding General Heflebower regularly occupied a table at Charlie's).

And there is little doubt there was plenty of drinking going on around the big concrete tables and little cozy booths that ringed the expansive, polished floor—and no doubt at all that most of the liquor that showed up under the tables was flatly illegal. Not all of it, however. Texas had worked out a face-saving convention that accommodated military thirsts despite state liquor laws. Abilene adopted the device of liquor by prescription, and it was legal enough to be blinked at by lawmen and popular enough to make significant contributions to the building of some pioneer pharmaceutical fortunes.

A doctor would simply write a prescription for liquor, and the druggist would bring the medicinal palliative from the back room where it was kept with the lesser (and greater) narcotics. At the height of the demand, some drugstores had resident doctors—often sitting at a card table in the lobby—who would write a prescription for a nickel or a dime. Presumably much of that "nerve medicine" ended up under the tables of Charlie's, where the waitresses would bring soft drinks and waxed cardboard buckets of ice to civilize the potables.

Most available sources agree Charlie's place—though admittedly scandalous on its face—was charming, exciting, the best place in town for food and often-live dance music, and notably orderly, particularly in the early days. The place always had a bad reputation, but most of it was apocryphal—at least as long as Charlie was running the place. Some of the bad reputation may have been earned after Charlie died in 1956, when his dream club tended to deteriorate into more of a country-western dancehall and beer joint.

When Dr. Virginia Boyd became the first woman doctor in Abilene, the news was announced on September 22, 1940, under a small headline on page 7 of the Social Activities section of the newspaper. Dr. Virginia Boyd Connally, as she was known after her marriage to attorney Ed Connally in 1953, practiced for more than forty years before retiring.

ABILENE'S FIRST WOMAN DOCTOR

LORETTA FULTON

The onset of World War II and the establishment of Camp Barkeley, twice the size of Abilene, proved to play a role in Dr. Virginia Boyd Connally's early years in practice.

Male physicians were going off to war, making Dr. Boyd's acceptance easier. "So many of them were leaving, and they were glad to see me," she said. And soldiers needing care provided by an eye, ear, nose, and throat specialist were counted among her earliest patients as she began to establish a clientele. "It seemed like I never lacked for patients," she recalled. "I worked from dark to dark."

On at least one occasion, a uniformed soldier even served as an impromptu bodyguard. Never one to say "no," she agreed to make an office call late one night. When she arrived at her downtown office in the Mims Building, a group of soldiers had congregated on the street. She was alone, and her office was on the eighth floor. A little apprehensive about being trapped upstairs with someone she didn't know, Dr. Boyd chose to enlist the aid of a young soldier. "I just grabbed one of them and said, 'I have to go up to see a patient—would you go with me?' " He did.

With Camp Barkeley filled with soldiers, and male physicians leaving for military service, it didn't take the doctor long to start building a patient base. In fact, she saw her first patient before even opening her office. A local pharmacist called and asked her if she would treat a woman who accidentally had put iodine drops in her eyes. She obliged, and her long career in medicine in Abilene had officially started.

In those early days, reception from male physicians and from patients varied from one day to the next. An attitude that only men were suited for the practice of medicine still prevailed among much of the populace. The federal government had a definite opinion. Nurses were highly sought after to serve in the military with war looming, but female physicians were another matter.

Dr. Connally remembered that practically every physician in town volunteered for military service, even though not all actually served. She did her duty, too, volunteering to serve alongside the male physicians. "They said they would let me know if they needed me, but I never heard from them."

Some local residents had the same attitude about women doctors. Early on, she was one of only two doctors in town who specialized in diseases of the eye, ear, nose, and throat. So she got her fair share of patients with cataracts, sinus infections, tonsillitis, or just in need of new glasses. She realized that she had actually "made it" into the male world of medicine when people started calling her "doctor."

If they didn't, she didn't like it. A soldier from Camp Barkeley came into her office one day seeking relief from a sinus infection. He made the mistake of calling her "Virginia" instead of "Dr. Boyd." He left with the sinus infection still raging and—perhaps—his ears ringing. She immediately dismissed the impertinent young man, mincing no words: "You don't come back. You get someone else to treat you."

Dr. Connally remembered another incident early in her practice—in the days when physicians made house calls. A woman called for an appointment, apparently not realizing the name "Virginia" was feminine. "I walked up with my case, and she looked at me and scowled. She was NOT going to have a woman doctor. I went and got right back in my car and drove off."

She was greeted by similar disrespect from a few physicians, including a medical school classmate who established a practice in a nearby community about the same time she opened her office in Abilene. The doctor had a tonsillectomy patient who was experiencing bleeding that the doctor was unable to stop. So he sent the patient to Dr. Boyd, knowing that tonsillectomies were her specialty. She cured the young patient and sent the bill to the county where the physician practiced, as he had instructed. "He was furious because I sent a bill," she said. The county treasurer balked at the bill, and in the end, nobody paid her for her service.

In those years, most of her practice was conducted from her office, but she still made some house calls, despite being rebuffed by occasional unsuspecting patients. Her daughter, Genna, often accompanied her mother on hospital rounds and house calls when she was a child. She still remembers the "last straw" for Dr. Boyd.

"Mother told me to stay in the car and lock it. She went up some unpainted steps and through the screen door of a two-story older house, calling on an elderly woman who was having eye pain. She wasn't there long. She told me as we drove away hurriedly that she would never make another house call and that the family frightened her with their rudeness."

Genna still recalls being upset because she saw something that she rarely saw. Her mother was scared.

Hoping to persuade Congress with money in the bank, Abilene civic leaders lobbying for a U.S. Air Force base set out to raise $500,000 in just one week in January 1952. With an estimated $1.5 million monthly government payroll potentially flowing into the local economy, the money was not difficult to secure. In fact, an extra $300,000 was raised over the next few months to ensure the base would be even larger than originally planned.

A TREMENDOUS BARGAIN

FRANK GRIMES

Hit while the iron is hot should be Abilene's slogan in the push to raise $500,000 to meet Air Force requirements for creating a permanent Air Force Base just south of Tye, six miles from the west city limits of Abilene as the jets fly.

The seven-man committee picked by the Chamber of Commerce with Morgan Jones Jr. as chairman has set up a 21-man executive committee to conduct the campaign for funds. To head this committee and spark the campaign, the dynamic Dr. Harold G. Cooke was named as chairman. Dr. Cooke, president of McMurry College, is a fund-raiser from way back, and the score of men who will assist him in overall management of the whirlwind civic enterprise are go-getters.

First, two things need to be kept in mind: The final decision to place the proposed base at Abilene has not yet been made. We have plenty of powerful rivals for this installation. The promptness and completeness with which the push for funds is met will go a long way toward winning final approval.

The other item to keep in mind is this: It has not yet been decided whether to make this a permanent or temporary base. Abilene wants it to be a permanent base. That calls for 3,500 additional acres of land at the Tye site, and Abilene has promised to raise the money for this extra acreage.

Of course we want the permanent base. That would be a powerful economic factor in the life of this city and its territory for years to come. A temporary base could be here today, gone tomorrow. Big point is this: Without the additional land, it can't be a permanent base.

Raising the funds isn't all Abilene will have to do, if the location is made. It will have to take steps to expand its school system to absorb an additional 1,500 pupils. We'd probably get some federal assistance with that. We would also get some priorities for other things we couldn't get otherwise—water and sewer pipe, construction steel, needed to expand the public service.

We are convinced it would be a tremendous bargain at whatever the cost. It is above all a patriotic enterprise.

[The exhausting effort of convincing the Pentagon and both houses of Congress to reactivate the former Tye Army Air Base came to a successful conclusion on July 14, 1952, when President Truman signed the military construction bill which gave birth to Dyess Air Force Base.]

Almost twenty-five years after the B-1B arrived in Abilene, an Abilene Reporter-News *article reflected on how the new bomber was warmly welcomed.*

THE DAY THE B-1B CAME TO TOWN

JARED FIELDS

Squinting from the glare of the sun along the flight line, an estimated crowd of 45,000 waited in the late June heat for a glimpse of the Air Force's newest bomber. A nine-year roller coaster process to bring the B-1B bomber to Dyess Air Force Base ended June 29, 1985, when the "Star of Abilene" surprised spectators by flying in from the east.

The day of arrival, and those leading up to it, were like few Abilene has seen. Part air show and part Super Bowl, the city and base prepared and braced for the expected onslaught of people.

On base, crews were tasked weeks in advance of the bomber's arrival. "If it didn't move, we painted it. If it (did) move, we picked it up," said Richard "Doc" Warner, curator and historian for the 7th Bomb Wing. "This place was a showplace to begin with, and we made it even better."

Warner said Dyess has not seen a crowd like it since. "This is the first new aircraft, especially a heavy bomber, that the Air Force had seen in twenty years. It was brand-spanking new. Everybody was excited about this."

The transition from the B-52 to the B-1 is what thousands came to see. "Here comes an airplane [the B-1] that you can sweep the wings back, and you're Mach 1 right now," Warner said. "The B-1 when they first got them, they could yank and bank that airplane just like a fighter. You can't do that with the B-52. This was all exciting, brand new technology."

Nightclubs and bars concocted new drinks called the "B-1 Bomber." Churches held prayer vigils. Vintage World War II aircraft were displayed on base.

The second biggest attraction that June day may have been B-1B merchandise. T-shirts, patches, posters, souvenirs—everyone wanted a reminder of what they had fought through heat and traffic to see.

Hundreds of vehicles were turned away from the Dyess gates. Protesters holding signs opposing the nuclear arms race elicited taunts, curses and mild threats. Most passers-by were polite, but a few were not. Two men leaned out of windows in a pickup as it passed five protesters a few hundred yards from the main gate at Dyess. "Commie bastards!" one screamed.

One protester, an Austin man who said he felt it was his duty to demonstrate against nuclear weapons, just smiled back. According to archives, there were no arrests but a few minor incidents. Three people were escorted off the base after entering in a black pickup with a circle and slash through "B-1B" on the hood. Department of Public Safety troopers were called when Abilene police asked for help dispersing three protesters handing out leaflets along Arnold Boulevard. Seven troopers, tucking billy clubs into their belts, asked the protesters to move. They did.

In another incident at 1:30 p.m., fifteen minutes before the B-1 arrived, three people climbed over a fence onto the base, causing officers to close the main gate. Officers let the three stay after determining they just wanted to see the bomber.

Many were unable to get on base. The base was to be open from 10 a.m. to 5 p.m., but Dyess officials closed it at 1:30 p.m. and then reopened from 2 to 2:30 p.m., leaving many frustrated and wondering why they were not allowed in.

One person not waiting in traffic was Darleen Miller. A soon-to-be sophomore at Cooper High School, Miller had won a naming contest for the first B-1 at Dyess. Miller now works on base at Dyess for Boeing and can still see her plane, the "Star of Abilene." "I remember the B-1 coming in, being put on the news and getting to meet all the bigwigs," Miller said. "Seeing the emblem, knowing I was the one that named it, that was just awesome."

The "Star of Abilene" is on display near the main gate of Dyess.

ABILENE AND DYESS

DOUG WILLIAMSON

Some call it a "love affair," but others just say we're being good neighbors. For going on six decades, Abilene has been best friends with its neighbor—Dyess Air Force Base.

Retired Air Force Col. Bill Ehrie has seen it from both sides of the fence. He was base commander, and after retiring, he joined the Abilene Industrial Foundation as its leader.

"In my twenty-five years [in the military], I've seen many good community-base relationships, but none like Abilene. The difference with the Abilene-Dyess relationship is that the level of interface between people carries down to the minutest activity. Elsewhere, it ended at social functions," he said.

When folks around town talk about Dyess personnel, they don't relegate them to "Air Force people." They are fellow "Abilenians."

Ehrie said the alliance goes much deeper than working well together. "I think it is a genuine concern that goes on between the two," he said. "It is not a thing that patronizes people. It is something that has been here since day one when the base was established. There is a deep assimilation between the two that is not there in other communities."

The connection is driven in part by a patriotic spirit and in part by pure economics. Dyess families shop in Abilene stores, dine in local restaurants, attend area schools and churches, volunteer their time, work for community causes, live and play and form friendships with Abilene neighbors.

The whole Air Force knows and respects the Dyess-Abilene partnership. "Everybody knows the [World's Largest] Barbecue. The reputation precedes itself. In fact, it comes up spontaneously in conversation. You'll be talking to an Air Force person, and he'll say, 'Oh, you're from Abilene. That's where the big barbecue is,'" Ehrie said.

Fred Lee Hughes, former chair of the Military Affairs Committee, agrees. "All cities support their bases in varying degrees, but Abilene just goes all out for them."

The Military Airlift Command presents an annual award for the best base-community relations. Dyess and Abilene won so many times that officials just renamed the award the "Abilene Trophy." Abilenians now help present it to the winning city and base.

The Abilene-Dyess bond is enhanced by activities such as the barbecue, an honorary commanders program, along with annual golf and tennis outings. Extensive joint projects, such as the base entrance, visitors' quarters and linear air park also demonstrate the close kinship between the two.

Abilene also works and invests behind the scenes to ensure its continued relationship with Dyess. The Abilene Industrial Foundation contracts with lobbyists in Washington to help. The annual investment of about $170,000 pays off. When other bases are closing or being downsized, Dyess has picked up additional missions.

Mike McMahan, president of the Abilene Chamber of Commerce and also a retired Dyess commander, said having these resources on the ground in Washington gives Abilene day-to-day presence in the halls of Congress and a constant ear to the ground at the Pentagon.

Six decades of living next door to a good friend has proven to be a winning connection for both. The love affair goes on.

GROWING PAINS
COMING OF AGE

John and Laura Guitar home at 1502 North First Street

Hardin-Simmons University Collection

As Abilene marked her fiftieth birthday in 1931, the population hovered at just around 25,000. By the time of Abilene's milestone centennial celebration in 1981, the census showed we had rocketed to become a city of 100,000. In that time, Abilene began to annex neighboring acreage as new neighborhoods were platted and paved. Over the same period, we came to accept our idiosyncrasies, overhaul our opinions of one another and better define our earmarks. The town of Abilene had come of age and had ascended into a modern city.

We firmly settled the issues of race and alcohol. Desegregation was swept away and beer sales were ushered in. We began to let television transform our lives and take us off of our front porches and into our air-conditioned dens. Mom and pop saw their eateries and stores paved over and undercut by shopping centers and big box retailers. We welcomed the men and women sporting Air Force blue.

If the city's sense of its history faltered occasionally during those years with the destruction of some landmark structures, the structure of downtown was wisely polished and preened into a revitalized city center punctuated with the proud exclamation mark of being named an All-America City in 1990.

A personal account of the early days of KRBC-TV, Abilene's first television station, by an eyewitness to this exciting era in the history of the Big Country.

WHEN TV CAME TO ABILENE

JAMES HALLMARK

The year was 1953. Our part of the country was smack dab in the middle of one of the worst droughts in decades. Lakes were drying up. The ground was cracked and dying of thirst due to prolonged lack of moisture. And the thermometer topped the 100-degree mark for weeks on end. Against this bleak background, technology was giving birth to a brand new industry that would touch the lives of all of us. As a twenty-year old college student, I never dreamed that I was about to embark on a career that I would still be actively involved with almost sixty years later.

In 1953, television was still in its infancy in the nation and Texas. WBAP-TV in Fort Worth was the first commercial television station to go on the air in Texas in 1948. During the next few years, a handful of stations began operating in major markets in the state. In the early fifties, the Federal Communications Commission lifted the freeze on new station construction and began issuing construction permits for medium-sized markets throughout the nation. Within months of each other, television stations signed on the air in Abilene, San Angelo, Lubbock, Midland, Amarillo, and Wichita Falls.

Getting people with television experience to staff the exploding number of new television stations in West Texas was understandably difficult. Those with any experience at all already worked for stations in the major markets and weren't terribly interested in moving to the smaller markets for less money.

In the spring of my sophomore year at Hardin-Simmons University, I registered for a course in radio and television as an elective. I was told that it was a snap course that had very little homework. Much to my surprise, I fell in love with broadcasting, and my career goal changed from becoming a fulltime preacher to a career in broadcasting. I became involved with KHSU, the campus radio station, and pulled shifts as a staff announcer and quickly was chosen to be the manager for this low-power radio station that barely covered the campus.

I went to work for KRBC radio on May 11, 1953, the day of the deadly Waco tornado that killed 118 and injured hundreds of others. That same day a tornado struck San Angelo, claiming eight lives. I was hired as an announcer and suddenly was covering breaking news of a major event for our radio audience. It was all quite exciting!

A couple of weeks after joining the staff of KRBC, the station manager called a staff meeting to announce that KRBC had been granted a construction permit for Abilene's first television station. He then asked if any of us had any television experience and would like to work for the new TV station when it went on the air a couple of months down the road. Obviously none of us had any experience. Half jokingly, I told the boss that a few months earlier I had been in Fort Worth and joined a crowd standing in front of a department store window intently watching the Today Show with Dave Garroway and Muggs, in black and white of course.

To promote the coming of television to Abilene, the station rented Rose Field House on the Hardin-Simmons University campus to stage an event that would prepare the people of this area for the advent of television. Thousands of potential viewers of our new station packed the venue. John Kelly, who was hired as KRBC-TV's first manager, had a closed-circuit television set up on the stage and asked me to volunteer to come up from the audience to be interviewed on stage for the cameras. The purpose was to give the thousands who were on hand some idea of what television would look like by seeing the interview displayed on four TV sets strategically positioned on the stage. Dealers, who sold television sets, were set up in booths around the venue and were doing great business. The event was a huge success.

And then the day came that we had all waited for—August 30, 1953—the day television came to Cedar Gap, Texas, and Abilene. We were told to report to the station's studio and transmitter site atop one of the mesas at Cedar Gap, about twelve miles south of Abilene on Highway 83-84. We were told that they would throw the switch at 4 p.m. so we needed to be on site no later than 3 o'clock.

As I approached Cedar Gap, I turned east off the highway and made my way up the side of the mesa. The road was more like a set of tire tracks, and the path was overgrown with weeds and overhanging mesquite trees. A herd of Black Angus cattle was feeding nearby and looked up briefly out of curiosity as I passed by in my 1939 Studebaker coupe. After a few trips up and down the "mountain," I learned that Black Angus cattle are interesting to observe during daylight, but they turned invisible when I was coming down the mountain around midnight and rounded a curve to unexpectedly meet some of them in the middle of the road. And rattlesnakes were everywhere! We appropriately dubbed our transmitter-studio site "Rattlesnake Mountain."

I arrived a little early the first day and parked near the putrid green concrete block building that housed our studio, control room, and engineering equipment. I walked over to the base of the television tower that rose about 700 feet in the air. An antenna on top of the tower added another forty-five feet to the overall height. Considering the fact that this was all atop a mesa which was about 500 feet above the average terrain, I had a spectacular view of Abilene on the horizon to the north.

Several others arrived shortly after I did, and we were chatting excitedly with each other when someone came to the door of the building and told us to come inside. We assembled in the studio to get our assignments. I was told that I, along with another young man, would be running one of the two television cameras. My only prior experience with a camera was taking pictures with a Brownie box camera. The TV cameras were huge Dumont cameras that produced black and white pictures and were about the size of a large suitcase. They were mounted on very heavy pedestals on wheels.

An engineer gave us a five-minute briefing on the use of these two electronic monsters. He then informed us that we would be hitting the air in about fifteen minutes with a five-minute live show for the Bootery Shoe Store. One camera was to follow the movement of a model walking down three steps, and the other camera would have a close-up of the shoes described as the model paused briefly at the bottom of the steps. My camera partner and I just stood there looking at each other with mouths open, but somehow we managed to get through the first live show without a major incident, other than the fact that most of our shots were out of focus.

Since I was hired as an announcer, I later went into the announcer's booth for the remainder of the evening to read voice-over commercials, program notes, and give station identifications. As I recall, our station break went something like this: "This is KRBC-TV, Channel Nine, where the viewing is fine." Very creative . . . or so we thought!

Later that same day, our on-the-air personalities made their debut with what we cleverly called our Six O'clock News. This was an event that our television audience had eagerly anticipated for weeks. Dub Bowlus was the newscaster. Larry Fitzgerald was the sportscaster. And a meteorologist from the weather bureau at the airport handled the weather. I think his name was Frank, but I'm not sure. It was an exciting moment for everyone since most of us, like the audience, had never seen a television newscast.

Back then our viewers were thrilled to watch whatever we could come up with. Our audience had nothing to compare our efforts with. If we moved and made noise, they were happy. They were very forgiving and fascinated just being able to see characters on a screen and hear them speak.

About two weeks after the station signed on the air, Harry Holt, KRBC radio's longtime farm and ranch director, began his long-running thirty-minute weekly television show, *On the Farm*. It was an instant hit with the large number of viewers who made their living in the farm and ranch business. Holt was the voice of agriculture in the Abilene area for more than fifty years. He was a living legend. Harry was my friend and my mentor in those early days. I couldn't have asked for a better teacher.

DEALING WITH RACISM

JANE McHAN

There's a large ivy plant in Dorothy Wiseman's living room—a reminder, she says, of the many children she taught over the years. This plant grew from a cutting of one she received as a gift in 1972, at the time of her husband's death. Returning to work, she discovered that a substitute teacher had accompanied her seventh-graders to a store on Grape Street, where they pooled their pennies and lunch money to purchase the plant for her. Mrs. Wiseman reflects that when she experiences difficult times, "I can just sit here and see my life and know that my children loved me enough to take their lunch money and buy me this plant. I am just hoping that their lives have blossomed like it has."

Dorothy Wiseman was born on March 14, 1931, and lived her early years with her parents, two sisters and one brother on a farm in Mount Vernon in East Texas. When she was a child, her father left the family, and her mother was unable to maintain the farm by herself. Mrs. Wiseman's mother came to Abilene, where she had a sister who was working at Camp Barkeley. She worked until she could earn enough money to return to Mount Vernon and bring her four young children back to Abilene with her in 1942.

Though the community was segregated, Mrs. Wiseman feels that her life was still good. "Once you live a certain way . . . you adapt to that environment and you know that everyone whose skin pigmentation is the same as yours lives in the same environment.

When I look back, I can't say that I regret it, because everyone who looked the same as I did lived the same way."

She attended Woodson School, which included grades one through twelve for African-American children. The school calendar was a bit different from "regular" schools because many of the children worked in the cotton fields and allowances were made so they could "maintain a living." Although her textbooks included "*Little Black Sambo* and all that garbage," she notes that her teachers "had the foresight to use the Bible for literature instead of the other textbooks," and she believes that her teachers instilled in her the same strength that her mother did.

Mrs. Wiseman's mother was a firm believer in education and always worked two, sometimes three, jobs to assure that her children's needs were met. She only made about $3.50 a week in wages. "It was poverty level, but she was such a strong character. I don't think welfare was around at the time, but she wouldn't have taken it. Some people thought, with four children, she should put us to work, but she knew what life was like without an education and she didn't want that for us. She said she just wanted to live long enough to see all of her children grown and educated." Because of her strength, her faith, and her unwavering support of her children, Mrs. Wiseman's mother is her hero and the person she chooses to emulate.

During those years, African-Americans needing health care often found that no doctor would see them or that they received substandard services. In Mount Vernon, a wagon wheel once ran over Dorothy's foot, but she was not allowed to go to the physician's office. Instead, he told her mother what to do to take care of the injury. Later in Abilene, the hospital reserved some rooms for blacks on the ground level with the machines and equipment. "If you had to go to the hospital at that time, you were down there with the mops and brooms . . . I can remember that very vividly." Many black children did not receive birth certificates. "It wasn't important because they were a nonentity."

If Abilene blacks went to a local restaurant, they had to enter through the back door and sit in the kitchen to eat. "I used to just accept it, but now I sometimes wonder what kind of people would do that kind of thing?" As a young girl, Dorothy would accompany her mother to pay utility bills downtown and remembers, "[When] we wanted to go upstairs, if there were white people on the elevator, we couldn't get on and ride with them. We had to wait until the elevator was clear of white people. Sometimes we would wait for . . . I don't know how long . . . ." Even on the sidewalks, "If you were going south and white people were going north, it was up to you to get of the way or risk being called the most negative things out of someone's mouth."

As a teenager, Dorothy had a job as a domestic for a wealthy local family and was once accused of stealing a fifty dollar bill from her employer's purse. The woman's husband threatened Dorothy and tried to scare her into admitting to something she had not done. She refused to quit her job because she felt that doing so would be the same as admitting guilt. Later she found out that the woman had dropped the bill at a local drugstore while buying cigarettes and that it had been returned to her. Neither the woman nor her husband told Dorothy about the mistake nor apologized for their accusations. She remains indignant. "Just imagine, going to work in that kind of environment! What that said to me was that I was not worthy enough of an apology." However, she believes that God intervened and gave her a way out of Abilene and off to college by letting her learn the truth. She says that otherwise, "I would probably still be doing domestic work because I wouldn't have ever quit as long as they thought I took that money." Still, after all these years, this experience with racism continues to hurt her the most.

After graduation from Woodson School in 1946, Dorothy worked at Thornton's Department Store for a year, saved her money, earned a scholarship from a church, and moved to Waco to attend Paul Quinn University. She obtained a degree with honors in Business Education in 1951 and returned to Abilene. After teaching one year in the public schools, she spent nine years working in business offices. As a child, she had accompanied her mother to pay bills, noticing office women who would type without looking at the keys, and thinking what a great job that would be. Eventually, she returned to teaching at Woodson, married and had one son.

In 1968, when the Abilene public schools integrated, the AISD superintendent came to Woodson, telling the students all the names they would be called and that "there wasn't anything they could do about it." Mrs. Wiseman remembers, "I really couldn't believe that. But there was a lot of truth to it—what comes out of your mouth, I can't control, so maybe it did help prepare them." She moved to Mann Junior High (now Mann Middle School) where she stayed until her retirement after thirty-two years of teaching.

Early on, she used experiential exercises to help her students understand prejudice and racism. One week she let all of the blondes go to lunch first, the next week all of the students with blue eyes. "Most of them were just livid and a lesson was learned. I wanted them to see what it's like to pick out a certain segment and give it a privilege over another."

Although Abilene Christian would not fully integrate until 1962, students on campus questioned the college's segregation policy as early as 1954 as evidenced by this letter to the editor of the campus newspaper. One of the students signing the letter was Joe Schubert, whose son Phil would go on to become president of ACU in 2010. Across town, McMurry admitted its first black graduate student in 1955 and first black undergraduate student in 1959.

 —————————————————————————— 

DISCRIMINATION POLICY CHALLENGED

Letter to the Editor, *The Optimist*, March 1954

Dear Editor:

During the recent issues of the *Optimist*, there have appeared numerous letters to the editor discussing the pros and cons of various current issues on the campus. While perhaps most of these issues are important and should be discussed, it seems to us that there is a greater, more serious problem that has not been mentioned as much as it should have been.

This problem is the Negro discrimination policy that Abilene Christian College is now following. In short, we feel that Abilene Christian College is following a policy that is un-Christian and dramatically opposed to New Testament teachings.

It would not be fair, however, for us to issue a statement of this sort without substantiating it with Biblical proof, and that is what we shall derive to do.

(1) Galatians 3:27-28 tells us that there is neither Jew nor Greek, bond nor free, male nor female, in the kingdom of heaven, but that we are one in Christ Jesus. Paul tells us that there is absolutely no

room for discrimination of any sort in Christ's church. We are all one in Christ Jesus. We are all one, yet we cannot associate with our dark-colored brothers and sisters in Christ on our campus. Why?

(2) In Matthew 11:19 we are told the story of Jesus' eating and drinking with the publicans, and how that certain ones murmured against him for this. The publicans in Jesus' day were considered the scum of the social cycle. Yet the greatest man that ever lived humbled himself enough to eat and drink with them. Can we, as mere mortals, do any less? Will we not eat and drink with our colored brethren on our campus? Why?

(3) Galatians 3:26 informs us that we are all sons of God through faith in Christ Jesus. Our colored brethren are sons of God. We, too, are sons of God. Are we any more sons of God than they? When we gather at the throne of God to sing praises to His name, will God want us any closer to His throne than they? If God will accept them in heaven, can we not accept them in school? If not, why?

(4) Finally, if we had no other scripture, this last one would be enough. We quote James 2:9: "If ye have respect to persons, ye commit sin." What else could be so plain? Regardless of all of the things that we have done for our colored brethren, including their own college, if there is only one dark-colored friend that wants to come to Abilene Christian College regardless of his reasons, and we say, "No, our doors are closed," James says we have sinned. Every race on the face of the earth is permitted to attend ACC except the Negro. Why?

There are many objections that one may raise to prohibit Negroes from coming to Abilene Christian College. When such objections are issued, it seems to us that the faith in God of the persons making the objections is not as strong as it should be. Will we lose financial support? "All things work together for good for them that love God." (Romans 8:28) "If God is for us, who is against us?" (Romans 8:31)

We realize that Abilene Christian College is not the church, but as its very name implies it is to be governed by Christian principles. Regardless of all the secular objections that we can raise against Negro equality, do we have one scriptural objection?

When we gather at the throne of God to sing praises to His name, will God want us any closer to His throne than the Negro? Every race on the face of the earth is permitted to attend ACC except the Negro. Why?

Signed:

Sonny Ellis
Ellis Long
Ted Pemberton
Howard Norton
Walter Kreidel
Joe Schubert
John Bailey
Larry Hornbaker
Kenneth Oller
Bob Barnhill

While Abilene School Superintendent A. E. Wells and the school board labored over a solution to the problem of how they could integrate Dyess Elementary School and comply with both state and federal laws, the school officials continued to receive letters of concern from black parents living on Dyess Air Force Base. Captain John P. Rice, a black Air Force officer, wrote the following letter, dated March 14, 1962, to Superintendent Wells.

A LETTER TO THE SUPERINTENDENT

CAPTAIN JOHN P. RICE, USAF

Dear Sir:

After a great deal of soul searching and contemplation, I have decided to write to you to get some firm, definitive answers to a question that has to be answered sooner or later.

To come at once to the heart of the matter: I am a Negro officer stationed at Dyess Air Force Base with on-base quarters. I have two children, the eldest of whom will soon be eligible to attend grade school. I am informed that solely because of color and because of the existing segregation policy my son will not be able to attend the William E. Dyess school which is only a few hundred yards from our home. He can look across the yard at this school and see the white, Latin-American, part Japanese, and so on, children attending this school, but he must or will have to ride a bus to attend the "colored" school which is about five or six miles away (this letter is not meant to disparage that school).

I would like to make it very clear at this point that I am not a "trouble maker." I am not trying to "create an incident." I have full respect for the laws of Abilene, Texas, and I am well aware of the extremely touchy "race issue" in many parts of the south. I am also aware of the gradual but orderly progress or evolution in race relations that is taking place throughout the south, and I would like to see some progress begin in the Christian community of Abilene. I also realize that it is sad but true that many of the enemies of American democracy use these segregation policies to discredit or embarrass our country abroad. I, myself, actually saw this happen when our former president was denied the chance to visit a certain foreign country, an important Asian ally, actually, as a result of left-wing riots.

With all due respect, I'd like to point out certain facts. The school (Dyess) is supported by taxes, and I make some small contribution in that direction. The school is primarily attended by the children of Air Force personnel, and, while I am definitely not an Air Force spokesman (I am writing as a private citizen), I don't believe the Air Force would interpose any objection to the admission of my son to the school. My son is a clean cut, healthy, well-mannered young gentleman from what I like to believe is a good home. My wife and I are both college graduates. I am a regular officer in the United States Air Force, and I graduated with honors from Harvard College with the class of 1950.

If the present policy is in favor of segregation, are there any plans to open this door in the near future? Please rest assured that I am 100% sincere in this matter, and, if you so desire, I would be glad to quietly discuss this with you at any time that is convenient. My sole motivation in this matter is my own sense of parental responsibility.

[Dyess Elementary was integrated in 1963.]

Hispanic students walked out of their classes at Abilene High and Franklin Junior High on October 21, 1969, in protest of discriminatory practices at both schools. Following a nine-day boycott, students returned to class wearing brown armbands in a show of cultural solidarity as the Abilene school board set out to address the grievances.

HISPANIC STUDENT BOYCOTT

ABILENE REPORTER-NEWS

In 1969, some Abilene school teachers called Spanish the "monkey language." It probably wasn't the first time educators had ridiculed the language, but this time it was enough to trigger a student protest on local campuses. And by the time the resulting controversy had run its course, most had learned a thing or two about Hispanic pride.

It was a lesson few would forget

Trouble flared not long after school had begun that year. Hispanic students in the Abilene Independent School District were admonished when caught speaking Spanish in the hallways. About 300 Hispanic students complained about the punishment and other problems they labeled discriminatory.

A boycott of Abilene schools in late October was the result. Mostly Hispanic students stayed out of classrooms for nine days while negotiations were worked out between members of the Abilene school board and leaders of the student protests. At the end of the boycott, an estimated 1,500 people marched through downtown Abilene, carrying signs that pledged Chicano power. And when students did return to classes, they wore brown armbands to remind others of their cultural pride.

While a handful of instances of students being admonished for speaking Spanish in school served to prompt the walkout, the protest picked up more steam when school officials threatened the student protesters with expulsion if they didn't return to classes. Lawyers from the Mexican-American Legal Defense Association and Education Fund became involved. Attorneys for the students later saw to it that a suit was filed in federal court alleging discrimination. The case was lost, but for some students such as Andres "Andy" Gamon, then a junior at Abilene High and involved in the protest, the battle was won.

"By the time it got into federal courts, we had felt we made our point," said Gamon, who was on the student boycott organizing committee. "We presented our grievances to the school board—they heard us out." The demands included the following:

*Allow Spanish to be spoken on school grounds.

*Encourage better Hispanic representation in student government.

*Hire more Mexican-American teachers and counselors.

*Establish workshops for teachers and administrators that would help them "appreciate, respect and understand" Mexican-American children.

*Form bilingual programs.

*Study the Mexican-American dropout problem and initiate steps to help curb the dropout rate.

A. E. Wells, AISD superintendent, was at a national meeting in Atlantic City when he heard about the boycott. Surprised at the news, he headed back to Abilene to find the cause of the problem.

The idea of student protests—already happening elsewhere in the country—happening in the Big Country never occurred to Wells, he recalled later. "Things were happening everywhere, but we never had any of this in Abilene."

Although it seemed there were a lot of people rallying behind the student group, Wells said he was convinced many were coming from out of town. Not all Hispanics here were in support of the walkout. "I started working with people I thought were leaders in the [Hispanic] community, and most of them were ministers," Wells said. "I found out right away that it was mostly people from the outside who came in and started the insurrection.

"They had little to complain about," Wells recalled. "That's why they had trouble getting the whole community to go along with them."

Wells did not support the boycott, and though he says he was sympathetic about their perceived problems, leaving school was not the answer. "We were trying to get them back in school. We didn't want them to lose out on their education. Even if they were dissatisfied with things, they should still be in school, instead of out on the streets rebelling."

Lucille Santana remembers being worried when her daughter Laticia participated in the walkout. She supported her daughter's stand. "A lot of parents were afraid they would lose their jobs if they spoke out," Santana said. "There were mixed feelings, but overall support."

Gamon says the students were fighting for more than just a list of demands. They were voicing pride in their culture, he said, and if the boycott had any long-range effect, it was that it brought the Hispanic community in Abilene closer together. "It was an identity period for a lot of ethnic groups," Gamon said.

No one particular incident triggered the walkout, Gamon recalled. A group headed by high school students Gloria Bryant and Johnny Sanchez were just trying to make things better, he said. "We had legal grounds," Gamon said. "It wasn't just a bunch of kids going wild."

Some students realized that without a good education their future would be bleak, he said. "We were starting to appreciate the value—the importance—of education. We wanted to make sure that the kids coming up after us had a chance."

If there were any doubts about speaking the so-called "monkey language" on campus, the Abilene school board cleared it up in its

November 1 meeting, telling the Hispanic student leaders there was no written policy prohibiting the speaking of Spanish on campus. School board members also assured students they were continuing to try to hire good Mexican-American teachers; that school officials had no objection to a Hispanic organization on campus if it had a faculty advisor; and that other ideas would be studied.

Following that meeting, students returned to their classrooms, though some administrators suggested the protesters should still be expelled for unexcused absences. Gamon, however, said their excuse was better than any note from a doctor. "We just said we were sick at heart."

Few issues have divided Abilene as much as whether to allow the sale of alcoholic beverages in the city. After decades of debate, the issue was finally put to rest in a tightly contested election in 1978.

ABILENE GOES WET

DAVID COFFEY

Abilene's early war against local saloons and its well-cultivated reputation for wholesome living in a powerfully Christian environment were as much a part of its identity as the railroad and the cowboy. Abilene wore its "dry" status like a badge of honor.

But there had always been a bit of fiction in the word "dry," especially so after World War II. The influx of thirsty soldiers and airmen during and after the war created new demands for alcoholic beverages. Bootleggers had long prospered by selling overpriced product to willing consumers. After the war, VFW halls could offer beer, and private clubs flourished. Members of the Abilene Country Club and the Petroleum Club could drink in high style. But for most Abilenians who desired a drink, high prices or memberships left them wanting—until some enterprising citizens fired the first salvo in what became a two decade war between the "wets" and the "drys." That first shot made Impact.

In February 1960, a group of citizens, headed by lawyer and landowner Dallas Perkins, submitted a petition to incorporate forty-seven acres in Taylor County just off the northern edge of the Abilene city limits. Impact was born. Its main purpose, indeed its only real purpose, was to become an alcohol oasis in dry West Texas. But that would not happen without a fight. Church and civic leaders in Abilene attacked with fiery determination, but the quest to sell alcoholic beverages for off-premise consumption pressed on. After a thirty-three month court battle, Impact won the right to sell package liquor, beer, and wine. Cars crammed the streets north of Abilene as Impact opened for business just days before Christmas 1962.

In 1965, residents of Buffalo Gap south of Abilene voted by a margin of one to approve on-premise sales of alcohol by restaurants in a small section of the village, making it a favored destination for many local diners. With Impact to its north and Buffalo Gap to its south selling alcohol, Abilene became known as "the city that was wet on both ends and dry in the middle." But these events marked only the beginning—Abilene's dry status, fictitious though it may have been, was on its last legs.

The oil boom and high-rolling times of the 1970s reinvigorated the wet-dry debate in Abilene. The city's few private clubs had all the business they could handle, and many new residents brought with them a desire for more available alcohol. During the spring of 1978, pressure mounted as Abilenians on both sides of the alcohol issue marshaled support for a scheduled June 17 referendum. A group called Update '78 pressed for the legal sale, both on- and off-premises, of liquor, beer, and wine. Update '78 faced stiff competition from the Citizens for a Better Community (CBC), who carried the dry banner. A compromise group, the Citizens for Moderation, advanced the on-premise only option, or liquor-by-the-drink. Heated debate preceded the vote. In a true sign that times were changing, the *Abilene Reporter-News* endorsed the wet position.

When the results came in, the wets had carried the day by a margin of some 130 votes out of more than 23,000 cast. But the issue was not settled. The CBC challenged the results, which led to a divisive legal battle that threatened to tear the community apart. Finally, with church and university leaders calling for unity and understanding, the challenge was dropped. Beer trucks lined the highways into Abilene in anticipation. On September 20, 1978, beer went on sale at local convenience stores. Liquor stores and new restaurants followed.

Growing up in Abilene, Jorge Solis became the city's first Hispanic lawyer, district attorney and district judge before he was appointed a federal judge by President Bush in 1991 and moved to Dallas.

JORGE SOLIS: A MAN OF FIRSTS

ABILENE REPORTER-NEWS

Jorge Solis grew up in an Abilene largely devoid of a Hispanic middle class. There were few Hispanic teachers in schools and few Mexican-American businesses catering to the dominant Anglo sector of the city. Most importantly for his future, there were no Mexican-American lawyers practicing in town and no Hispanic elected officials.

"We just didn't have many Hispanic professionals here. We weren't successful in politics," recalled Solis, whose family moved from San Ygnacio, near Laredo, to an Abilene barrio near Fannin Elementary School when he was five. "When I was going to college, I was already thinking I wanted to see that change."

Twenty years after moving to Abilene he was part of that change. After getting a law degree from the University of Texas in 1976, he became Abilene's first Hispanic practicing attorney. In 1982, he was the first Hispanic and first Republican to be elected Taylor County District Attorney. In 1989, the first Hispanic district judge in Abilene. In 1991, the first Hispanic federal judge in the Northern District of Texas.

Like most Hispanics in Abilene during the late fifties and sixties, Solis noticed the prejudices that came with growing up Mexican-American in an Anglo society. He remembers kids getting in trouble at Fannin Elementary for speaking Spanish even though most children at the school were Hispanic. "By the third grade, I was just getting away from Spanish being my dominant language," he said.

He enrolled at McMurry College in 1969 where he studied political science and history, graduating in 1973. "I began to feel that we needed to get more Hispanics interested in politics and in some positions of authority," he said. "I was aware that we weren't getting anywhere from a political point of view."

After getting his law degree from UT, he and wife Rebecca decided to return to Abilene despite enticing offers from firms in San Antonio and Houston. As the first Mexican-American attorney in town, he had to look over his shoulder somewhat. "When you know you're the first one, there's a feeling that they are watching you. I take pride in being Mexican-American. I wanted to do well because I was the first one."

Like most people in Abilene, Solis voted in the Democratic primary because, before the 1980s, "that was where the action was." But that was about to change. In 1981 he quit his position with the DA's office and joined a law firm that included then-Taylor County Democratic Party Chairman Jess Holloway, later county and district judge. Holloway's political preference aside, Solis signed up in 1982 to run as a Republican for district attorney against his former boss, Patricia Elliott. He decided to run as a Republican, he said, in part because of the party's perceived more conservative philosophy.

The year 1982 wasn't a good one for Republicans who were routed across the state by Democrats in the November election. The shining star for the party in Taylor County was Solis, who won rather easily, just the second Republican elected in the county. Four years later he was unopposed for re-election.

Although many historic downtown buildings have been restored, Abilene allowed one of its singular landmarks to be torn down, a decision that continues to haunt a community now recognized for its preservation efforts.

RAZING THE GUITAR MANSION

RAY HOLLIS, as told to SAM PENDERGRAST

I had seen and felt the depth of public emotion that gets hung onto a building with some historical significance in Ballinger, but I was still not prepared for the firestorm of sentiment that faced me within hours after the announcement that I had a contract to raze one of the most familiar and beloved—although private—landmarks in Abilene.

It was the palatial old Guitar Mansion on North First Street that had served for half a century as the ultimate goal for the would-be rich and powerful of the Key City. It wasn't that old. The family had moved in about 1907. And it wasn't as palatial as some of the private estates I've torn down over the years. I guess it was mostly a symbol, and a very visible symbol at that.

Half a dozen blocks from downtown Abilene, it fronted on both the Texas and Pacific Railroad and old Highway 80 that was traversed by everyone who passed through Abilene as well as most local citizens regularly. It was within the sight of old Abilene High School, so that schoolboys grew up with the idea that the one unquestionable sign of success in life would have to be the ability to own such a residence as the Guitar Mansion (the word "mansion" was as much a part of the title as the family name; I never heard it referred to by any other word except by members of the family).

It was rich brown Roman brick perfectly laid and marble trim with other hand-worked stone highlights and ceramic tile roof in a façade that suggested the palaces of Spain. On a lot nearly half a block in size, it boasted one of the better coach houses in West Texas—and even a cast-iron cage for an eagle nobody recalls having seen. Corners were marked by winged lions standing upright and holding—what else?—stone guitars.

I'd been a wrecker for years, but, even to me, it was almost unthinkable that the Guitar Mansion could—or should—be removed from its familiar corner near downtown. But it had been vacant for some time. The familiar signs of decay and vandalism were appearing. The grounds had gone to weed, the juniper bushes wild at the corners.

I got in touch with Earl Guitar, who was handling the estate. And, yes, the house seemed doomed—the familiar drain on taxes and insurance and the developing possibility of an eyesore that would reflect as badly—worse probably—on the family name as local memories of what had been and was no more. I made a deal with Guitar to buy the structure for $2,500, with a ninety-day contract to clear the lot. I gave him a cashier's check for that amount. And found myself immediately in the midst of a heated campaign to "save the mansion."

As soon as word got in the paper that I was preparing to tear down the Guitar Mansion, I was the villain. It seemed everybody in town had a different idea about what to do with the "white elephant" except to come up with the surprisingly little money it would have taken to preserve what would have been the most beautiful showplace in West Texas.

I suggested it would make a fine museum and at one time offered to turn over my interests for $10,000. By that time I had commitments amounting to some $8,000 in addition to my original cost. I was paying hands to look after the place that was suddenly the object of everybody's attention including souvenir hunters. It was already costing me money.

The Guitars and I could have been bought out entirely for about $100,000. Earl had a buyer talking about a $90,000 price tag for the building site. But he had already taken a $5,000 loss to call off a prior wrecker because of somebody's attempts to "save the mansion," and I would have been only too happy to see the fine old mansion preserved as a sample of the best in home building at the turn of the century.

It came out in the paper that I was expected to make $25,000 on the wrecking deal, and everybody suddenly wanted to figure out how to keep me from making any money. Somebody got the Internal Revenue interested and the State Comptroller. The tax people came up with the novel idea that I ought to be taxed for money I was expected to make in addition to money I had made.

Everybody wanted a piece of me. But I agreed to wait as long as possible to give various individuals and groups a good chance to come up with something concrete to save the mansion. There was one group that wanted to save it for a home for a psychiatric retreat. I attended a meeting at the Evangelical Methodist Church to organize a drive on behalf of the landmark. But I had signed the ninety-day contract on May 18 [1964], and it would take several weeks to clear the site. I had to begin wrecking the outside walls no later than July 2.

As the deadline approached for beginning the destruction, the activity was feverish among would-be saviors of the Guitar Mansion. A Dallas oilman was said to be interested in buying it, and the mental health people had one last emergency meeting, but nothing came of either initiative.

I gave the order to start tearing down the great old home with as heavy a heart as there was in Abilene, with the possible exception of the members of the family who had grown up in the protection of its sturdy walls. It was the best-built structure I ever encountered, I guess. Every brick was perfectly set with quarter-inch grouting. And nothing was spared in finishing, trimming, and decorating the massive brick home. All the baseboards and window trim were birch, and the cherry was around the fireplace and the pantries. Three mantels were cherry collector's pieces.

I sold the massive front door for, I think, $250, and the stained glass pieces were worth money, but I didn't make anywhere near that $25,000 they were saying I would make and the tax people were wanting to bill me for in advance. In fact, this is going to be a revelation about one of the great mysteries of Abilene trivia. What became of the lions-with-guitars figureheads that were on the principal corners of the old mansion?

We were coming down to the deadline to deliver the Guitar lot leveled to the ground, and I didn't have any place to store the surplus material. So I ordered a big hole dug at the back of the lot with a big bulldozer, and we filled it up with left-over materials I hadn't been able to sell. And that's where five of the familiar winged lions with guitars rest for posterity—in a rough grave at the back of the historic lot. All but one. I have Repp's guitar, one of the massive crests, as a memento of his childhood home.

Somebody probably ought to dig up the rest of those lions with guitars. They'd be nice in a museum that the old house should have become.

[The Guitar family donated several architectural relics from the house to the Grace Museum, including a stone guitar that is in the museum courtyard.]

Abilene may have been slow to embrace historical preservation, but once it got started it became a source of civic pride, especially downtown. And one woman quietly took the lead in making it happen.

THE WOMAN WHO SAVED DOWNTOWN

GLENN DROMGOOLE

Judy Matthews almost single-handedly saved downtown Abilene from ruin. She would probably argue with you about that, but not many other people would.

Matthews and the Dodge Jones Foundation, established by her mother Ruth Legett Jones in 1954, poured millions of dollars into downtown renovation beginning in the 1980s when they rescued and restored the Paramount Theatre.

The Grace Museum, the Elks Building, the T&P Depot and right-of-way, the Cypress and Compton buildings and others stand today as monuments to the vision and generosity of Julia Jones Matthews and the foundation.

And for all of that, she never sought recognition. Gradually, it came to her anyway—selected with her mother as Abilenians of the Millenium in 1999 by a citizens committee, as well as other accolades. But Matthews and the foundation—named for her brother Dodge Jones, who died at a young age—were best known for many years as "Anonymous." It wasn't too long before everyone knew who Anonymous was.

"In the entire history of Abilene," said Tucker Bridwell, president of the Dian Graves Owen Foundation, "no one person or entity has done more positive things for this town than Judy Matthews and the Dodge Jones Foundation," a sentiment that would be echoed by virtually every civic leader in town. "Abilene is so fortunate to have had a foundation and a lady that has largely improved the quality of life and the entire look of the downtown area over the last fifty-plus years."

The foundation, presided over for three decades by Joe Canon and grants administrator Larry Gill, funded countless other civic endeavors, including $750,000 in 1985 to launch the Community Foundation of Abilene, which twenty-five years later reported assets of more than $85 million.

Mrs. Matthews came by her philanthropic interests naturally. Her mother, Ruth Legett Jones, was known before she died in 1978 as "the quiet philanthropist" who founded the Dodge Jones Foundation. She scrupulously avoided the spotlight. Once, when Mrs. Jones donated land to the city for a new park, the city proposed to name it for her. She said she would withdraw the offer in that case. So, instead, Abilene's largest park is named for her favorite tree—the Redbud. Judy Matthews' grandfather, K. K. Legett, who died in 1926, helped establish Simmons and McMurry colleges among many other Abilene civic contributions.

"It's easy to make a difference in Abilene," Mrs. Matthews told an interviewer. "It seems like there are so many things that we need."

The downtown facelift may well have been the showcase for her and the foundation. By the early eighties downtown Abilene, like many downtowns around the country, was looking grim and deserted. Most of its retail business had headed out to the malls and strip centers, hotels were vacant and vandalized, buildings were boarded and decaying. The wrecking ball had already torn down several theaters and landmark sites, and it threatened to take out others, including the historic Paramount Theatre, once the pride of Abilene.

That's when Judy Matthews stepped in, not only saving the theater but restoring it to its original grandeur. "Everyone my age or older, or even younger, enjoyed the Paramount Theatre and the movies there when we were growing up," she said. "For many years, that was the only thing you could do, go to the movies. Now, it wasn't the only movie theater [in town], but it was the nicest. And it just looked like it was going to go."

Thanks to her, it didn't go. It stayed. And it led to numerous other downtown improvements, most significantly the Grace Hotel, which became the Grace Museum, and the T&P Depot, housing cultural and visitor bureaus. Other foundations, organizations and individuals caught the vision, including the Tax Increment Finance District, charged with reinvesting downtown tax funds into central city improvements over a twenty-five year period. Abilene gained a reputation statewide for its revived downtown.

"When someone asks how Abilene has been able to preserve so much of its downtown history," said one downtown business owner, "I tell them there is a long answer and a short answer. The short answer is Judy Matthews. The long answer is that she inspired a lot of other people to get involved in downtown preservation."

Or as foundation executive director Joe Canon put it, there has been "a ripple effect that Judy's interests have helped crystallize."

HOWEVER YOU SPELL IT

ABILENE REPORTER-NEWS

The most misspelled name in Abilene is the name Legett. The city of Abilene misspells it on dozens of street signs. So do all the business firms that report on signs or on stationery that they are located on "Leggett Drive."

The family for whom the post-war street was named has only one "G." But the family has made and will make no effort to get the error corrected.

The two daughters of the late K. K. Legett, one of the giants of early Abilene, were Mrs. Percy Jones and Mrs. Julia Legett Pickard. They were out of town when the misspelled street signs went up. When they discovered the error, they discussed whether they should point out the mistake to city officials. Their decision was: "The Judge wouldn't care. He wouldn't think it was worth the bother."

Judge Legett was a lawyer, a church leader and an educator. He was one of the small group that founded Simmons College and served the school as chairman of trustees many years. He was for many years chairman of the board of Texas A&M College and was instrumental in the establishment of Prairie View Normal. He was one of the pillars of First Baptist Church.

"The Judge didn't think you should mourn for the dead too long," his daughter, Mrs. Pickard, recalled. "He said such mourning was not in keeping for a Christian. He wouldn't want to make a fuss over the spelling of his name."

Mrs. Pickard said that in signing her checks, she spelled the "Legett" in her name with one "G" and the "Leggett" in her address with two.

For years, however, the *Abilene Reporter-News* stuck to the one "G" spelling in its news columns.

A term for committee miscommunication earned Abilene dubious distinction in behavioral management programs across the country.

THE ABILENE PARADOX

ROBERT W. SLEDGE

Abilene gained some unwanted notoriety in 1974 when an article titled "The Abilene Paradox" appeared in the journal *Organizational Dynamics.*

Jerry Harvey, the author, told the story of a family in Coleman sitting around the house playing dominoes on a hot Sunday afternoon. One of the group suggested that the others might like to drive to Abilene to eat at the cafeteria. Another chimed in that that was a good idea, while others, who wanted to stay where they were, agreed to go along with the notion. They made the trip in an un-air-conditioned car "across a godforsaken desert in furnace-like heat and a dust storm to eat unpalatable food at a hole-in-the-wall cafeteria in Abilene, when none of us had really wanted to go . . . we'd done just the opposite of what we wanted to do."

The essay was a meditation on "groupthink," the notion that committees can decide the wrong things because everybody wants to agree with what others seem to want.

Soon after "The Abilene Paradox" first appeared, a short film of the same title appeared as a case study for management programs. Ultimately, the author included the essay in a book of "meditations" with that one as the featured article. The concept became a regular staple of discussions on organizational behavior and, in time, a shorthand term for committee miscommunication. For example, the author speaks of a "relatively small industrial company that has embarked on a trip to Abilene." When an organizational analyst speaks of "going to Abilene," everyone immediately understands that the term is meant as a criticism of the decision-making process.

Abilenians might not appreciate this kind of publicity for their hometown, even if it was not intended as an attack on the city's reputation. In 2008, a Waco editorialist likened the Iraq War to Harvey's model. "Ultimately, the only justification that sticks [for the Iraq War] is that although on false pretenses, we're there. We're stuck—in the Abilene Paradox." The writer did not explain that the proverbial trip was from Coleman to Abilene, so a reader assumed that he meant from Waco to Abilene and retorted with a letter titled "the Waco Paradox" and concluded: "the paradox isn't that Abilene and good times are somehow contradictory. Rather, after such a nice day in Abilene, who in the world would want to go back to Waco?"

In management circles, Abilene is famous—whether we like it or not.

For a generation of Abilene teens, everything changed one Friday evening in 1958—it was on June 20 that Mack Eplen opened his Drivateria at North First and Shelton. Although he didn't intend to, Mack created a mecca for Abilene's ardent youth.

CIRCLIN' MACK'S

JAY MOORE

Mack Eplen was a lifelong Abilenian and restaurateur extraordinaire. He grew a single root beer stand on Grape Street into a stable of local eateries—from his Cypress Street cafeteria and Ticker Tape diner on Pine to the Starlite, Jamaica Inn, Chicken-on-the-Run and even Old Abilene Town, he fulfilled his trademark phrase: "Where Abilene Dines." But for Abilene teens of the '60s and '70s, there was just one Eplen establishment that mattered; it was simply known as Mack's and you circled it.

The full name was Mack Eplen's Drivateria and the concept allowed you to either dine in or park your car in one of the twenty-one canopied spots and order over the intercom. The speaker would alert you when it was time to drive to the window and collect your charcoal-broiled Squareburger and signature Chewy Brownie. Along North First, the big Drivateria sign featured Eplen's iconic walking chef and a clock reminding all it was "Time to Eat." The old building still stands, serving as offices for a used car lot punnily touting itself as the "Loan Arranger." But Mack's property was surely unrivaled as the "Date Arranger." It was *American Graffiti* Abilene-style.

The geometric allure wasn't the Squareburgers being made on the inside, but rather the circle wheeling around outside. Circling

Mack's was a coming-of-age custom. A place to set your young life in orbit, drawn by the gravitational pull of possibilities. With your windows rolled down, the slowly passing parade offered you a real-life social medium for exchanging winks, smiles and sentences cut short. The resulting tingle was innocent and actual. And, with no turn lane, the possibility of rear-ending someone slowing to turn off First was real, too. To have a wreck was to commit social suicide.

For many years, the railroad tracks partitioned Abilene's high schools, but Mack's offered a hole in the fence, a place to enter the other world. And, throughout the 1960s and '70s, Cooper and Abilene High met at Mack's most every Friday and Saturday night. We Cougars went hoping to catch the eye of an Eagle while Eagles arrived confident of charming a Coog. We both peacocked our best strut with youthful naiveté convincing many guys that a cigarette upped their cool factor. The girls modeled best they could while seated in a car.

I'm not sure how things worked early on but by the mid-'70s, guys typically drove counter-clockwise while the girls hugged the curb and made the four right-hand turns along Green, Second, Shelton and North First. The primo spot in the car was just behind the driver. That meant you didn't have to handle the driving and didn't have to lean over to see and be seen. You were sitting pretty.

Should a girl turn away as you came alongside, you were left to wonder if it was personal or a ploy of hard-to-get. Occasionally you passed a carload of over-excited junior high kids who had implored a parent to enter this spiraling epicenter of high-schooldom. Without a doubt, the ultimate gift for any eighth-grader was an invitation to ride along with his older brother (*but keep your mouth shut*) and after getting caught pointing and mouthing "*He likes you*" to the girl in a blue Chevy, you were mystified that he didn't get mad.

And so you would spend a hot summer evening circling and looking, laughing and talking life while over the radio another band of Eagles convinced us all—"One of These Nights."

And, when a carload of engaging Eagles exited the parade, crossed the tracks and parked at Taco Bueno, you went, too, swaggering in under the pretense all was coincidental. Sometimes a daring bravado prevailed and you wound up at the same dark-stained picnic-style table—you and your friends on one side, she and hers opposite. Posting face looks in real time. Mostly you poked fun at the other's school just to keep the conversation going, but still it was a verbal dance requiring instant wit. You felt light-headed as you got up to leave and stepped back outside, dizzy from having plucked a possibility out of the evening air.

By the late 1970s the ritual of circling was slowing and soon disappeared altogether, just as the Drivateria itself did in 1998. But the groove left on the Abilene scene was etched too deep to have been forgotten. For thousands of past Abilene teens, the rite of passage known as Circlin' Mack's lingers; certainly it inflames an occasional longing to circle back, just once more. To return—deep into a Friday night—and go up North Second, to turn back down Green. To roll the windows down, to let the bliss of youth blow in your face. To again feel the Abilene summer wash over you as you turn up Shelton. To slowly roll past a Pontiac full—you are quite certain—of Eagle cheerleaders, bathed in red brake light, and know once again that innocent tingle as a dark-haired girl catches you square on, slowly sending out a smile, sitting primo in the back.

In 1990 Abilene was one of ten cities to be named an All-America City by the National Civic League, sparking considerable civic pride throughout the community—but also a little fun from a San Antonio newspaper columnist, as Abilene Reporter-News *writer April Nixon related.*

ALL-AMERICA FUN

APRIL NIXON

The recent hoopla over the All-America City award has set off a humorist who has been poking fun at Abilene for more than a decade. Roddy Stinson, a columnist for the *San Antonio Express-News,* has been writing tongue-in-cheek columns for years about "one of the most quintessentially chauvinistic cities in the state."

Stinson has been known to write, "I once suggested that the concept of hell was invented by an Abilene preacher who was trying to convince his flock that there was some place worse than West Texas."

Stinson's latest target is the city's winning an All-America City award a few weeks ago. In a recent column, Stinson stated that he must have been wrong about his previous criticisms of Abilene if the National Civic League had given the city the award. "Obviously," he wrote, "there is more to the city than dust storms, tumbleweeds, fundamentalists and the other scourges of West Texas."

One of the projects that won the award for Abilene was the attraction of the new maximum-security prison. "It's hard to understand why no one thought of it before," wrote Stinson. "Abilene is pretty much escape-proof. Once you leave the city limits, there is nothing but miles and miles of godforsaken wasteland and an occasional Campbellite church."

When contacted by the *Abilene Reporter-News*, Stinson said his columns were all in fun and he hopes Abilene residents took them in jest.

"Oh, I think Abilene is wonderful," Stinson said. "I might even retire there. You have a lot of churches and when I'm close to dying, I'd like to be closer to heaven."

From the first time his father, Tobe Christian, left him in charge of the barbecue restaurant that would someday bear his name, to the business's last day on July 30, 2011, Harold Christian served generations of Abilene families.

★———————————————————————————————★

THE LAST DAY AT HAROLD'S

GREG JAKLEWICZ

Anticipation. You almost could hear Carly Simon singing about it Saturday morning before eleven, when Harold's Pit Bar-B-Q was to open for perhaps the last time. As expected, folks were lined up outside, the earliest to arrive seated on a bench on the shady west side of the cinder block building.

Among the first through the front door, which was unlocked a few ticks past eleven, were Crystal Millican of Fort Worth and her buddy Kristin Brewer of Farmers Branch. Talk about anticipation. They got up just after sunrise, packed Kristin's six-month-old into the van and began their one-day trip west. Kristin had suggested coming to Abilene to eat at Harold's one last time.

By the time the two Abilene Christian University grads exited their van in the parking lot and smelled the cooking, they were ready for lunch.

Which didn't come quickly for anyone except the very first in line. From the front door to one of the tables covered with a red-and-white-checkered vinyl tablecloth, it was a good hour. Much of the final week, lines were out the door, around the building and sometimes to the field behind the restaurant on Walnut. With people waiting hours and hours to eat Friday, Russell Christian said the restaurant stayed open until 5 p.m. — two and a half hours longer than usual.

Those coming Saturday knew full well there would be a wait. But this is Abilene. It's something to do. Some brought umbrellas to block the hot sun. Harold's crew set out a cooler filled with iced bottles of water. No one seemed put out by the wait or the heat.

Many orders were to go, and many of those included a bottle of the restaurant's famous sauce. Smartphone cameras flashed and those lucky enough to get in quickly saw Harold himself. Still recovering from a stroke, he hasn't been able to stay long at the Pit.

Brandon McAuliffe was not shy about stepping behind the cash register and posing with Harold for a photo. McAuliffe was first in line, arriving a good seventy-five minutes before Harold's opened. He put on headphones and listened to music and texted his friends.

While others took home pounds of beef and quarts of cobbler, he left with a load of Harold's signature hot-water cornbread. "I have lots of memories," he said, looking at the restaurant that has operated in Abilene for more than fifty years.

Duwain Houston was second in line. He had waited until closing day to eat there for the first time since he heard the news that Harold's was shutting its screen door at 2:30 p.m. July 30, 2011. "I'm a Southern boy from Alabama. I love barbecue," he said.

Next were friends Jessica Thompson and Jennifer Oliver, who chose barbecue over a girlie lunch. It was Jessica's first time at Harold's. "No one ever told me about it," she said. "I've lived here since I was three." "Well," Jennifer said, "you're fixin' to find out."

They were there an hour early and passed the time talking. "That's not hard for us," Jessica said. Then she let it slip. Her sister's mother-in-law, she said, is a competitor. Who? "Betty Rose's," she said. "I feel like I'm cheatin' on her." Surely Betty R. would make an exception for Harold's.

Steven Santana looked fit and trim and ready for lunch. Must be all the walking he does delivering the mail. He said his former route included Walnut and the downtown area. "I ate at Harold's every day for thirteen years," he said. He'll always remember Harold's singing at the restaurant and his charity to those who had a death in the family.

Steven said that in Lubbock, a statue was erected to honor C.B. "Stubb" Stubblefield, who founded the popular barbecue joint and music venue Stubb's Bar-B-Q there. That was a few years after Stubb died. Steven told Harold recently a statue should be put up here, too. Not of Stubb, but Harold Christian.

"But I hope he lives to be a hundred," Steven said. Steven was to be joined for lunch by his wife, Gloria. She would've come early, too, but she was helping with a project at church.

"For lunch, they were serving barbecue," he said. "She told them, 'Sorry, I'm going to Harold's.'"

SETTING THE TONE
CHURCH & SCHOOL

First Methodist Church Abilene Collection

First Methodist Church completed in 1883

It shouldn't be surprising that Abilene would turn out to be a city known for its three church-related colleges and a church on virtually every corner. Although the ranchers who named the town envisioned it as a cattle center like Abilene, Kansas, they couldn't have been more prophetic. The name "Abilene" comes from the Bible, mentioned in the same chapter (Luke 3) as John the Baptist (not a Hardin-Simmons graduate).

Abilene's first church—First Presbyterian—was organized on February 27, 1881, more than two weeks before the town lot sale officially made Abilene a town. Before the year was out, Methodists and Baptists had also organized, and soon there were Episcopalian, Catholic, Lutheran, and black Baptist and Methodist worshippers. Baptists founded Simmons College in 1891; Church of Christ leaders, new to Abilene, organized what would become Abilene Christian College in 1906; and McMurry, the Methodist college, opened its doors in 1923.

The civilizing influence of the churches and colleges has long been noted. "Abilene is a church town," Fort Worth writer Silliman Evans observed in 1921. "The churches, the schools and the moral appeal have more influence in Abilene than any other consider-ations." That sentiment was confirmed almost three decades later by Jack Yeaman, writing for *Texas Parade* magazine. Calling Abilene a "family town," he noted: "Its churches inspire you. Not just their number or their size, but the hold they have on nearly everyone in the community."

Keeping that in mind, we present a few stories here specifically related to church and school—some serious, some not-so. But the pervasiveness of church and school, through the years, has also set the tone for other aspects of community life here, from politics and economics to sports and culture, even weather.

PARSON'S GIFT

JAY MOORE

Without a doubt, one of Abilene's greatest treasures is a gift brought back home from Europe in 1926. Curiously, it was a gift we didn't know we had until it was set down in our midst thirty years later. It took that long to build it.

It was after three summer months spent strolling the streets of England, absorbing the art and gardens of Italy and France and standing in architectural awe throughout Europe, that a fellow Abilenian returned in October of 1926 and brought with him—a beautiful building.

Six years prior, in 1920 (Friday, February 20, to be exact) a bespectacled, energetic thirty-year-old bachelor—standing barely over five feet—stepped off the T&P and into the life of Abilene, spending the next sixty years—the remainder of his days—in his adopted hometown. And it would be this Tennessee-transplant who would bequeath to Abilene a solemn gift.

Greeting him at the Abilene train platform was the secretary of the Radford Grocery Company, Mr. Ernest Batjer, who escorted the newcomer across North First and into the lobby of the Grace Hotel. Abilene's newest resident set down his bag and registered as a guest for three days. He had hoped for a longer respite but due to an oil boom in Eastland County the hotel was in high demand and three days was the best he could negotiate. (Years later he would quip that upon his arrival in Abilene, he was given "just three days Grace.") Taking up the pen, he signed the hotel register—Mr. Willis

P. Gerhart (the "P" for Piedmont). But, soon enough, as he imprinted his life on this city, he would be known to nearly everyone as, simply, Parson.

Parson he was, since he would live in a church parsonage for twenty years, but more accurately, he was Rector—Rector of Abilene's Episcopal Church of the Heavenly Rest. The parsonage was right next door to the church affectionately known as the Little Stone Church, located at North Third and Orange, as it had been since 1884.

He would move from the church parsonage in 1940 and astonish everyone with the reason. Abilene tongues were feverishly set a waggin' in October of that year when the fifty-one-year-old Parson returned from a church convention in Missouri and brought home a wife. The parsonage would be left behind as the Gerharts set up their family home on Highland Avenue.

But it was early in his tenure, after serving Heavenly Rest for just six years, that parishioners granted Parson a three-month leave to study in Oxford and to take in Europe in 1926. Visiting museums ignited an appreciation for art—an appreciation which would manifest itself in Abilene a decade later as he instituted an art museum, now known as The Grace.

He would also visit the great churches—Christ Church in Oxford, the cathedral at Canterbury, St. Paul's and Westminster in London, and Notre Dame in the heart of Paris. He would walk on the stone floors polished by the years; feel the craftwork in the finely-fitted, soaring colonnades. He would gaze at windows painted with the faces of saints. He would stand in naves of brightly scattered sunlight. And he would sit in silence where he would find the concert between architecture and serenity.

But it would be a pivotal trip to Chartres, fifty miles outside of the French capital, which would firmly imprint the young parson's mind with a sublime vision. Approaching Chartres, and visible from all directions, is a church; the Cathedral at Chartres dominates the rise in the heart of that ancient city—rightly crowning the city's highest point with a place of worship. It is an echo of reverence for the people of Chartres. A soaring sanctuary to hear God.

Parson Gerhart would never become a man of means. His home was modest and the car he drove for years was one given to him by parishioners. Those same good people often outfitted him with credit at local stores and bought his meals. The Wooten Hotel provided a room for him to pen his sermon each Saturday morning. His lack of material goods was famously self-inflicted as he gave away his coats, his money, his food, his kindness and, frequently, the spare bedroom. His charity was not focused on just his parishioners; it was cast out to any Abilenian in need. Parson not only lived "do unto others" but he wisely groomed goodness in others—often dispatching church acolytes on missions of mercy to ease hunger and sorrow and, in doing so, bestowing the gift of compassion on the unsuspecting errand boys.

Willis Gerhart was a cross between Mitford's Father Tim and Capra's George Bailey—always defender and friend, never judge or prosecutor. He was the kindly, somewhat unorthodox, little man who tucked daily reminders and notes into his hat band and who drove badly. Those who knew him well would claim that his sparkle-eyed demeanor masked a mischievous bent. The sort who could happily manipulate and who was not above annexing one of your many hospital room flower arrangements and transferring it down the hall to a patient with none.

One Abilene agnostic admitted to a church member, "That parson of yours is enough to make even me believe in God. That may be one of the finest specimens of gracious manhood I've ever met." And, when Parson stepped down as Rector after thirty-seven years, *Abilene Reporter-News* editor Frank Grimes paid him homage, writing, "He was welcome everywhere and he fit perfectly everywhere. He made no vain display of his high moral principles or his unshakeable integrity; he just lived them seven days a week, twelve months a year, twenty-four hours a day."

✶ ✶ ✶

As Heavenly Rest grew in the 1940s, the Little Stone Church was proving too snug. With First Baptist offering to buy the property, Parson gently persuaded his congregants to take them up on it. Needing a new location, Parson knew exactly the spot he wanted— not another downtown site crowded in amongst other denominational First Churches—but out in a neighborhood, specifically a neighborhood with a crowning elevation; a hill at South Sixth and Meander known as Alta Vista—High View—and the site of the old Legett Mansion.

To no one's surprise, Parson Gerhart did indeed get the Legett property in 1949 and—as only Parson could—convinced the people of Heavenly Rest to build a Gothic church, straight out of medieval Europe, right smack dab in the heart of Abilene up on a hill.

At a parish meeting in June of that year, he offered his reasons for taking on such a labor. Parson's mind must have travelled back to Chartres and Canterbury as he spoke, reminding parishioners that "Divine worship is most clearly known among lofty arches on piers of stone, shadowy vaults, golden light coming in shafts from windows painted with faces of saints and angels." He was describing the church he had kept tucked in the back of his mind for three decades. A church he had brought back to Abilene in 1926.

Parson had just one man in mind to design the new church and he wouldn't take "no" for an answer. He wanted Philip Frohman. Frohman was the architect of Washington's National Cathedral, which was a very full-time job, consuming fifty years of Frohman's life. But with a kindly persistence, Parson deftly spaced his calls and letters—knowing just when to stop short of irking and offending Frohman—before convincing him to give some of his attention to a hill in Abilene. To read a list of Frohman's architectural accomplishments and stumble across "Abilene, Texas" is to know there has to be a story buried there.

The construction job was seen as so complex that just one contractor dare bid. Oscar Rose was the sole person willing to gamble on erecting such a unique structure. Even in his years of building experience, he had not faced such a rare challenge. The church was not only Gothic in architecture but it was to be built as Parson wanted, "honest construction with no tricks, imitations, not pretense of any kind." So, the massive limestone walls would not be mere cladding for a steel frame, they would bear their own weight and rest on deeply dug foundations stacked high and wide with brick and stone, with many of the stones coming from the dismantled Little Stone Church. The flying buttresses would not be built as embellishments; they would keep the structure erect. Stone carvers from far away would need to be brought in to do their job just as the stonecutters of Chartres had done centuries before.

Parson saw to it that the builder incorporated a rock from Canterbury Cathedral as well as a brick from America's first church in Jamestown. He included a door panel from the first Episcopal congregation in Texas along with stone from King Solomon's quarry and others brought here from Mount Sinai. And he made sure that carved into the capital of one column was the likeness of Philip Frohman.

Finally, in 1956, following seven years of planning and building—and thirty years of dreaming—Parson's gift was set in our midst. The city's highest point was crowned with a solemn place of worship. Astonishingly, here, in the middle of our Abilene, stands a medieval-inspired church with elements from old English and Spanish architecture. Here is a church whose stone floors are slowly being polished by the years and where you can feel the finely fitted, soaring colonnade resting on massive foundations. Where you can stand in a scattered spectrum of Abilene sunlight. Where you can gaze at windows painted with angels. A place to sit in silence. An echo of reverence on top of a hill. A soaring sanctuary for hearing God.

THE ORIGINAL TONIGHT SHOW

JIM WILSON

On a night when everyone
was reasonably healthy
and you didn't have cause
to fear for your safety
a spring evening on the prairie
sleeping on the ground
next to the wagon
watching the universe light up
is probably why
you don't hear about
too many pioneer atheists.

STOP THIS COLLECTION NOW

(and Other Church Stories)

Colonel James H. Parramore, who had fought with the Texas Rangers, became a loyal and enthusiastic supporter of First Baptist Church and Simmons College. He contributed generously to both.

One Sunday in 1912 the pastor was seeking to raise $1,500 in a special collection after the Sunday sermon. Commitments went very well for about a thousand dollars and then there was a stall. While the pastor was appealing with fervor, Colonel Parramore rose and said:

"Dr. Coleman, I am hungry and I think everybody else here is too. If you will stop this collection now, I will pay the unsubscribed part."

"Oh no, we will not do that. You have already promised your part," the pastor said, and continued, "Now brethren, we must not leave this burden to Colonel Paramore. Let's raise this money here and now."

"Dr. Coleman," the veteran ranger and cattleman said, "I stated a moment ago that if you would stop this collection now I would pay the unsubscribed part. If you are going on with the collection, I will withdraw my offer."

Whereupon the collection ended. —Rupert N. Richardson, *This I Remember*

During a long drought, there were prayer meetings for rain at the various churches in town.

One night it was at the Presbyterian Church and gentle, much-beloved Dr. Knox opened the meeting by asking the Heavenly Father "to send the gentle rains of heaven upon the parched and thirsty earth."

Then he called on Colonel Locke, who bounded to his feet, shut his eyes tight and in loud, forceful tones said, "Oh, God, with all due respects to Dr. Knox, what West Texas needs is a good FOUR INCH rain." —Ruth Gay, *Abilene Reporter-News*

When he was a student at Abilene Christian College, John Stevens preached at a congregation in Brownwood to help pay his tuition. Stevens didn't have a car and hitchhiked from Abilene to Brownwood for his Sunday preaching duties.

Once he caught a ride from an innocent looking man and woman. When John climbed into the back seat and made himself comfortable, the man started the car and announced he was leaving his wife. Then the man's wife came into view. She was running down the street with a pistol in her hand. "Everybody duck!" the man shouted as he hit the gas pedal.

On another hitchhiking trip to Brownwood, Stevens discovered too late that the driver was gulping whiskey. The bottle leaked on the seat and soaked John's suit. When he walked into the Brownwood church building to meet with the brethren, he loudly announced, "It's not in me; it's on me." —David Ramsey, *The ACU Century*

I was a guest speaker in Abilene, Texas, at a beautiful church, leading a three-day series. We had concluded our last event, a gathering for senior citizens. A tall, regal-looking elderly gentleman, age eighty-two he said, came down the aisle with his beautiful wife.

"Nine years ago, Preacher," the man said, "my wife died from a long and awful bout with cancer. So I sat there hour after hour, day after day, glumming and glooming. I was scolding the Lord, too. Night after night, same song, next verse: miserable me.

"One evening as I was up to my usual negatives, I suddenly came to myself. I got up from the couch and said out loud, 'This has to stop. I'm hurting no one but myself. I'm living in a miserable world of my own making. Disliking everyone and everything, including myself. Maybe the Lord, too.'

"I went immediately to the telephone and dialed a lady I had dated once or twice. Without even saying who I was, I roared into the phone: 'DO YOU WANT TO GET MARRIED?'

"To which the sweet little voice answered, 'I most certainly do. May I ask who's calling, please?'" —Charlie Shedd, *I'm Odd, Thank You God*

R. L. Paschal, for whom Paschal High School in Fort Worth is named, taught at Simmons College from September 1892 to December 1893. He reminisced on those days in a letter to Dr. Rupert Richardson in 1940, including these vignettes.

RECOLLECTION OF SIMMONS COLLEGE

R. L. PASCHAL

I reached Abilene by train from the east early in September 1892. I found Rev. W. C. Friley and three beautiful daughters at the train to meet me. Others, numerous enough to populate a large town, were there also to see the train go by. This train then, with the exception of a telegraph line, was the only means of communication with the outside world.

After Mr. Friley had received his mail, we drove out to the college, about one and a half miles from the railroad station. The houses extended about half a mile north of the station. On the east of the street were the Presbyterian and the Baptist churches. The streets were not paved, but there were board sidewalks as far as the houses extended. A few blocks to the west the rather pretentious home of J. H. Parramore was pointed out.

As soon as we had left the city, we entered a village of quite another sort—that of the prairie dogs. It was in a mesquite grove extending nearly half a mile along the road and perhaps nearly the same distance east and west. At first glance, I saw the prairie dogs busily engaged in eating grass or grass roots. Then the sentinels, who were standing up, gave the danger signal, when all went scurrying to their holes, where they sat barking at us. As we drew very close to those beside the road, they would go down into their holes with a growl of annoyance.

The cistern at the college was at times exhausted of its supply of water, when water had to be supplied from tanks. Later in the year Mr. Friley determined to put down a well. He wanted to drill where he was sure to get water, and fresh water at that. He told me of his purpose to get a man to witch for water. In vain, I tried to argue him out of it. A fine old gentleman from Roby by the name of Dr. Keiffer was sent for.

A student, Isaac Patterson, said he had the ability to witch for water also and got him a forked plum tree switch. He located water a few steps in front of the boys' barracks, which had been built on the grounds, and said fresh water could be found at a depth of one hundred feet. He drove down a little peg, which he covered with sand.

The next morning Dr. Keiffer came. He said he had no confidence in witching but that the switch would turn down in his hands despite any effort to prevent it—always at the same place on repeated trials even if he were blindfolded. The first place he tried was where Patterson had witched the afternoon before. The end of the switch turned down. He gave it a smart swing downward and then held it until the vibrating end came to rest. Then he scratched away the sand and found Patterson's peg driven there the afternoon before.

I do not know whether water could have been found there or not. Dr. Keiffer made another location nearer the college, where he said the switch indicated that fresh water could be reached at a depth of one hundred feet, and Mr. Friley had a hole drilled there. It was a "duster."

Soon after the opening of the college, a baseball team of our students, with Ross Douglass as captain and Quincy Lowery as pitcher, played a game with a team of city boys on a diamond south of the railroad somewhere in the eastern part of the city. We won this first game. The next spring there were several games.

Frank Kelly explained a defeat of our team in one game by the elusive curves of the opposing pitcher. Mr. Friley told Frank that it was mathematically impossible to throw a curved ball. Frank replied, "I know nothing of the mathematics of it, but I do know that if you had faced that pitcher you would have no doubt about his curve balls."

Mr. Friley's physician advised outdoor exercise for him. He bought a Winchester rifle and drove about the prairie and shot jackrabbits. At times he would ask me to accompany him on these hunts. He was a fair marksman. Jackrabbits and wolves had not yet deserted their ancient haunts and were frequently seen in the neighborhood of the college.

Mrs. Friley had some chickens which roosted in trees to the northeast of the building. Wolves would come in the early morning before day, lie down in hiding until the hens came off the roost at daybreak, when each would grab a hen and make off.

One morning Douglass Friley, who slept in the attic on the third floor, heard a hen squall. He jumped up, grabbed his father's Winchester and ran to the window and saw a wolf running away with a hen about one hundred fifty yards away. He drew a bead on the wolf. The ball hit the wolf in the back of the head, and he keeled over dead. Douglass was a proud boy and had every right to be.

Mrs. Friley and Mrs. Thatcher [wife of Professor Thatcher] were pretty good doctors, able to diagnose the various physical troubles of the girls.

One morning one of the girls who attended some kind of party the night before came to my class making a terribly wry face. She said, "Mr. Paschal, I'm unprepared. I am feeling bad this morning. I went to Mrs. Thatcher and asked her to excuse me from class. She felt of my pulse, looked down my throat, and then mixed up some quinine and some brown truck and poured a teaspoonful on my tongue [the "brown truck" was probably rhubarb]. Oh you don't know how bad it tasted. She then ordered me to report to class, saying that if I did not feel better soon to come back and she would give me another dose."

Word was passed around among the other girls. They had fewer complaints after that.

For the first fifteen months, the college was not a financial success. We were in the midst of the panic of '93. In December 1893, Mr. Friley told me that he could no longer pay my salary, already several months in arrears. So armed with recommendations from him and from Dr. H. T. Harrington, then president of the board, I came to Fort Worth.

On January 22, 1894, I became principal of a Fort Worth school and served in that capacity for forty-one years, when I retired as a principal of the high school now named after me.

Abilene Christian University traces its origins in Abilene to 1906 and a fortunate gust of West Texas wind.

A TIP OF THE HAT TO ACU

DON H. MORRIS and MAX LEACH

A. B. Barret came from Tennessee to Oklahoma and Texas in 1903 to preach, and the idea began to "jell" for a Christian college in rapidly growing West Texas. In going over prospective sites, Barret narrowed the field down to three locations: San Angelo, Ballinger and Abilene.

He took a T&P train out to Abilene, and since it was nearly an all-night trip, took a berth. Being able to sleep well under most circumstances, Barret slept right through Abilene to Sweetwater. He woke up in time to get off at Sweetwater and catch the first train back to Abilene. He said that when he saw Abilene, he was convinced it would be a "mighty good place" for the school.

However, not wanting to make a snap judgment in such a serious matter, he decided that he also should survey San Angelo and Ballinger.

To get to San Angelo, he rode a "bobtailed" train, consisting of one or two passenger cars tied to the end of a freight train. Being a man of action, Barret found it necessary to move around during the train trip and went to the coupling platform at the end of the passenger car to get a better view of the scenery. Underestimating the power of the West Texas wind, Barret suddenly saw his one and only hat go sailing off in one direction while the train kept merrily sailing on in the other.

In 1906 for a man to go hatless to a business appointment would be equivalent to his going to one today shirtless. It just wasn't done. On arriving in San Angelo, Barret found that he was really in a tight spot. He had only fifty cents more than enough to pay for his fare back to Denton, and he had to have a head covering of some kind before he met with the committee concerning the establishment of the school. So he took his extra fifty cents and bought a cap.

In those early years of the twentieth century, caps were for children, not men. Occasionally a man of adult years would be seen wearing a cap, but he certainly belonged to a peculiar fringe.

"All the time I was talking to the committee," Barret related years later, "I had the feeling of a lack of warmth there. That is, they were definitely cool to me and so to my proposition. I think that they must have thought that a man who didn't know any better than to wear a cap wouldn't know enough to run a school."

So it might have been San Angelo Christian College all those years instead of Abilene Christian College if the wind hadn't snatched brother Barret's hat, or if there had been more than just a lone fifty-cent piece over his fare back to Denton in his pocket.

In Ballinger, Barret found the committee "rarin' to go" when he put his proposition before them, cap and all, but during his stay there he had consumed some of Ballinger's water. He didn't like it. On his way back to Denton, he became convinced that Abilene was the place.

Childers Classical Institute, the forerunner of Abilene Christian University, opened in September 1906.

McMurry University opened in 1923 to a "record attendance" of about two hundred students and a host of proud local dignitaries.

THE FIRST DAY AT MCMURRY COLLEGE

PAUL D. LACK

The rain of the previous day cooled the air on Thursday morning, September 20, 1923, as the cars from the city and many parts of West Texas rolled out to the far reaches of southern Abilene and sought parking places close to the "magnificent" new administration building, the grander of the two permanent campus structures of the new Methodist institution. Visitors caught the air of excitement as they filed into the building past some of the two hundred students who chattered nervously while jostling for positions in the Registrar's office to arrange their class schedules.

The number who came to enroll seemed impressive rather than sparse; in typical booster fashion the Abilene *Daily Reporter* described it as a "Record Attendance." Editor Frank Grimes strained to hear the first word spoken when J. W. Hunt stood at ten o'clock to begin the proceedings. "Now, Ladies and Gentlemen," said the President, and the reporter concluded that "now" provided an "ideal motto for Abilene's newest educational institution because its conception, its construction and its fruition wholly eliminated the numbing presence of procrastination."

Actually, the students had the first word. Perhaps anticipating an excessively solemn celebration, they gathered and rent the air with their college yell before Dr. Hunt could make his historic utterance.

Local dignitaries delivered the major addresses and also helped set the tone that dominated the school for the next few years. In his welcome, Mayor Charles Coombes paid tribute to President Hunt and proclaimed grandly that the opening of McMurry began a "new epoch" in southern Methodism and in the intellectual life of Abilene. "I am glad this institution stands foursquare with the Old Jerusalem Gospel and the Bible of our Fathers." Earlier, in a speech to students, he had described Abilene as the ideal setting for such an institution because it was a city of churches, free "from vice in every form." President J. D. Sandefer of Simmons College followed the mayor with a mainly upbeat address, predicting a great future for McMurry. And then, as if in warning, he spoke of the troubles and struggles of his institution in its early years.

Abilenians who read about the opening ceremony in the evening paper encountered, too, other stories—of bootlegging, controversies about "Bobbed Locks" for women, articles of the "Shortcomings of Modern Boys," and of demonstrations by the Ku Klux Klan. Those who had been following the headlines in even a passing manner knew too that the mayor had exaggerated the purity of the local environment. Though Abilene may not have roared as much as other communities during the "Jazz Age," in 1922 the city police commissioner had warned of threats to the city's "reputation of being a moral upright Christian town."

As a leader of the religious establishment, President Hunt shared these concerns, which he viewed as part of a dangerous trend toward modernism and secularism. He believed that McMurry College would help fulfill what an associate called Hunt's "dream of an empire of purity." McMurry, in his vision, would provide "that closer relation to God among its students through Biblical training in the classroom and the wholesome influences of a strictly religious environment."

TOO MUCH JAZZ AND NOT ENOUGH JESUS

GERALD McDANIEL

In 1920 when the Eagles, a local semi-professional baseball team, tried to increase its earnings by playing on Sunday afternoons, the preachers sent up such a hue and cry that the idea was dropped. Babylon would not come to Abilene. But the Jazz Age spirit could not be suppressed that easily.

On the night of Friday, September 30, 1921, the local Masonic Lodge sponsored a street dance on Cypress between North 2nd and 3rd. The pulpits of the city resounded with denunciations, not only of the street dance but the portents it showed of future sin.

Most vociferous in denouncing it was Dr. Millard Jenkens of the First Baptist Church, who claimed that he was not upset with dancing per se, though we suspect he was, but by its being done on public property. For him it showed "a spirit of Bolshevism [and] the beginning of doom." Dr. Jenkens preached, "The city is paving the way for Sunday picture shows followed by a public dance pavilion from which the notes of the jazz would float into church windows as the sons and daughters went off to Hell."

Dr. W. O. Dallas told his congregation at First Christian that the modern dance was the first step to prostitution and that public dancing would allow "the lowest down rankings of the earth to dance with the very best people."

The one clear message from all the city pulpits was that such public immorality was even more degrading in a city that prided itself on its social morality. The Jazz Age had come to Abilene. The question in 1921 was: What would Abilene do about it?

By 1923, the moral decay had become so threatening to the status quo that eleven Abilene preachers—four Methodists, three Baptists, two Presbyterians, one Disciples of Christ, and one Church of Christ—joined their voices in a public resolution, a "Jeremiah ad" against the sins of the modern world, or as a more slogan-conscious Abilene preacher had put it a couple of years earlier in his sermon titled "Too Much Jazz and Not Enough Jesus."

Heading the list was the modern dance, condemned as "revolting and disgusting to the spiritually-minded." Then came gambling, especially among women playing cards for prizes. Drinking came third. Fourth, the most modern of the evils, joyriding, tempted innocent girls to their ruin, miles from the city. Last were indecent shows.

There is no way, of course, to discern just how much good this resolution did toward stemming the tide of evil, but at least these eleven could rest assured that the city would not continue unwarned and unscolded down the primrose path.

Probably no dog in Abilene was more celebrated than the pup Fritz, who became widely known around the Simmons College campus as Dam-it.

DAM-IT THE DOG

RUPERT N. RICHARDSON

In January 1920 Simmons College suffered its great loss in the death of Dam-it, the college mascot.

Brought from the east side of town as a pup in 1916 by Gib Sandefer, Fritz, the pup, grew up with the class of 1920. How he got his un-Baptistic name is still a matter of speculation. I used to suggest that, since the name came about the time his tail went, the name was in keeping with the thoughts that must have welled up in his canine brain when he was deprived of that appendage.

The dog was a natural clown. He was taught to retrieve sticks and rocks; then for good measure he began to carry rocks around, the bigger the better it suited him. He would attach himself to a certain student at certain times each day, go with that student to class or chapel, and lay himself down at the same spot consistently day after day. At times in chapel or in class he would go to sleep, his jaws would relax, the rock would roll out with a clatter, he would awaken and leap for the rock, and there would be still more commotion before he had it firmly in his jaws again and had lain down. In class he would sometimes utter a sort of yawn and groan that imitated almost perfectly the exaggerated performance of a person advertising the fact that he was bored.

Why did we put up with such nonsense? one naturally asks. The fact is that everybody was having so much fun out of the dog that any talk of suppressing or eliminating him would have created a veritable riot. Dam-it just belonged. In any college crowd he had as much liberty as a newspaper photographer. He went where he pleased, did what he pleased, and was especially in evidence at pep rallies and games, where his barking contributed to the performance.

But in the third week of January 1920 the delightful mascot was seized with pneumonia and died in less than seventy-two hours.

News of his death spread over the campus as a blanket of sorrow. His fellow classmen, the seniors, arranged for a funeral, freshmen uncomplainingly dug the grave, in the center of the campus. The band led the funeral party, playing an appropriate funeral march, and the procession proceeded to the grave. The greater part of the faculty and students were present. Four seniors served as pall bearers. Class chaplain Ira Harrison delivered the funeral oration, speaking from the text "Every Dog Has His Day."

Telegrams of consolation were received from Dallas, Austin, Fort Worth, and other places. The dog's death inspired at least three poems that were published in the *Brand*. Typical is this verse:

Dam-it, old dog, we bid you farewell.

We loved you much and you loved us, tis said.

We're sad that you no longer with us dwell;

We all say, 'dam-it! Dam-it's dead.'

The plain marble slab that marked the canine's grave was roughly used by souvenir hunters and vandals. About 1950, when nothing was left of it save a few fragments, Merle McCasland, an alumnus who had attended the mascot's funeral, paid for the metallic plate that is now firmly fastened to the huge limestone rock sunk flush with the earth.

In a worthy effort to replace the lamented all-college dog, the senior class presented the college with "Twenty," a well-bred young Dalmation; but the student body took little interest in the new dog. There could be no successor to Dam-it.

Prof Bynum, credited with organizing the first high school marching band in Texas while at Abilene High, later conducted the McMurry College band for twenty-six years. The band hall at McMurry is named for him.

THE FIRST HIGH SCHOOL BAND

BILL WHITAKER

Six days before turning ninety, Raymond T. "Prof" Bynum conducted the combined Abilene and Cooper high school bands during public school convocation ceremonies.

That little fact should surprise no one acquainted with Prof. If the regal-seeming gent generally credited with pioneering the institution of high school marching bands across the Southwest has any biorhythms at all, they likely keep time to "Stars and Stripes Forever."

Other than convocations and the occasional Fourth of July concert, when he's invited back into the limelight for as long as it takes to conduct John Philip Sousa's most rousing American march, Prof carries on a quiet routine.

Although he still has the proud demeanor about him he's always had, he also displays an ability to poke fun at himself. Sometimes he suggests his success in the realm of area band music—including two decades of conducting Abilene High's band—was just a lot of luck and a lot fewer sour notes than one might've naturally expected. After all, the only instrument he had in his home growing up was, he said, an Edison phonograph. When, as a young high school Spanish teacher, he agreed to form and lead Abilene High's band in 1926—the first all-school band in Texas and probably the entire Southwest—Prof couldn't even read bass clef on the sheet music.

What little experience Prof had in band came at Hardin-Simmons University, then Simmons College. "The director didn't know anything more than we did," he said, recalling his student years there from 1922-26. One of the guys said to me, 'Why don't you play in the Cowboy Band?' and I said, 'I don't play an instrument.' And he said, 'Yeah, but most of us can't play, either!'"

Raymond was given an old, beat-up bass horn, but whenever one of the football players was free, he took over the horn and Raymond had nothing at all to play. Eventually, Raymond's dad—a teacher— helped procure him a saxophone. "After that," he quipped, "I was doomed to the sax.

"I had no lessons," he recalled. "I was just self-taught. I sat next to a kid named Austin, and when we played, it sounded real good. And when he stopped playing, it didn't sound so good."

Prof even admits his reason for organizing Abilene High's band was less than noble.

"Back then, Abilene High football games were played at Simmons, and there was a fence around the field and all the male teachers were supposed to keep the kids from climbing over that fence. Well, I was 135 pounds, and if some big ol' boy your size climbed over that fence, I'd say, 'Hey, you can't do that!' Well, he'd say, 'Who says?' and I'd say, 'Well, you're not supposed to climb over that fence.' I think that's why I started band, so I wouldn't have to do that anymore."

Prof said he decided to introduce marching after seeing some of the ridiculous pursuits in play at halftime. "At halftime at the Abilene High football games, the pep squad would come out and march and do a snake dance. And at Hardin-Simmons at halftime, they had what they called a shirt-tail parade. They'd let their shirt-tails out and run around the field. It wasn't very exciting except maybe for those who were doing it. They thought they were really whooping it up."

Prof scored many firsts during his early days with the Abilene High School Band—among them, ensuring the band didn't have to pay admission to play at the games.

He remembered, on one occasion, Superintendent R. D. Green becoming irked by the band's tracking mud into the school during a rehearsal. "We just won't have band if we can't do any better than that!" Mr. Green proclaimed.

"Band was kind of a stepchild," Prof said.

Prof said he enjoyed his days teaching band, both at Abilene High and another twenty-six years at McMurry University. He doesn't claim he ever became a great musician or even a good one, but he always had a keen understanding of what crowds might enjoy.

"You know, when I got up that band [at Abilene High], we'd play at ball games, but we couldn't begin till the second quarter because our main cornet player was the only one who could play well enough to know exactly what he was playing. The rest of 'em would just kind of follow along. Well, he'd take advantage of that and never show up on time!"

Douglas Fry, band director at ACU from 1953-69, led the band in a concert at the end of his first year that would not soon be forgotten.

HOWITZER ON THE HILL

JOHN C. STEVENS

The most spectacular band concert in the history of Abilene Christian University took place on Friday evening, May 21, 1954. The place was Sewell Auditorium. The band was the Wildcat Band—not yet known as The Big Purple. The director was Douglas "Fessor" Fry. It was the end of Fry's first year as band director. A 1940 graduate of the college, he had been hired away from Brady, Texas, high school, where he had won all sorts of honors for his high school band.

Fry knew how to run a band. He had organizational skills and discipline. He knew how to develop a good marching band for halftime at football games. He also had an outstanding concert band, and this was his first spring concert at ACC. If some people had been making the decisions, it would have been his last spring concert.

On the day of the program, the *Optimist* [student newspaper] carried a short notice: "The ACC Wildcat Band will present its spring concert, Friday, May 21. Both heavy and lighter types of music will be played." Little did the campus newspaper know how "heavy" it would be. One of the numbers was Tchaikovsky's "1812 Overture." The reporter did not know that the grand climax, with sounds of cannon fire in Moscow, would not be the usual rolls of drums but the real thing.

Fry had made a deal with a local unit of the National Guard—the 131st Field Artillery of the 36th Division—to set up a 105-millimeter howitzer at the rear of Sewell Auditorium. He had two cousins—Neil and David Fry—who were members of that unit and who had special responsibilities. David, with a walkie-talkie, was stationed off-stage with the conductor in view. Neil, with a walkie-talkie, was outside with the gun crew. As the concert band reached the exact point for the thunderous response, the conductor gave the signal to his off-stage man, who relayed it to the gun crew outside. The result was described in the next issue of the *Optimist*, under the headline "Novel Band Concert Creates Disturbance."

"To some it was the end of the world; to some it was a Russian attack; to some it was an explosion in the Science Building; and to some it was the dormitory going up in flames.

"And yet to many others it was the climax of a marvelous band concert in Sewell Auditorium. Thanks to the nine booming sounds from the National Guard cannon, last Friday's program was considered extremely effective.

"Indeed it was! Whole dormitories shook. Windows fell out. Babies were awakened. Parents ran out in the street. Cars stopped. Neighborhood people called city police sixteen times and the *Reporter-News* about ten times. As far as attracting attention, the concert was a howling success. We only hope most of the reaction was favorable."

Not all of the reaction was favorable. Rex Kyker of the Speech Department, who lived a half-block south of the big noise, had just succeeded in getting his children to sleep, only to have them jarred awake by the noise. He proposed organizing a march on the president's home with a petition to fire Doug Fry immediately. However, he soon got over it and became a strong supporter of Fry and his band.

Some window panes in McDonald Dormitory, Julia Hall, and the semicircular formation over the door in the east end of the auditorium had to be replaced. Bursar Lawrence Smith had them installed and charged the band's budget. The howitzer was firing blanks instead of projectiles, but inevitably remnants of the bags that held the powder came out and started some grass fires where the shreds fell. They were quickly extinguished by guardsmen.

So ended Bonaparte's takeover of Moscow, and so began his retreat. Neither Fry nor any of his successors tried a repeat of that notable performance.

Tipi Village has been a popular McMurry tradition and attraction for more than sixty years.

A TIPI TRADITION

LORETTA FULTON

Despite an exploding bonfire years ago and, more recently, an NCAA ban on the mascot name "Indians," McMurry University's unique homecoming, with its centerpiece Tipi Village, endures.

In 2011 the university marked the sixtieth anniversary of Tipi Village, the collection of authentic Native American dwellings erected by student groups each year in Wah Wahtaysee Park on campus. The scene is easily viewed during homecoming at the corner of South 14th Street and Sayles Boulevard.

The village, first built in October 1951, has attracted thousands of students from Abilene and area schools to learn the history behind each structure and the tribe it represents. It also attracted photographers from *Life* magazine in October 1956 and *Texas Highways* magazine in October 1982.

Jack Darnell was a freshman at McMurry in the fall of 1951 and remembers the first Tipi Village. Like other McMurry alumni, Darnell, an Abilene resident, was disappointed when the NCAA ruled that McMurry had to drop its Indians mascot or be prohibited from hosting postseason athletic events. McMurry's founder and first president, Dr. J. W. Hunt, grew up on a Kaw Reservation in Oklahoma Territory, where his father was a government physician. Hunt chose the name "Indians" out of respect, and alumni said that's why it was disappointing that the NCAA took the name away.

"That's what we tried to emulate," Darnell said of Hunt's respect. "There was nothing that was negative toward the Indian culture."

McMurry chose to go five years without a mascot before unveiling the "War Hawk" in 2011. Homecoming materials feature the fierce-looking hawk with the motto "Traditions Reign, Spirit Unchanged" underneath.

Perhaps almost as threatening to the survival of Tipi Village as the NCAA ruling was the explosion in 1975 that injured ten people and rattled windows on campus and in neighborhood buildings.

An Abilene Fire Department lieutenant said a lack of wind and high humidity apparently caused vapors from the igniting fuels to collect around the pile of wood. An arrow with a flare was fired from the top of Radford Auditorium, traveling along a wire to the bonfire. When the flare hit the bonfire, it was supposed to ignite the fuel. About ten people were injured, none seriously, by flying debris.

The idea for a "Reservation Theme" homecoming, with "one big teepee" encircled by smaller ones, was adopted in October 1951 by McMurry's Student Council. Darnell, who was a freshman that year, remembers that the idea wasn't enthusiastically embraced at first. "There was a little bit of consternation at the outset," he said, "because at that time everybody had a bonfire and the Tipi Village idea was something totally new." But by the time the tipis started going up, "everybody was on board," with student organizations competing to see which group could erect its tipi the fastest or which structure was most authentic.

Just five years after it started, Tipi Village had grown in stature to the point that *Life* magazine sent photographers to campus for a photo spread under the heading "Texas Blows Its Top Over Football." More fame came to McMurry in 1982 when *Texas Highways* magazine carried a story and photos under the heading "Tepees Rise Again."

It wasn't until 1994 that the university published a "Tipi Village Handbook" that standardized the spelling of "Tipi Village." The handbook noted that, "In regard to the spelling of 'tipi,' a universal spelling of 'tipi' will be used. 'Tipi' is a Sioux word formed of 'ti,' which means to dwell or live, and 'pi,' meaning 'used for.' "

Authenticity has been a hallmark of Tipi Village from the beginning. The handbook states that, "The purpose of Tipi Village is, and was begun, to commemorate the American Indian with dignity and integrity." Native American judges are chosen to evaluate the structures each year. Each structure represents a different tribe, and a student from the sponsoring organization relates the history and culture of that tribe to schoolchildren who tour the village.

A PRAYER FOR ABILENE

GLENN DROMGOOLE

(To the tune of O Waly, Waly.
Chorus arranged by Greg Young)

O, Lord, we ask your grace on all
Those here and those foreseen;
Make this a place where wisdom reigns,
That's our prayer for Abilene.

Give us great joy and peace of mind,
Let kindness rule supreme;
Make this a place that you ordain,
That's our prayer for Abilene.

    A prayer for Abilene,
    A prayer for Abilene,
    Make this a home for hopes and dreams,
    That's our prayer for Abilene.

O, Lord, bestow on us your love,
Young and old and in between;
Make this a place your love sustains,
That's our prayer for Abilene.

We ask your blessing on our town,
Let service be our theme;
Make this a place that is humane,
That's our prayer for Abilene.

A prayer for Abilene,
A prayer for Abilene,
Make this a home for hopes and dreams,
That's our prayer for Abilene.
That's our prayer for Abilene.

PRAIRIE RENAISSANCE
ARTS & CULTURE

Slim Willet, 1953, songwriter of "Don't Let the Stars Get in Your Eyes"

The long-standing belief of the 1800s was that the Wild West began beyond the 100th meridian. Past that imaginary line, lawlessness prevailed, lascivious lifestyles were lived out and culture came to a screeching halt. One-hundred degrees marked the place where land turned from green to tan and society switched from cultured to crass. Although Abilene lies just shy of the 100th longitude (99 west, to be exact), the hardy souls who dared to carve out a life at the edge of the frontier packed in some strong aesthetics along with their household goods.

As Katharyn Duff has noted, literature, music, dancing and the social niceties were cultivated in Abilene right from the start. The early sound of cowboy gunfire was soon replaced with a community band serenading the dusty streets of Abilene. The ladies quickly formed what is recognized as the oldest literary society in Texas, the Shakespeare Club. It would be the daughters of those early pioneers who would promote the idea of a library into existence and, in turn, their daughters who would gracefully give us an art museum.

And more recently, the Center for Contemporary Arts, the National Center for Children's Illustrated Literature, Frontier Texas!, and ArtWalk have joined the Abilene Philharmonic Orchestra, Abilene Community Theater, and branch library locations as Abilenians continue to promote "Catclaw culture."

Of course there's culture, and then there's culture . . . with a beat: the champagne music of Lawrence Welk, the hillbilly swing of Fraley's Butane Boys and Slim Willet, the rockabilly rhythms of Elvis Presley, and the iconic couplets of a song entitled "Abilene."

Art and culture did indeed take root in the windswept soil out on the edge of civilization.

Katharyn Duff wrote a front page column for the Abilene Reporter-News *and was one of Abilene's best known historians and commentators.*

A BETTER PLACE TO LIVE

KATHARYN DUFF

Early Abilenians would never have used the now-popular expression, life style. That combination of words is only lately in vogue. But the notion that this town should make itself attractive physically and philosophically, financially and socially was popular among community leaders from the first days. It echoes from the oldest papers and speeches and publicity pieces. Pamphlets and broadsides sent to newcomers declared Abilene a good place to live. Promoters of civic improvements argued that their causes would make this a better place to live.

The urge of early Abilene to improve life style out on the dusty (and in some lucky years, muddy) prairie was natural for some. It was the town's good fortune to attract in its first years an unusually large number of educated men and women. Many were college trained. Many more were self-educated. There were enough of these two groups to create a community climate where even the unlearned respected schooling.

The urge to improve the town was not purely altruistic, however. All who helped organize schools, who supported the town band, who raised funds to get the Carnegie Library were not motivated solely by yearnings for culture. Rather, they saw such efforts as good business. The opera house, the little college that Baptists started out on the north end of town, the lending library, the band concerts—such as these set Abilene apart from other drab towns struggling to get started. Such causes as these were assets to dangle before immigrants eyeing this new country where rains were not tightly scheduled. And good business they proved to be, as good business as a Philharmonic Orchestra, an Abilene Community Theatre, a Fine Arts Museum, parks and schools and Civic Center and Coliseum proved later to be.

Pioneers who gathered for the town lot sale in March of 1881 laid down foundations on which community philosophy still rests. They organized churches. The first Abilenians, before they moved from tents into their first boxed houses, passed the hat and raised six hundred dollars to build a public school. While the one-room schoolhouse was being erected, classes were held in a tent pitched between Hickory and Cedar streets.

Right away these first Abilenians opted for law and order. When the community was two years old it incorporated and adopted a rigid code outlawing all sorts of rowdiness. In 1884 the town fathers hired John J. Clinton, former marshal of Dodge City, to see the law was enforced.

While establishing order, the townsmen also opted for the positive as well as the negative in life style. The first Abilenians enjoyed a party as well as their grandsons. And tastes varied then as now. While cowboys might head for a gambling session with town boys at one of the many saloons, other young bachelors imported a dancing teacher from Fort Worth to teach them new steps "so as to get away from the old square dance timed to hoe-down fiddle music."

Women had much to do with setting the cultural tone of the young town. The Shakespeare Club, still active, was formed in 1883. It is recognized by the Texas Federation of Women's Clubs as the oldest study club in the state. Other clubs interested in music, literature and art followed the first one. Through these organizations or through individual efforts the women promoted the lending library that grew into the Carnegie Library that grew into the present library. They supported the other arts, and saw that reluctant husbands did, too. Women began the first beautification project—a drive to "pen old Bossy," to get off the streets roaming cows that munched the flowers women were trying to grow.

The culture the first Abilenians began cultivating on Catclaw Creek was distinctive in one respect. It was a participant, rather than a mere spectator, activity. If Abilene had a town band, Abilenians had to play in it. If the local theater efforts survived, local folk participated.

In that respect, at least, Catclaw culture has not changed. It is still in many respects a participant undertaking. And such participation may make for a better life style. Certainly it makes this a better place to live.

'PRETTIEST TOWN I'VE EVER SEEN'

JOE W. SPECHT

Singers and song writers have long waxed poetic about the towns and cities of the Lone Star State, with the likes of Amarillo, Austin, Dallas, El Paso, Fort Worth, Houston, and San Antonio receiving numerous musical accolades. Few Texas burgs, however, have garnered more tuneful recognition than Abilene. And certainly the most famous song associated with the Key City of West Texas is "Abilene," as recorded by George Hamilton IV.

The story behind the tune that topped *Billboard*'s Hot Country Singles chart in 1963 (it also reached Number15 on the pop chart, *Billboard*'s Hot 100) is an engaging, if contradictory, one, and it is pieced together here with the assistance of Kees Vanderhoeven, the webmaster of a site devoted to John D. Loudermilk, one of the song's credited co-writers.

While the source of the original verse (or chorus) remains a matter of speculation, the couplet itself has been floating around in the air of the public domain for some time: "Abilene, Abilene, prettiest town I've ever seen/Women there don't treat you mean in Abilene." To these memorable lines, various other verses have been attached by a variety of performers.

"Abilene," in the version with which most listeners are famil-iar, first appeared on a Bob Gibson album, *I Come for to Sing*, in 1957. Now often overlooked, Bob Gibson was an important mover and shaker on the national folk music scene of the 1950s and early 1960s. His singing and performing style, on both twelve-string guitar and banjo, influenced numerous young folknicks, including Roger McGuinn and David Crosby.

Working out of Chicago, Gibson became acquainted with Lester Brown, the co-owner of the Gate of Horn folk club, and the two became friends, with Brown even filling in as Gibson's manager for a while. Lester Brown later recalled that he and Gibson were in New York City strolling around Washington Square Park when they ran into a fellow musician who was plunking on a banjo and "mumbling" something about "Abilene, Abilene, prettiest girl I've ever seen" or was it "Abilene, Abilene, prettiest town I've ever seen"? According to Brown, "[I] pulled Bob aside and told him to learn the chord progression, because [I] was going to write the rest of the lyrics."

When they returned to their hotel room, a bottle of cheap booze proved inspiration enough for two verses to flow from Lester's pen while he reclined in the bathtub. And the phrases about sitting alone each night watching "those trains roll out of sight" in a crowded city where "there ain't nothing free" are the ones that have stuck with the listening public ever since.

In his autobiography, *Bob Gibson: I Come for to Sing*, Gibson tells the story of the song's composition somewhat differently. Instead of the Big Apple, Bob recollects that he and Les were in Chicago killing time at the bar in the Gate of Horn, talking about a movie Gibson had seen on television. "It was Abilene [the actual name of the film is *Abilene Town*, a 1946 oater set in the Kansas railhead located at the end of the Chisholm Trail], and it starred Randolph Scott. Like all good Americans, I got most of my ideas from the movies, and then later from television . . . . All there was to begin with, was 'Abilene, Abilene prettiest town I've ever seen,' to which I added the verses as they are now, with Les Brown . . . ." Gibson concludes, "John Loudermilk's name is on the song, too, and it belongs there, but that's another story."

"Abilene" remained mostly neglected, however, until 1963 when entered the aforementioned John D. Loudermilk, a name now often identified with the song. In 1963 Loudermilk was well on his way to becoming one of Nashville's most successful songwriters, with credits that included "A Rose and a Baby Ruth," "Waterloo," and "Ebony Eyes"; plus he had a recording contract with RCA Victor. Loudermilk's association with "Abilene" began when he made a promotional stop with fellow RCA Victor artist George Hamilton IV at a radio station in Franklin, Tennessee.

While there, the disc jockey played Bob Gibson's "Abilene," which prompted John D. to advise George, "If you don't cut this, I will." Hamilton eventually decided to record the song, and Loudermilk was in the studio, although the session sheet filed with the musicians union does not list him as being present. Loudermilk remembers, "Though Chet Atkins was RCA's producer of record for the session, I basically arranged and produced it . . . . I worked the board from the control room."

George Hamilton IV cut "Abilene" on March 20, 1963. The song debuted on *Billboard*'s Hot Country Singles chart on June 15, 1963, and the next week arrived on *Billboard*'s Hot 100. "Abilene" remained on the country music play list for twenty-four weeks, including four weeks in the Number 1 slot, and fourteen weeks on the pop chart, topping out at Number 15.

Loudermilk's account of how his name became permanently linked to the song offers insight into what goes on behind closed doors in the Nashville music publishing business. Soon after George Hamilton IV recorded "Abilene," John D. received a telephone call from his publisher, Wesley Rose of Acuff-Rose, asking him to come over to the Acuff-Rose offices. There Loudermilk found Bob Gibson and Lester Brown in conference with Wesley Rose. "I was informed that they had made a deal whereby Wes would publish the song and my name would be added as writer . . . . Wesley would get all the publishing (half the royalties) and we three would divide the other half (the writer's share) . . . . we all shook hands, and that was the end of it."

In time, Loudermilk reached the conclusion that "the fairest way I could have been acknowledged and repaid for my efforts in helping the song become the hit it was would have been for Wes to recognize that I actually did the work of the publisher . . . . my royalties really should have come from the publisher's share." Nevertheless, Loudermilk copyrighted "Abilene" under his own name in 1963, and on his 1971 album, Vol. 1 *Elloree*, he again took sole credit for the song.

Lester Brown's explanation of exactly why Loudermilk garnered a share of the royalties diverges considerably from Loudermilk's. According to Brown, a friend alerted him to the fact that "Abilene" was racing up the *Billboard* charts. Brown then contacted his publisher, Acuff-Rose, to check on things. Only later did he learn a third name, John D. Loudermilk, had been added to the writer credits. In addition, a couple of words had been changed in the lyrics. Brown decided not to protest or take legal action because Loudermilk "played a more important role—he found the song and made it a hit." Conflicting accounts aside, one thing is certain. Lester Brown, Bob Gibson, and John D. Loudermilk ended up sharing composer credit for "Abilene." And it is apparent, too, that Brown and Gibson understood the significance of Loudermilk's involvement.

Since 1963, more than forty performers have covered "Abilene." Sonny James' version reached Number 24 on *Billboard*'s Hot Country Singles in 1977. Other interpreters include Academy Award-winning actor Walter Brennan talking his way through a rendition, Meridian Green (Bob Gibson's daughter) crafting a vampy, jazzy clarinet accompaniment to spice things up, and Josh Roy Brown (Lester Brown's son) tendering a most doleful rendition.

In later years, Bob Gibson tinkered with the words, substituting "people" for "women" as in "people there don't treat you mean." He attributed this to consciousness raising. "I got my act together, let me tell you. See I attended meetings of N.O.W.—that's the National Organization of Women .... You learn a lot—change a lot of your basic attitudes. You meet some great broads there, too, I'll tell you!"

As for the ultimate question—is "Abilene" about a town in Texas or Kansas—both Lester Brown and Bob Gibson were vague, even though Gibson said the song was inspired by the movie *Abilene Town*. When asked the question, Gibson's standard response was, "I don't know." At least that's how he answered until he performed at the Kerrville Folk Festival in 1978. Gibson recollected, ". . . the first time I got on that stage at Kerrville and sang 'Abilene,' and 5,000 Texans stood up and put their hands over their hearts, I knew right away I'd written it about Abilene, Texas!"

Two years later he finally came to town with a busload of Kerrville Folk Festival performers to play a benefit concert for the Hendrick Home for Children at the Hendrick River Ranch. *Abilene Reporter-News* entertainment editor Bill Whitaker had an opportunity to chat with Gibson, and the singer ruefully confessed he had never visited the Key City, or for that matter, Abilene, Kansas, either. When Whitaker inquired about writing "Abilene," Gibson rejoined, "Abilene—it's a great name. Things rhyme with it. It's a pretty name," and besides, he chuckled, "nothing rhymes with Chicago."

PIANO LESSONS

KATHARYN DUFF

Cultural endeavors required some imagination for early West Texans, living as they did in a desolate region of sandstorms and rattlesnakes. Many thought the way of life was no excuse for uncouthness. They simply made do, best way they could.

Mr. and Mrs. John B. Clack, uncle and aunt of Miss Tommie Clack, moved here by covered wagon two years before there was an Abilene. The wagon was packed with the necessities the family would need. Certainly, pianos and organs were not included, but Mrs. Clack was determined that her children would learn music.

Once the family was installed in a log cabin near Lytle Creek, she found a plank, painted on it a piano keyboard and set her children "to practice." She taught them the position of the notes, the timing, the chords. Since the plank was soundless, she sang so they would be familiar with the notes.

After a few crops were made, the family could afford an organ and, lo, the children already knew how to play it!

OLD MUSICIAN

MAUDE COLE

He plays the violin on Chestnut street;
Down by the crossing of a railway track.
Where cinder dust surrounds his twisted feet,
And needle pointed sun rays pierce his back.
He cannot see the faces, but can hear
The people as they hurry on their way,
And when their rhythmic footsteps patter near,
He lifts the violin in haste to play.

Old tunes, that he has learned long, long ago,
With trembling hands are drawn out mournfully:
"Tenting Tonight," "Sweet Home," and "Old Black Joe;"
But many pass who never seem to see
The bent old man, in ragged clothes, and blind,
Who echoes days the world has left behind.

WEDDING OF THE CENTURY

GERALDINE SATTERWHITE

It happened in 1926, but it's still remembered as the wedding of the century. And the local parties generated by the announcement that Abilene's Mildred Paxton was to become the bride of Texas gubernatorial candidate Dan Moody have not been topped in number, size or elegance since. "A maze of social affairs unprecedented for brilliance in the annals of Abilene society," the *Reporter-News* termed them.

Moody, who had become Texas' youngest attorney general at age thirty-one, had been dating Mildred, the daughter of longtime Citizens National Bank president George L. Paxton and Mrs. Paxton. He had proposed marriage and she had accepted. But fearing a bitter campaign to unseat Miriam A. "Ma" Ferguson as governor would subject a bride to a great deal of campaign flak, Moody suggested they postpone the wedding until after the election.

Mildred Paxton, who had been the *Reporter-News'* first society editor, would have none of it. The date was set, April 20 (Mildred's twenty-ninth birthday). The engagement announcement was to have come through Leltie Faucett, a friend of Miss Paxton's who had succeeded her as woman's editor. But news leaked out in Austin and the local paper was scooped on the story.

The wedding, although it drew political and social notables from all over, was Abilene's own production. A huge reception was hosted on the night of April 17 at the Abilene Country Club by Bernard Hanks, *Reporter-News* publisher, Mrs. Hanks and Leltie Faucett. They had expected a crowd, but not the one that turned out. Guests poured in, the food ran short, and crisis after crisis arose as the Simmons Cowboy Band played on.

Since Moody was in the midst of a political campaign, no invitations to the wedding at First Baptist Church were sent. "Everybody come," the *Reporter-News* had invited, and everybody did. The Paxton house was next door to the church, so the couple walked over.

To give Abilenians up-to-the-minute news of the wedding, Frank Grimes, longtime editor of the paper, and Howard Barrett had the front page made over. Wendell Bedichek, a young reporter who would later become managing editor, wrote a past-tense lead for the Associated Press describing the wedding, then went down to the church and climbed up to a south side window to see that things went as he had reported.

A happily-ever-after finale to the storybook courtship and wedding was the fact that Moody did indeed win the governorship.

Before performing at a concert in Abilene in 1974, the legendary band leader Lawrence Welk spoke with a writer for The Abilenian *about the time he lived and performed in Abilene in 1932.*

WHEN LAWRENCE WELK LIVED IN ABILENE

LINDA HONEA

"I'm kind of an unusual man in that I don't seem to remember the bad things," Lawrence Welk remarked in a pre-show interview, the lights surrounding his dressing room mirror a bright background for his words. "I seem to be a man that constantly thinks of the positive side, the good things. If something bad happens to me or if someone gets extremely mad at me, I won't remember what happened or why the person was mad in about three or four years."

His face turned thoughtful as his mind's eye focused inward on memories of a time long ago—The Great Depression. "Conditions were so bad in those years when we were in Texas that I don't remember very much—just a few little minor things," he said.

Welk and his then small band spent much of the Depression era in Texas, playing a series of engagements at the Baker Hotel in Dallas, the Hilton Hotel in Lubbock, the Hilton Hotel in Abilene, and the Texas Hotel in Fort Worth. In addition, they played for as many dances in the outlying area as possible.

Earl Guitar, Abilene rancher and businessman, was manager of Abilene's Hilton Hotel (now the Windsor) at the time. "Back in 1932 when Lawrence Welk and his band came into Abilene, his car had broken down, and they were stranded here," Guitar recalls. "Lawrence came into my office for a conference one day to see if there was anything they could do to earn their meals and rooms for a few days. There were six members in the band—all very clean-cut men. Two of them, including Lawrence, had wives with them. He said they needed a job badly.

"I told him that we could not pay him or his band a salary, but that we would furnish each of them a room and $2.50 per day for meals if they wanted to play during the evening meal at the hotel."

A meager offer? By today's standards, yes. In light of Welk's present reputation, yes. But Welk himself reminds us: "Things are entirely different now. Nobody knew us when we came into Abilene that time—just no one. We were completely new and fresh. When I came into Abilene, I came in completely broke. Earl Guitar, a very kindly sort of man, felt sorry for me and the rest of the boys and gave us room and board. Now today the folks may think that's horrible just to pay people room and board. For us, it was saving our life, so we looked at it in a little different sense.

"In those days, I slept later than I do today. I would usually sleep until eight or nine or ten o'clock in the morning," Welk smiled and locked his hands behind his head. "We were playing for lunch at the hotel until about 2:00 or 2:30 p.m. We rehearsed an awful lot in the afternoons, and then we would start up again in the evenings.

"In those days," he continued with a twinkle, "I didn't play golf. Today, whenever I have a little time, I sneak out and play golf—but in those days, I didn't!"

While Welk was busy meeting the people and playing the music they wanted to hear, Abilenians were quick to adopt this new group into their local scene.

"Lawrence and his band were very popular here," Earl Guitar affirmed, going on to reveal: "Our food business picked up so much that in two or three nights we had a waiting line and could not accommodate all the people. At the end of two weeks, we begged him to stay; so they stayed in Abilene for about six months. We were surely sorry when he left. In their spare time, they practiced continuously in the ballroom, and on the weekends they played for various dances in town and also in surrounding towns. The highest class of people came to hear them."

When Welk and his band left Abilene, the big time was still a long time coming in spite of local popularity.

"It took us longer to make the grade than any other band in the United States," he has said. "We didn't hit the big time until 1951 when we got on television in California. And we didn't get on coast-to-coast television until 1955. From 1927 to 1955—that's a long time."

BOB WILLS AND THE BUTANE BOYS

ARCHIE JEFFERIES with BETTYE PEARCE

While playing at dances, it was very common to have guys who were "feeling no pain" come up to the stage and ask if they could "sit in" with the band. Most would claim they'd played with Bob Wills or some other big band. At first I used to fall for their stories and invite them on stage, then get a big disappointment when they started to play or sing. I finally learned to make some excuse not to let them sit in.

It seemed like everybody always wanted to say, "I played for Bob Wills." When people asked me if I ever played for Bob, I'd answer, "No, but Bob once played for me." They probably walked away thinking that was a big lie. But I wasn't lying. It did happen.

For several years as the Butane Boys, we did our daily broadcast live on air. Around 1948, one of the announcers said, "Why don't you boys tape a week of shows so you can take a vacation?" The manager okayed it, and we set the recording session for a Saturday afternoon.

The radio studio was on the top of the Hilton Hotel. We got there about one o'clock, and one of the boys found out Bob Wills was staying in the hotel. Bob's band, the Texas Playboys, was to play that night at the old Camp Barkeley.

We were big admirers of Bob Wills and played his music at all our dances. One of the boys said, "Archie, why don't you go down to his room and see if he'll come up here and help us make the tapes?"

I said, "Bob wouldn't play with a bunch of country hicks like us." But they kept insisting so I said I'd try. I went down, knocked on the door, and he yelled, "Come in." Bob was in bed with just his shorts on. I told him what we were doing, and to my surprise, he said he'd be glad to come up and play with us. There in his natural state I saw that what I'd heard about his appearance was true. He was almost completely bald except for a few patches of bristles on top. When he got out of bed, I saw he had the biggest, most saggy stomach I had ever seen on a man of his size. He put on a corset, finished dressing and put on his hat.

He never mentioned his stomach but said, "I guess you noticed my hair, or where there should be hair. Tell you how that happened. When I first started out, I played medicine shows as a black-faced comedian. I used black greasepaint to cover my face and rubbed it way back on my high forehead so no white skin would show. Each night after I finished playing I'd go back to my room and be too tired and sleepy to wash it off, so I'd just take a towel and try to rub most of it off. What I was doing was clogging up the pores in my scalp, and after a while, the hair began to fall out. I'm very self-conscious about it—that's why I always wear a hat."

When he was dressed and ready to go, we went up the stairs to the studio. I introduced Bob to the boys, and we got started making those five tapes. Bob had brought his fiddle. First he'd play, then Popcorn [Earl Deatherage] would play, then they'd "twin fiddle" together. I was singing a lot of his songs, and he'd give that famous Bob Wills' "Ahhh, haaa," "Tell me more," "Let's evabody ride." I'd heard him do this on his record for years, and it was such a thrill that here he was doing it with me. After about two hours, we had the five tapes cut. But instead of quitting, we just kept playing.

With that big grin on his face and smoking his cigar, Bob seemed to be having the time of his life. We'd started about 1:30, and around 6:30 I said, "Bob, I sure hate to end this, but we've got to go about seventy miles to play tonight. He looked at his watch and said, "Lord, I didn't know it was that late. I haven't enjoyed myself this much in years. Our playing is so cut and dried now it gets to be a chore, but today we just let our hair down and got after it, doing tunes I haven't played for years."

I really liked Bob Wills, and he must have liked us because after that whenever Abilene people would go to one of his dances, he'd always say, "Tell ole Archie and Popcorn I said 'Hello.'" I didn't think at the time to get those tapes from KRBC, and it's too late now. But I'd give almost anything to have them today."

Long before she became Reporter-News *society columnist MizCheevus, Roy Helen Ackers was active in the city's social circles, where she crossed paths with legendary society editor Leltie Faucett.*

LELTIE FAUCETT AND MIZCHEEVUS

ROY HELEN ACKERS

Has Abilene always been social? This reporter would vindicate her positive answer with the following example:

The March 20, 1950, issue of *Life* magazine revealed the startling story of Abilene *Reporter-News* society editor Leltie Faucett, a sixty-three-year-old widow, as she enthusiastically covered assignments and delivered volumes of fascinating stories for the 55,000 people in Abilene, Texas (often viewed as the social center of the US!).

She and Eva May Hanks (co-owner of the paper with husband Bernard Hanks) as early as 1919 wrote social news and delivered it via buggy to the editor before she became the official society reporter.

While the big dailies from Fort Worth and Dallas could do their coverage of national news, the *Reporter-News* (circ. 36,000) went in heavily for local chitchat and rural items—making Leltie more than just a society reporter. In her thirty-one years with the paper her job mushroomed to cover everything from upper crust parties to fashion notes, a daily recipe and even agricultural doings (she once wrote that cattle are "Abilene's real aristocracy.")

The general feeling of Abilenians was, "It isn't a party unless Leltie is there." But when asked about the result of this hyperactivity on her health, her answer was simple, "Why, it's just seeing my friends."

Life went with her on her social rounds—taking pictures of people—some of whom are recognized as being: Mrs. Bea Haney; Mrs. L. W. Hilgenberg, who married R. A. Bible; Elbert E. and Mary Eldridge Hall; Mrs. Rupert Harkrider. On a busy day she got to as many as six events, either on foot or in her car, got tips on new parties from people who stopped her on the street, ran in and out of her office to turn in copy, and wound up baby-sitting for her grandchild Lenda—now Lenda Delk who lives with husband Steve Delk in Whitney, Texas.

Then there is available via courtesy of Frances Hill Cooper Daniel (widow of Judge J. Neil Daniel) Leltie's "Tops On Calendar" column from the Thursday evening, November 17, 1938 edition—entitled "Chrysanthemum Tea for Bride" describing the Grecian Gown Banded in Gold Sequins Worn by Honoree Mrs. George (Mary Pittman) Minter, Jr. when Mrs. George (Mabel Lockett) Minter, Sr. presented her as bride of her only son George L. Minter, Jr. to Abilene's high-crusted guests. Dress and table décor is described in detail. It is thought that the only two guests still living are the said Frances Hill Cooper Daniel, whose mother Mrs. O. T. Cooper wore wine crepe with white chrysanthemum corsage, and Mrs. Lance Sears, whose black dress was a straplesss model. The descriptions are vivid enough to envisage attendance.

I first met Leltie in the early '40s at a luncheon given in the home of Ann O. Smart, another socialite, caterer, etiquette teacher, radio personality and mother of the late Hudson Smart. Leltie portrayed authority, impressed with her position, in asking me, "Who gave you license to wear COLOR?"—to which my answer, "No ONE but LIFE!" seemed to annoy her.

MizCheevus once asked Judy Jones Matthews what Leltie was like: "She was a lot like you—knew everybody—everybody thought they knew her and liked her—and we told her all our secrets which she would promptly tell to her readers."

Perhaps the biggest difference between the long success of Faucett's career and the relatively short one of MizCheevus (only twelve years) is that her cost to attend those many functions was minimal compared with current fundraiser expenses. Also, the *Reporter-News* does not encourage detailed apparel and table descriptions, although some are tried. And MizC often attends four events per day—changing wardrobes each time—while Leltie apparently always wore black.

Records show Leltie died September 30, 1960, probably in her seventy-fourth year. MizC just celebrated her ninety-first birthday.

Abilene continues to be social—and enjoys seeing it in print.

A request from a young G.I. in 1951 inspired a million-selling song that has been recorded by more than one hundred performers.

'DON'T LET THE STARS GET IN YOUR EYES'

JOE W. SPECHT

In the fall of 1952 and well on into 1953, the nation's radio airwaves and jukeboxes were filled with the sound of "Don't Let the Stars Get in Your Eyes." The song, penned by Abilene disc jockey Winston Lee Moore—better known as Slim Willet—was all the rage with four different versions in *Billboard*'s Country & Western Top Ten. On *Billboard*'s Pop chart, Perry Como took the song to Number One, selling over one million copies.

According to Willet, the inspiration for his opus came from a letter he received sometime in September 1951 from a young G.I. stationed in Korea. The soldier asked the deejay to spin a platter for his girlfriend who lived in the area and listened to KRBC: "Play her a song, tell her to wait for me, and tell her not to let the stars get in her eyes."

The phrase stuck with Slim, and he soon began work on a song. Willet's wife, Jimmie Moore, remembers her husband sitting on their bed strumming his guitar, piddling with the lyrics—Don't let the stars get in your eyes, don't let the moon break your heart, love blooms at night in daylight it dies—while the reflection of "the stars and moon would shine through [an open window] and splash on our bed."

Willet eventually got around to recording the song, now appropriately titled "Don't Let the Stars Get in Your Eyes," in the spring of 1952. He moved equipment into Fair Park Auditorium. And at the conclusion of the *Big State Jamboree*, a musical variety show hosted by Willet every Saturday evening, Slim with an aggregation of local musicians including members of Shorty Underwood's band, the Brush Cutters, got down to business. Buck White tinkled the ivories in his inimitable honky-tonk piano style, Smokey Donaldson supplied the lead flattop guitar picking, Shorty Underwood took the fiddle breaks, James Wood handled the steel guitar duties, Mack Fletcher and Jean Stansbury were on rhythm guitar, and Georgia Underwood played bass. The rollicking, freeform results were, in Slim's words, "an off meter song [in which] the band could play as long as they want between phrases, and the singer can begin singing whenever he feels like it."

By the time he recorded "Stars," Willet had a working arrangement with Bill McCall and 4 Star Records, located in Pasadena, California. Don Pierce, McCall's second-in-command, describes his first exposure to "Stars." "I was at a little studio in downtown Los Angeles making some masters for custom manufacturing when a tape came in from Slim Willet. When I heard that song I about jumped out of my skin." Bill McCall was not impressed, however, and he told Slim in no uncertain terms that the song was "offbeat, off meter, off everything."

Willet went ahead and paid eighty-five dollars to have three hundred copies pressed for release on his own Slim Willet label. He also hired a salesman to help promote the record in Texas. Initially they plugged the flipside, "Hadacol Corners," but listeners soon discovered "Stars." When McCall realized the song he had panned was "getting terrific requests" in the Lone Star State, he exercised his option and re-released it on 4 Star in June 1952. *Billboard*'s review of the disc proved oddly lukewarm: "Nothing special or exciting here."

Nevertheless, crossover was in the air, and record producers were acutely aware of a country song's hit potential when recorded by a pop performer. This was an era, too, when record companies still were convinced the song, not the recording or performer, was what counted most. It wasn't unusual, then, for several different versions of the same tune to be available to the buying public at the same time. And "Stars" joined the list. At one point, there were four versions of "Stars," including Willet's, in *Billboard*'s Country & Western Top Ten.

On the pop side, there were at least fourteen competing versions getting some play, but it was Perry Como's mammoth selling chart-topper that insured the song's immortality, something that Slim readily acknowledged. "The break I got on 'Stars' was when Perry Como recorded the song. That's when it took off like a rocket. Without Como's record, it probably would not have hit the big time." Perry was a reluctant participant at first. He later told Don Pierce, "They [RCA Victor producers] played it for me, and I didn't think much of it, and I didn't think I could sing it." Como's record sales were in a bit of a slump, however, and with juke box operators, dee-jays, and record dealers urging him to step up the rhythm, he agreed to record one take of "Stars" with Hugo Winterhalter's Orchestra and vocal backing by The Ramblers.

Yet, Como never took to the song. As he admitted to the Associated Press in a 1988 interview, he considered "Stars" just one of the "awful novelty songs" his concert audiences expected him to perform. "Me and Sinatra and all the rest of the singers used to talk about all the (junk) we had to sing . . . . I still do ['Stars'] onstage once in a while . . . but I say 'yech' afterwards." One wonders what Mr. C's reaction would have been if he could have read his own obituary as posted by Reuters News Service. In noting that Como sold more than fifty million records, Reuters singled out three songs for mention. "Don't Let the Stars Get in Your Eyes" was one of them.

Willet continued to record in Abilene and release his records on 4 Star or on the Slim Willet label, but the follow-up hit remained elusive. The royalty checks on "Stars" were not rolling in as expected either, validation of Bill McCall's exploitative reputation. Or as Faron Young, a future member of the Country Music Hall of Fame, put it: "Bill McCall screwed everybody in this town [Nashville] once, or tried to."

Faron also commented on Slim's plight. "Slim Willet . . . was owed over $100,000 in 1953 and received only $1,500. If you got in McCall's office past his ten secretaries, he was such a smoothie he could talk you out of killing him. God knows, enough of us tried! But Slim just walked in there, reached over McCall's desk, grabbed him by the neck, and like to beat the (stuffing) out of him. He left with a check for $60,000 in his pocket."

An exaggeration perhaps, but Bill Mack, the famed "Midnight Cowboy" and late night disc jockey, offers a similar account about Willet heading out to California to confront McCall over the royalties due him. "Really it was a scene similar to the one . . . in the film, *The Godfather*. Utilizing a weapon he had brought from Texas, Slim made McCall 'an offer he couldn't refuse' . . . ." Even more apocryphal and perfectly scripted for a Max Sennett slapstick comedy is the tale of a passel of Willet's "oil rigger buddies" dangling McCall out of a hotel window until he agreed to pay up.

Within the Moore family, Slim's older brother, Omar, told the story something like this. "Winston arrived at Bill McCall's office wearing cowboy boots. To make his point, he jumped up on McCall's desk, and he stomped his feet so hard he shattered the glass on top of the desk." Suffice it to say, Slim's visit left an indelible impression on Bill McCall—not to mention his desk—and the royalty checks commenced to flow without interruption. In 1958, Willet could boast that the song had earned him "more than $230,000" which, if accurate, is the equivalent of $1,600,000 in today's currency.

In 1997, on the twentieth anniversary of Elvis's death, writer Greg Jaklewicz caught up with some Abilene fans who saw Presley in concert.

FIFTH ROW FOR ELVIS

GREG JAKLEWICZ

Kathy Swaim was in line at the Expo Center at 4 a.m. for tickets to Elvis Presley's concert here in 1974. Tickets sales were to begin six hours later. Crazy? A hundred others already were in front of her. Tickets cost just ten dollars each. For the best seats.

Swaim waited and waited and waited. Finally, the box office opened, and the line inched forward. Suddenly, she saw a figure in another box office and ran to the window.

"I broke out in a sprint for the ticket booth," Swaim, a receptionist at West Texas Rehabilitation Center, recalled. She cashed in on her mad dash, securing six tickets to the first show in Abilene by the King of Rock'n'Roll in nineteen years.

Fifth row.

The wait—and the run—was worth it. "It was great . . . it was super. I was more of an Elvis fan than they were. My sister (Tommy Waggoner) asked me once what was wrong with me because I was just sitting there in awe. It was such a thrill."

"They screamed all night," Gerald Waggoner, Swaim's brother-in-law, recalled. "My ears rang after the show."

"He came on stage and did this," Waggoner said, mimicking Elvis strumming his guitar once, "and they went crazy."

The crowd of 8,606 for the October 9 concert broke the record for a concert at the five-year-old Taylor County Coliseum. The record was just seven months old—band leader Lawrence Welk attracted 8,331 in March. Only two concerts by the rock group KISS in 1978 have drawn larger crowds in the twenty-three years since.

Elvis returned to Abilene on March 27, 1977, attracting an estimated 7,500 fans. Premium tickets had skyrocketed to fifteen dollars each.

Five months later he was found dead at his home, Graceland, in Memphis. He was just forty-two. Ironically, the *Reporter-News* reviewer at the show noted how relaxed and healthy the King looked on his last visit to Abilene.

Swaim chose not to go. "By that time," she explained, "he had gotten so big. I wanted to remember him when he was young and active. He never slowed down that night."

The 1974 and 1977 concerts were Elvis' fourth and fifth in Abilene. The first three were in 1955, a year before Elvis did his first show in Las Vegas where he was called a flop.

Where did Elvis play when he first came to town? Fair Park Auditorium in those days was Abilene's entertainment center before it was demolished.

A story told time and again around town has been that someone scratched Elvis' new Cadillac parked outside the building. It infuriated Elvis so much he vowed never to return. It was millions of records and almost nineteen years between concerts.

Realtor Pat Garren wasn't familiar with that story though she was there for Elvis' February 15 show in 1955. A sophomore at Abilene High, she was one of a carload of girls who went to see this "extremely good-looking boy" in a ducktail. Garren described herself as a "closet hillbilly music" fan who listened to Hank Snow and Hank Thompson on a Coleman station on the car radio or under the sheets at night so her parents wouldn't hear.

"It was full of screaming teenagers, like it was later when the Beatles came (to New York City)," she recalled. Her biggest impression, one that "embarrassed me greatly," was Elvis' gyrating. "I was naïve. I never had been exposed to that kind of overt sexuality," she confessed.

It didn't bother her "wild and crazy" friend Becky Willingham. To the contrary, Willingham got backstage and obtained Elvis' autograph. On her brassiere.

A hometown boy returned from the big city to become known as the Archduke of Art and have a lasting influence on the local art scene.

PRAIRIE RENAISSANCE

MARY HELEN SPECHT

After so many years away from Abilene, I had almost begun to believe that the stories I told about my hometown were the only stories there were to tell: my elementary school teacher who convinced thirty fourth-grade students the Soviet Union had taken over the U.S. earlier that morning, causing half of us to burst into tears—a lesson meant to help us appreciate our freedom. The biology teacher who kept a picture of an aborted fetus on his office door. The time in high school when fellow students scrawled "Vegetarians Have Sex with Animals" in big letters on our driveway.

To me, the city was immutable: my Bible Belt, backwater hometown. But even back then, Abilene had a lovely, eccentric side. I remember the first time I walked into the downtown studio of local art celebrity, Clint Hamilton, and was shocked that such a magical room could inhabit this conservative, Protestant place. Hamilton had lived for years in New York and worked among the biggest names in Pop Art—there were several early Andy Warhols on his wall, one inscribed, "Happy Birthday, Clint." He didn't just make collages (or assemblages, as he would say, using the French pronunciation), his studio was one: Art and photos covered every inch of wall, bits of glittery paper or cut metal hung from the ceiling, surfaces were strewn with small objects collected from junk shops.

But despite my love of his curio-filled studio, I wasn't particularly impressed by Clint. To a girl whose primary ambition was to see Abilene fade away in the rearview mirror, I couldn't fathom why anyone who made it into the Manhattan art scene would willingly return to West Texas. I decided Clint must be a failure. But the story of Clint Hamilton, and the art scene in Abilene, was more complex than I, a cocky teenager, understood.

Clint Hamilton graduated from Abilene High in 1947. By all accounts, his talent was apparent early on. He won scholarships to study art and created window displays for Sanger department stores in Dallas and, after moving to NYC in his early twenties, for Bonwit Teller and Tiffany & Co., where he presented pieces by other struggling artists as part of his creations. Andy Warhol's first exhibit was in a Clint Hamilton window display on Fifth Avenue—unveiled for the first time, like all big windows back then, at 5 p.m., just as Manhattanites began walking home from work. In an interview with the *Abilene Reporter-News*, Hamilton said, "I was living in a garret on 10th and Hudson, and I got greatly hungry. I found I could make a living in window display."

After sixteen years of helping break down barriers between high and low art in the emerging Pop Art scene, Clint Hamilton returned home in 1967 and moved in with his parents. It's not easy to get folks in Abilene to talk about why Clint moved back to his roots and his family. Official biographies attribute his flight to illness. A photographer friend of his said he was "overstimulated" by the New York scene. The truth is, Clint struggled with demons, including alcoholism and closeted homosexuality. Letters written to him over many years from his friends and intimates hint at how fraught with complicated emotions his self-exile really was.

It might seem strange that Clint went back to live with his family, but they were clearly kindred spirits. His parents were pack rats and collectors of clutter; playbills and earrings and arrowheads were stacked in every nook and cranny. There was hardly a place to sit, much less walk. The Hamiltons would let you take something you needed for a project as long as you promised never to bring it back. When Clint died, the theater department of one local university received twenty-five Hawaiian shirts and a real phone booth from this Hamilton house of treasures. But there are benefits to a small town, and despite living in mystical squalor with his parents, Clint was a star in Abilene. Known as the Archduke of Art, he became the unofficial mascot for the local art community. Dozens of people around town considered him their best friend in the world. He was an entertainer—always quick with a groan-inducing pun—and loved to make fun of his odd appearance by exaggerating it, strolling around the Center for Contemporary Arts in elf shoes, a Cyrano de Bergerac nose and palmetto fans behind his ears.

The pieces he created in Abilene were often playful, including one collage titled "Escargogo," featuring a series of doll legs in a kick line topped by seashells. He created a Francophile manger scene with the star of Bethlehem sitting atop a model of the Eiffel Tower, porcelain dogs playing instruments, and a red frog. Clint would poke fun at how the bourgeoisie collected art in the titles of some of his assemblages ("You Said You Wanted a Fish Above Your Bed"), but in general Clint's persona was warm, not pretentious. When he was in the hospital toward the end of his life, one nurse said she'd heard he used to work for Tiffany's and that she'd always wanted to eat breakfast there. Clint told her he thought she would enjoy it.

Clint Hamilton was also perpetually strapped for cash, so he would curate exhibits for museums and galleries in the area, or create displays for debutante balls, theater openings and society Christmas parties. His centerpieces often rivaled the events themselves. His favorite trope was the headdress, and he put elegant, glittery tinsel ones on mannequins for department–store window displays. For the Paramount Theatre, he made an assemblage headdress from cut-out photos of stars like Garbo and Valentino and lit-up marquees; for a particularly adventurous patron, he made a hot pink straw hat with purple net bows and hen eggs. He said, "Nobody can ever begin to imagine the work which went into creating, bit by bit, each of the headdresses, each of the decorative units."

He didn't consider these projects beneath him but rather their own kind of art, one that involved the community in a way that museums and galleries couldn't. In an interview, he snorted with disdain at the thought that "some people will walk by the windows and think that things were just stuck there, any which way, by chance." As Judy Deaton, art historian and curator of exhibits at Abilene's Grace Museum, argued, Clint made art seem welcoming and accessible to average people because "he didn't see it as an elite, intellectual process." Or as Lynn Barnett, director of Abilene's Cultural Affairs Council, told me, with Clint, people had a chance to see how art happens. He would pick up a piece of junk at your garage sale, and "the next week it would look magnificent in a display or in his next work of art."

Maybe because of his roots in Pop Art or his window-dressing past, Hamilton didn't seem to worry about the permanence of his creations. Deaton said that he would take collages apart and remake them, paint over them, and thread them with organic materials. Clint gave a wonderful piece to friends of my parents after they had starred in a production of *Who's Afraid of Virginia Woolf?* It's a woodblock print of Woolf herself surrounded by beads and pencil marks and delicate insect wings, pieces of which had disintegrated over time and collected in the bottom of the frame like fairy dust.

While much of Clint's tangible work is scattered or falling apart, his real legacy may be the Abilene art scene he left behind. Before his death in 2001, Clint taught art to hundreds of kids and adults in Abilene, mentoring a string of young artists and gallery curators who came through town. Hardly the failure I'd once thought him to be, Clint ultimately made more of an impact here than he probably ever could have in New York. He was the first director of the Center for

Contemporary Arts, a cooperative that still holds monthly art walks that bring more than 500 people to museums, shops and galleries in Abilene's once-deserted downtown.

Clint was not alone in these efforts. Officials realized early on the potential for the arts as an economic driving force, so they used the city's tourist tax to create and support a Cultural Affairs Council with a professional staff. Wealthy local philanthropists have chipped in to support artists and museums. Thanks to these efforts, the boarded-up Drake Hotel, built in 1909 in the Mission Revival style and fallen into disrepair over the years, blossomed into the stunning Grace Museum with world-class exhibits. Across the street, the old railroad right-of-way has been landscaped and now sprouts outdoor sculptures.

In 2010 the Texas Commission for the Arts named Abilene one of five designated "cultural districts" in the state, a program that highlights cities with thriving art scenes. When I heard that news, I was surprised. And then I wasn't. Abilene was not just my Bible Belt, backwater hometown. Like the collages and windows of Clint Hamilton, cities revive and fall away and transform into something different. In Abilene, Clint saw the raw materials for art.

On a recent trip back to town, I attended the senior art show of Hannah Capra, Clint's last student. A willowy young woman with long black hair, her work was both glossy and dark, butterflies and gas masks. At one end of the hallway hung a crayon portrait she drew of Clint when she was six. He was in poor health by this time, and she drew the lines of oxygen coming out of his nose like tentacles. She said walking into his house was like walking into a dream, a broken bottle from the street standing next to a fine vase. He would turn to her and say, "Make something."

Afterward, I stopped by the hip new coffee shop across the street from where Clint's studio used to be. It sells T-shirts with slogans like "Keep Abilene Boring" or "What Happens in Abilene, Leaves

Abilene." Pretty much my sentiments when living there as a young person. Drinking my Fair Trade coffee, I remembered what Hannah told me about a piece Clint did, made up of pennies with tiny vintage photographs on them, and how they made her "see pennies for the first time." That was a little bit how I felt now, like seeing my own Abilene in an entirely new light.

The inspiration for the National Center for Children's Illustrated Literature in Abilene came from a story that happened to be set in Abilene, even though the author had never even visited the city.

DONE WITH DISTINCTION

GARY McCALEB

James Michener wrote many wonderful works of fiction, including his Pulitzer Prize winning *Tales of the South Pacific*. But from one of his few non-fiction works, entitled *The Quality of Life*, comes this challenging statement: "In every city there is some new thing that waits to be done with distinction."

Great art is often the result of new ideas done with distinction. Today, painting a ceiling is not a particularly remarkable or novel idea. But Michelangelo executed the idea with such distinction that for almost five hundred years tourists by the thousands have traveled to Rome to view the Sistine Chapel. Every year we see evidence that tourists can be attracted to new things done with distinction.

A few years ago a children's book titled *Santa Calls* was published. The nationally acclaimed children's author and illustrator, William Joyce, told the fictional story of three children and their personal encounter with Santa. In this book, the children's hometown just happened to be Abilene, Texas. That simple serendipity was the beginning of a project which some talented and dedicated folks set about to do with distinction.

Today, Abilene is home of the National Center for Children's Illustrated Literature. Each year the National Center presents exhibits featuring original works from award-winning children's books.

The exhibits then go on tour to cities throughout the country, including museums in places such as Houston, Dallas, and Indianapolis.

As a result, thousands of elementary school children are developing an early appreciation for art and art exhibits. They are also spending more time with books, and the younger ones are enjoying more books read to them by parents and grandparents. A beautiful bronze sculpture depicting the three children from *Santa Calls* now graces the newly landscaped park in the center of town.

The great idea done with distinction does more than attract visitors—it pulls the community together and it lifts people up—it inspires, nourishes, and enlightens.

OPEN MINDS
LITERATURE &
LETTERS

Abilene's Carnegie Library opened in 1907 and was demolished in 1958

Although he was not widely known outside of Abilene, Frank Grimes
was the town's most prolific and, locally at least, most prestigious
writer over a forty-year period when he presided as editor of the
Abilene Reporter-News, turning out perhaps twenty million words

on the newspaper's editorial page and setting the tone for civil discussion in the community. In the larger world of letters, A. C. Greene carved out his reputation in Dallas and throughout Texas as a commentator on, and chronicler of, Texas life and literature. Yet Greene acknowledged that it was Grimes' influence that greatly shaped his own career.

While few Abilene writers have been prominent on the national stage, one did achieve a certain amount of notoriety only to mysteriously vanish into obscurity at the height of her fame. Gertrude Beasley's one book created quite a stir internationally, and then for years the question was, "Whatever happened to her?"

Featured in this section, as well as throughout the book, are some of the writers who have put pen to paper and left an impression, whether they practiced their craft exclusively in Abilene or were just passing through.

Longtime ACU journalism professor Charlie Marler has been an avid student of the writing of legendary Reporter-News *editor Frank Grimes. The following profile is taken from a much longer article in the 1972* West Texas Historical Association Year Book.

THE PROPHET FROM ABILENE

CHARLES H. MARLER

Frank Grimes produced the editorials for the *Abilene Reporter-News* from 1918 to 1960—some twenty million words in all. He wrote with more accuracy, insight, variety, humor, and depth than did numerous editors of larger daily papers in the nation.

Ichabod-like in appearance, Grimes disclaimed any prophetic vision. On occasion he would own up to his mistakes, realizing that volunteers from among his readers could rise up to call him a "punk prophet," one of his preferred labels for United States senators who fell from his favor.

Strangers would not expect prophecy to emerge from the mind of the tall, soft-voiced, two-finger-typing Texan. But day-after-day reliable commentary worthy of note poured from the typewriter of the watchman. Prophecy marked his work significantly for two reasons: first, the nature of the editorial writer's function and second, because of the rare qualities possessed by Frank Grimes.

He was a maverick. Grimes quit school at the end of the eighth grade. He educated himself. No one can safely estimate the amount of background reading and study he plowed into his editorials. Also, Grimes grasped the nature of his job when he wrote in 1943, "Jeremiah was a most unpopular prophet because he was brutally frank."

He wrote his first editorial for the *Abilene Daily Reporter* on the Armistice of 1918. Grimes moved to Abilene from Brenham to become city editor of the *Daily Reporter* December 4, 1914.

As he checked into Abilene, he had already begun omnivorous reading habits. Probably not a book in Abilene's old Carnegie Library escaped his attention; nor did he miss the magazines of the day or the exchange newspapers or the *Daily Reporter's* library. He also draped himself over the wire service printers and read every word of news daily, yards and yards of it. Katharyn Duff, one of Grimes' protégés, described the information gathering system of her chief as the process of bringing incredible amounts of reading material into "contact with a mind that soaks up facts like a blotter."

At the peak of his career, Grimes wrote six editorials daily, three each for the morning and afternoon editions with an estimated word count of 2,500 each day. In 1950 and 1952 Grimes narrowly missed winning the Pulitzer Prize for excellence in editorial writing. Herschel Schooley, former director of information for the United States Department of Interior, wrote at the time of Grimes' death in 1961 that only "understandable unwillingness of selection board members to accept the fact that one man could produce so much of high quality denied Frank Grimes that deserved recognition."

A diversity of writing techniques helped Grimes attract and hold his readers forty-two years. He was a master craftsman who could shift easily from technique to technique—including explanation and definitions, metaphors, literary allusions, questions, poetry, comparison and contrast, and the forecast. His prophecies, or keen perceptions, were amazingly accurate, whether they were about Abilene, Texas, the Southwest, the nation, or world affairs.

Frank Grimes always acknowledged the possibility of error, but he felt an editorial writer should follow his best judgment and give "it forth with all the assurance of a Moses on Sinai." In his early years, one of his editorials on editorials humorously described some of the pitfalls of the editorialist-prophet: "It is extremely unwise for an editorial writer to read anything he has written in the past ten years; it brings on profuse sweating, nightmares, sciatic twinges, and an inferiority complex."

Right or wrong, he felt newspapers without editorials were "journalistic eunuchs." He believed in the marketplace of opinions; "otherwise this would be a land of Schmoos, not a great democracy." Grimes' singular preparation for this task was compensation for his eighth grade education, in all probability. His yearning for knowledge was absolutely insatiable. And, like Ezekiel, the prophet from Abilene served as an alert watchman for his community and region.

Edward Anderson, newspaper reporter and editor who worked briefly for the Abilene Reporter-News *in the early 1930s, published two Depression-era novels,* Hungry Men *(1935) and* Thieves Like Us *(1937). The following piece is taken from Patrick Bennett's biography of Anderson,* Rough and Rowdy Ways.

YOUNG MINDS OF ABILENE

PATRICK BENNETT

When his back grew weary after hours at the typewriter, Edward Anderson got up and walked out, east, toward the library. In 1930 the Carnegie Library was Abilene's Mermaid Tavern, Kit-Cat Club, Bloomsbury salon, and Algonquin Dining Room. The town's young writers hung out there because the Carnegie librarian welcomed anyone with a claim, no matter how vague, to being a writer.

When Anderson caught sight of fellow writer John Knox sitting at their customary table in the southeast corner of the reading room, he ambled over. It was there that John introduced Edward to many of Abilene's literary hopefuls. Writing was just a temporary enthusiasm with some of them—the poet Oswald Babb, for example, whose father would soon put him to work in the grocery business. Babb eventually became an investment banker in France.

A more serious writer was Files Bledsoe. Only twenty-three at the time, Bledsoe later would work as a publicist for dancer Ruth St. Denis in England, collaborating with her on *An Unfinished Life*. He would also write for the *Daily Worker* in New York and be investigated by the FBI; help edit the magazine of the Partido Revolucionario Institucional in Mexico, where he would also publish a successful novel, *Lluvia y Fuego*.

Through Knox, Anderson got to know Houston Heitchew, the great-grandson of General Sam Houston. Heitchew never mentioned his great forebear, in fact flared up in anger if anybody mentioned him. A gangling youth so thin he looked even taller than his six feet, Heitchew had the sallow complexion of those whose faces are seldom turned from their books. When Heitchew had finished high school, a group of Abilene men offered to pay for his studies at Yale or Harvard, but he would have none of it.

Heitchew was the shrewdest analyst and critic of the Carnegie group. "Houston was like this," explained Knox. "He would work harder for something that didn't make money than for something that was profitable. If you happened to wonder aloud what part of the Great Pyramid of Egypt the bricks of the Wooten Hotel would make, Houston would show up in a week with it exactly figured."

On occasion Heitchew applied his knife to an overgrown Knox short story, trimming without sapping it. He was just the critic to make intelligent suggestions on Anderson's early tries at fiction and just the type to end spectacularly. On September 2, 1943, Heitchew plunged mysteriously—many believed he jumped—from an open window on the fourteenth floor of the Wooten Hotel. He fell to his death on the Paramount Theatre roof.

Edward was not long at the table with John and others before the librarian came over to say something pleasant. Her name was Maude E. Cole. She was fifty-one, a plain-faced woman, kind looking, with a smile over a firm jaw line. She wore rimless glasses, and her dark hair was cut short, parted, styled carefully but practically.

A widow since 1921, Mrs. Cole had first operated a hat shop and then a hotel flower shop before finding her real calling at the Carnegie. Being a librarian harmonized with her sense of order, and more important, it stimulated her creative juices. She had begun writing verse, which appeared in the *New York Times*, the *Chicago*

Tribune, and other newspapers and magazines. She believed it was her duty to fan every spark of literary activity in town.

The '30s, of course, was the era of the shushing librarian. Libraries banned the spoken sentence in favor of the printed paragraph, in favor of deep meditation, or even an occasional snore, so long as it was soft. Because of its jangle, a telephone had not been installed in the library. Yet while she kept most of the Carnegie's patrons to a whisper, Mrs. Cole let the city's writers talk at their own special table.

Some afternoons Mrs. Cole brought down her six-year-old grandson, A. C. Greene, a future author himself, who may have become a writer because he was impressed with the way his grandmother treated those writers at their special table. "My grandmother was very protective of the young writers who hung around at the library," Greene recalled. "The writers would get fairly loud, and I'm sure they would use four-letter words. She told me they were older, that they were grown up and could use that kind of language but for me not to use it."

When other Carnegie patrons complained about talk at the writer's table, Mrs. Cole put the complainers firmly in their places: "They know what they're doing at that table. They're really using the library." Eventually, however, some of the complaints reached the library board. For Mrs. Cole, the board's day of solemn deliberations each month was a period of terror. She got up those mornings sick with apprehension, her fingers clumsy as she dressed herself, her temper short with her grandson.

At the climactic board meeting, the chairwoman would save this hot item for last on the agenda, under "other business," in order to get through routine matters smoothly, before any unpleasantness. Nevertheless, she finally came to it. Someone, she would begin hesitantly, had mentioned that certain young persons who gathered in the Carnegie now and then were, well, perhaps without realizing it, talking loudly, sometimes rudely, and thereby disturbing scholars poring over texts. Of course, it should be understood that the library staff should in no way discourage young persons from coming in and reading to improve their minds, but . . . .

At every whim of these hoity-toity guardians of Abilene's culture, Mrs. Cole had knuckled under. But not this time. These young persons are what the library is for, Maude Cole told them. They are using their minds. They are serious people who read books seriously. Only in the library do they have a place where they can openly discuss the intellectual questions of the day. Mrs. Cole felt deeply about it, and she spoke with obvious emotions.

The board backed down. The issue never came up again.

Gertrude Beasley grew up in and around Abilene, attended Simmons College, and made a very mysterious name for herself.

THE DISAPPEARANCE OF GERTRUDE BEASLEY

MARY HELEN SPECHT

In 1987, my mother received a letter from Larry McMurtry inquiring about an obscure Texas author named Edna Gertrude Beasley, and another family obsession was born. My mother, Alice Specht, dean of libraries at Hardin-Simmons University in Abilene, and my father, Joe Specht, then director of the McMurry University library across town, love to investigate historical and literary puzzles most people could care less about, including my childhood self. This mystery turned out to be different.

According to my mother, McMurtry's letter "was the first time the world knew there was a mystery as to the ultimate whereabouts of our Beasley," an alumna of Hardin-Simmons. Here is what was known at the time: Gertrude Beasley's memoir of growing up dirt poor in and around the Bible Belt town of Abilene, *My First Thirty Years*, was released in 1925 by Contact Press in Paris. That's the same press that published James Joyce, Ernest Hemingway and Gertrude Stein. H. L. Mencken hailed Beasley's book as one of the best coming-of-age books ever and "the first genuinely realistic picture of the Southern poor white trash."

Despite these accolades, her memoir is largely unknown. Its violent and sexually deviant material caused it to be banned in Britain, where Beasley was living at the time. Most copies were destroyed by

Scotland Yard and U.S. Customs. The few that made it to Texas were mostly yanked off shelves by the Texas Rangers, probably on the orders of prominent Texans maligned in her book. Then the author vanished. She was thirty-five.

My First Thirty Years was Beasley's only work, but it stands the test of time. In his letter, McMurtry writes that her memoir "is one of the finest Texas books of its era; in my view, the finest."

"Thirty years ago," it begins, "I lay in the womb of a woman, conceived in a sexual act of rape, being carried during the prenatal period by an unwilling and rebellious mother, finally bursting from the womb only to be tormented in a family whose members I despised or pitied."

On the second page, Beasley recounts her first memory, age four: An older brother holds her down in the horse stall attempting to rape her. As the memoir progresses, her sister is fondled by a circuit preacher, another sister is beaten by their father until she defecates blood, and a brother is whipped for being "caught in the barnyard with the old cow."

It's not all sensationalism. The book is primarily about the hardscrabble and intelligent author attempting, and often failing, to retain her dignity as she strives to overcome the hardships of her roots. Beasley's mother eventually divorces her father—unheard of at the time— and moves to Abilene, where she hopes to get her thirteen children an education. Only Gertrude is interested. She writes that "it was like cutting me with a knife to say that I could not go to school."

She teaches while earning her bachelor's degree from Hardin-Simmons, then Simmons College. Eventually she enrolls in graduate school at the University of Chicago, where she attends lectures by luminaries like Margaret Sanger, Alice Paul and Emma Goldman. Beasley becomes a political radical herself, a socialist and supporter of women's rights. *My First Thirty Years* ends with Beasley sailing off to Japan, where she writes for *National Geographic* and travels to places like China and Russia before publishing her autobiography and disappearing for good.

McMurtry had written letters to every Beasley he could find in West Texas phonebooks in a futile attempt to gather more information for the afterword he was writing to the Book Club of Texas' reprinting of Beasley's memoir in 1989. Could she still be alive? Had she written anything else? Nobody seemed to know.

My mother, who became what she calls "a trader of information" on Beasley, kept a file of what she and a few others turned up over the years: school records, passport photos, the article Beasley published on women's birth control in Russia. She earns a brief mention in the memoir of her publisher, Robert McAlmon. "Only two authors got 'temperamental' and they were both Gertrudes, Stein and Beasley." My mother found clippings about Beasley's deportation hearing in England and a letter she wrote to the U.S. State Department on January 7, 1928, from a ship bound for New York. She complains about her treatment by British authorities, but still no sign of what became of her after that ship docked.

When I finally read *My First Thirty Years* around the time I turned thirty myself, I was surprised at how Beasley's tales of Abilene reflected some of my own experiences growing up there in the 1980s. I laughed in recognition as she recounted endless debates trying to reconcile evolution with the book of Genesis. Like me, Beasley was attracted to the leftists and rabble-rousers sprinkled into even the most conservative communities.

The book club's reprint of *My First Thirty Years* aroused the interest of Don Graham, a professor at the University of Texas in Austin, who included selections from the memoir in his *Lone Star Literature: A Texas Anthology*. Graham told me that after every public reading, a handful of women would come up to say they were buying the anthology for Beasley's passages alone. Those passages inspired actor and native Texan Veronica Russell to put together a one-woman play about Beasley called *A Different Woman: A True Story of a Texas Childhood.*

Beasley's memoir is important as an historical, regional and feminist document. Graham argues the memoir contains some interesting literary firsts: "Beasley introduced the confessional memoir into Texas writing long before Mary Karr," he says, "just as she introduced bestiality as fact and literary discourse thirty-six years before McMurtry came on the scene."

Those are not the only reasons this memoir deserves to be more widely read. *My First Thirty Years* is a very good book. The voice is compelling, dark and full of complex motives. The setting is vividly rendered, the dramatic moments heart-wrenching and bold. It transcends its time to tell us the still-relevant story of a woman overcoming often brutal circumstances in the search for a different way to live — even if her own success was partial.

In 2000, one of my mother's Beasley collaborators brought her attention to a 1930 New York state census that had just been made public. It listed a Beasley in a Suffolk County mental institution. In 2008, a grandniece of Gertrude Beasley, having seen a column in the Abilene newspaper, contacted my mother wanting to know more about Beasley's story. Together they were able to obtain a copy of the death certificate from New York, and it became official: Edna Gertrude Beasley, "our Beasley," was institutionalized ten days after her ship landed in New York. She lived out her last twenty-seven years in gulag conditions, until her death from pancreatic cancer in 1955. She was sixty-three.

Beasley "friends" and family have since located her grave, marked only by a number, and erected a headstone there. While Beasley's body may be at peace, her story isn't. New York State will not release details of her commitment hearing, even to family. The question remains: How did she end up there? The family has found a dictation from one of Gertrude's brothers claiming she was committed by

William Randolph Hearst, for whom she briefly worked as a journalist, though the brother claimed "she was no more crazy than you or I." My mother found no mention of Beasley in the Hearst papers at the University of California at Berkeley.

Maybe Beasley was crazy. The letter she sent to the U.S. State Department from the ship is full of grandiose suspicions regarding "a conspiracy against myself." Beasley also claims to be "completing a work which I believe to be one of the most significant of its sort ever written." She accuses British police and "certain people in Texas" of trying to stop her. She implies that once she disembarks from the steamer, her life will be in peril. She was never heard from again. My mother asks, "Is it paranoia if they're really out to get you?"

Gertrude Beasley wrote about the hardships of her first thirty years, but we can't begin to imagine what her last thirty must have been like. She wrote in her memoir that "it is perfectly clear to me that life is not worth living, but it is also equally clear that life is worth talking about." It seems the only thing she held dear was wrenched away: the chance to keep telling her story.

In an article for Hearst's *International-Cosmopolitan*, Beasley writes about her generation of women "who have been great warriors in a mighty battle, in a battle so horrible that if they told the truth about life it would take away the last breath of the censors."

Watching the final stages of Beasley's mystery unfold, I realized that while the Abilene she describes might have seemed a simulacrum to the city of my own youth, the eighty years separating us had made an enormous difference in the lives we lived there. My mother could become the dean of libraries because of hardships overcome by women like Beasley. Women like me inherited that privilege.

Bernard Hanks, longtime publisher of the Abilene Reporter-News *and influential civic leader who helped Abilene land both Camp Barkeley and Dyess AFB through his Washington connections, began his career delivering the newspaper by pony. He later co-founded Harte-Hanks Communications and was the father-in-law of publisher and community benefactor Stormy Shelton.*

FROM PONY TO PUBLISHER

ED N. WISHCAMPER

"Bernard Hanks and his pretty little pony have undertaken to deliver the *Daily Reporter* on the north side," the *Abilene Reporter* announced on September 17, 1897. "As soon as they learn the route they should do the job to a turn. Should anyone fail to get the paper please be patient and report the matter to us, though Bernard thinks he found all the readers this morning. The rain yesterday afternoon prevented the usual delivery at that time."

After he was a successful publisher, Hanks told how he got his start with a pony-delivered newspaper route. His father, pastor of the First Baptist Church in Abilene, told him he would have to earn the money to buy the horse. Young Hanks made his first business deal. Besides carrying the newspaper route, he drove neighbors' cows to the pasture of Colonel J. H. Parramore located at the edge of town then, but now almost in the center of the city. He charged a dollar a month to drive the cows to pasture in the mornings and return them home in the evenings. He split each dollar with Parramore.

After mastering the northside paper route, young Bernard was promoted to delivering the southside and raised to five dollars a month. W. J. Fulwiler, who later became Abilene's Ford dealer, a financier and another leader in the city's development, delivered the other side of town.

Ten years later he was a stockholder and partner with his mentor, George S. Anderson, in Abilene Printing Company. In 1923 Anderson and Hanks divided their operation, with Anderson taking over the commercial printing business under the name Abilene Printing and Stationery and Hanks heading Reporter Publishing.

Years later Anderson said that in their long association, which spanned more than fifty years, they never had a harsh word or misunderstanding. "I never knew him to do a dishonest thing," Anderson said, "and he possessed one of the brightest minds I have ever come in contact with."

Hanks was credited with picking the couplet from Lord Byron's "Don Juan" in 1927 which [for seven decades] ran on the front page of the *Reporter-News* as a statement of principle: "Without or with offense to friends or foes we sketch your world exactly as it goes."

A. C. Greene relates how the railroad helped him get his first newspaper job, which would lead to a long and productive writing career. The A. C. Greene Literary Award is presented every year by the Friends of the Abilene Public Library to a distinguished Texas author.

GETTING A JOB RIDING THE RAILROAD

A. C. GREENE

In the spring of 1948 I got my B.A. in history from Abilene Christian College, but the market for history teachers was slim. So I went to work in the Coca-Cola bottling plant, where I had worked before spending three years in the Navy and Marines in World War II.

One day at noon I was in downtown Abilene heading for Luby's cafeteria when I encountered another Class of '48 graduate who was enrolled in the University of Texas law school. He looked at my Coca-Cola uniform and asked why I had graduated if a bottling plant job was my highest ambition. I turned around in the middle of the street and went to the *Abilene Reporter-News* where I marched into the Managing Editor's office and asked for a job. He asked if I had attended J-school. I said I'd taken three hours of journalism and I thought that was sufficient. He wasn't too pleased with my cocky attitude but he relented and said if I'd write him a local feature story he would consider my application.

Being an Abilene native and already a railroad buff, I decided my best story would be a ride on the Abilene & Southern, from Abilene to Ballinger. I went to the A&S station and said I wanted to buy a round trip ticket to Ballinger. The clerk shuffled around in his desk drawer and finally admitted he couldn't find any passenger tickets.

"We don't get many passengers except for an old colored preacher who rides on a ministerial pass." The clerk told me just to come down when I was ready and I would not need a ticket. I think I paid him six dollars, which really strained my budget.

The train departed quite early in the morning, so I went aboard the old combine coach Number 52 which operated as a post office, baggage and passenger hauler (with "White" and "Colored" sections) and waited while the crew of engine Number 20 was making up the train.

Leaving Abilene, we passed behind the cotton oil mill by the A&S "round house," crossed South 11th Street just south of the casket company, and left the city limits. It was a part of Abilene I'd never seen, yet just on the other side of those sites was my familiar town. Going south we passed Iberis, by then only a store, a cemetery and a siding, and at Tuscola halted so the conductor could raise the gate that allowed us to cross the Santa Fe (AT&SF). There was a mild bit of business at Tuscola, and we steamed on through "the mountains" (the Callahan Divide) to Ovalo, dropping off a mail sack, then Guion where David Guion, President Roosevelt's favorite songwriter, was born. We paused at Bradshaw with a car, and at Winters we set out a car and I thought two women were getting on but they were just getting packages for their store. Hatchel got a mail sack and a few boxes, and at Ballinger most of the cars were either dropped off at sidings or were interchanged with the Santa Fe for San Angelo.

I wrote the story in the first person—which the M.E. had said not to do—and it ran several hundred words longer than he had suggested, but after he read it (admitting to me he had forgotten the A&S still ran) he said, okay, he'd give me a job: thirty-five bucks a week before taxes. That was cheap, even for 1948, but I took it and have been in the newspaper business, in one form or another, most of the years since.

As for that A&S story that got me my first newspaper job—it never ran!

*On a visit to Abilene in 1973, San Antonio poet Naomi Shihab Nye found
herself thinking about cows.*

THINKING ABOUT COWS AT TEN O'CLOCK IN THE MORNING, ABILENE

NAOMI SHIHAB NYE

The marker reads: "Western Cattle Trail"
for a second you remember Western movies,
dust rising up around hooves,
the wild driven look of their faces

Now it's tires
Sky Hawk, Gremlin,
a stampede of Rabbits and Pintos
in appropriate lanes

Lately my favorite absolute involves cows—
wherever you go, cows are eating

Across Texas, their slow bodies punctuate fields
You can depend on their bowed heads,
the little ones close by the mothers

When I didn't eat meat
I could look a cow in the eye
Now I say
Forgive us
for using you
to drive ourselves
where we think we need to go

Over a five-year period from 1987-1992, Jack Boyd wrote a weekly short story set in the fictional town of Cedar Gap, south of Abilene, for the Saturday edition of the Abilene Reporter-News. *Three collections of the stories were published by Texas Tech University Press, and the stories even spawned a full-blown musical,* Cedar Gap Homecoming. *Here is one of his favorites.*

WHAT A DARLIN' BALLPEEN HAMMER!

JACK BOYD

There's a wedding shower due in about an hour. It will be a nice event. They always are. The women will hang up streamers and fix finger sandwiches and stir up some lemonade punch featuring a big round chunk of pink ice. But it will NOT have certain innovations tried earlier this week. Of that you can be sure.

A few months ago Debbie Sleeton finally cornered Jay Joe Honniker and let him talk until he convinced himself he'd proposed to her. Tribal traditions being what they are, a wedding shower was immediately scheduled in the Activities Room at the Baptist Church.

Eudora Sleeton, Debbie's mother, called IrmaLynn Honniker, Jay Joe's mother, to finalize the plans.

"IrmaLynn," Eudora gushed, "you'll just love this! I heard about something everybody's doing over in Dallas." She paused dramatically. "All of the showers are for men and women both."

IrmaLynn hoped she'd heard wrong. "You mean we have to send two presents?"

"No, I mean the men have to come to the shower, too." Eudora waited. "IrmaLynn, you still there?"

"Yes," IrmaLynn said slowly. "I'm just thinking how I'm going to get Johnny and Jay Joe both to come to a shower."

Eudora snorted. "Do like I'm going to do with LeRoy. Just tell him he's going!"

It didn't exactly work that way.

LeRoy, Eudora's truck driver husband, exploded. "I'm not gonna waste a whole night sittin' around while you women ooh and ah over a hot pad the size of a tractor wheel or a place mat made out of Taiwan weeds."

"Oh, yes, you are," Eudora said firmly. "Just like the rest of the men."

LeRoy folded his arms. "Awright, who else is goin'?"

Two minutes later LeRoy stood yelling into the phone. "I tell ya, Johnny, I don't think I can handle that sorta party. That's woman stuff."

"Awright, who else is goin'?" Johnny Joe Honniker asked. LeRoy listed seven or eight men. "OK, LeRoy, here's what ya do."

Last Tuesday night thirty or so people stood awkwardly trying to balance plastic plates and cups. Each man used up at least ten printed napkins the size of cigarette papers trying to get the stuffed crab off his fingers. Finally a hostess led Debbie and Jay Joe toward two overstuffed chairs. A huge pile of brightly wrapped gifts overflowed a nearby table.

"Here," the hostess said, handing Debbie a striped package. "The first gift for your new home." Everyone applauded.

Debbie smiled as she pulled the paper off an electric can opener. "Oh, what a darlin' color" and "They can really use that" echoed around the room.

"Here's your second gift," the hostess said.

Debbie's eyes sparkled as she carefully slit the metallic paper. Then her jaw dropped as a huge adjustable end wrench appeared. Her mouth was a thin line as she read the card: "For those hard to reach pipes under the sink. Good luck, Jay Joe, from the Mayor."

The men applauded. The women smiled thinly. One man whispered "What a darlin' color," but he covered his mouth so his wife couldn't spot who said it.

A matched set of place mats woven out of Taiwan weeds and napkin holders with Hawaiian motifs elicited more traditional "Those are SO handy" and "Can't have too many of those around."

The very next gift box disgorged a chromed spinner lug wrench. The men mumbled "Those are SOOOOOO handy" and "Cain't have too many of those around." The women glared.

Debbie glanced sideways at Jay Joe, who was finally seeing some validity to that tradition called the wedding shower. "Here," she said through clenched teeth, "you open these two."

A plastic squirrel with a clock in its belly produced "That'll be just darlin' in the bedroom." It was followed by a matched set of rat traps and a Roach Motel. A husband started "That'll be just darlin' in . . ." but his wife's elbow in his ribs terminated any further comment.

For the women, the shower went downhill from there, but the men found it a great source of muttered inspiration. A garden hose was described as "the sweetest thang!" and a claw hammer as "just like the one my Mama had."

The Sleeton-Honniker wedding shower provided a jump start for every Palace Cafe conversation for the rest of the week. Today, the jungle telegraph tells us that only women will be at all future showers.

Fourteen men snapped their fingers and said "Rats!" Then they all grinned.

*Robert A. Fink teaches creative writing at Hardin-Simmons University
and is the author of six books of poems and one collection of essays.*

CALLED TO POETRY, ABILENE

ROBERT A. FINK

Squeezing into the DC-9's middle seat of three between two frequent flyers and introducing yourself as a poet means you know who will be first to be jettisoned if there is engine trouble and the pilot announces the necessity of lightening the load. The only calling more isolating than that of a poet is being a poet from Abilene. Texas, not Kansas. Everyone knows that Abilene, Kansas, has a heritage of gun-toters like Wyatt and Doc and drunken trail drivers shooting up the place. An acquaintance of mine from a state north and east of here wrote me that he knew my Abilene: "Didn't somebody back in the sixties have a song about women not treating you mean in Abilene?" He also recalled hearing something about preacher boys from three, small, denominational colleges erecting a church on every corner. And isn't Abilene the town with the Cadillacs half-buried nose down like something Aliens left overnight in a cotton field? I told him that was Amarillo. We're the one with the plastic pink flamingoes and the all-weather jig-saw Holsteins positioned prominently along the I-20 loop. I explained that our next piece of civic art will be an inflatable missionary, prominent as the Goodyear Blimp. I said our Visitor Center is also considering a series of wax poets-in-residence melting next to the population sign. He asked if I was kidding.

I'm proud to be an Abilenian. I'm resigned to being a poet. It started long before I turned into a West Texan. It started a hundred miles east of Dallas in a piney woods community that beat up anyone who wrote poems anywhere other than the stalls in the boys' gym, poems that began, "There once was a contortionist named Sal. . . ." It was here I learned rhyme and meter. It was here I overcame my fear of standing before a high school classroom of bootleggers' children and May Beth Linwood (who claimed to have seen the 1962 football team naked) and reciting, while focusing on the framed photograph of Longfellow on the back wall, "Thanatopsis," "The Village Blacksmith," and "The Cremation of Sam Magee." And once, only once, on select-your-own-poem day, rendering all seventeen quatrains of "The Face on the Barroom Floor." May Beth loved it.

Because I went out for football, basketball, and track (baseball not being offered, the school board uneasy about a sport in which a piece of required equipment could be used as a weapon) and played fast-pitch, church-league softball in the summers, most people forgave me poetry. They were almost certain it was something I would outgrow—like glass-pac mufflers and praying in public. There was only one incident when, my senior-year track season, I had to tell the coach I would miss the next day's practice. I would be participating in the district Interscholastic League poetry interpretation. Yes, I would be reading a poem. No, I would prefer not to recite it for the coach and the rest of the track team circled around me. Yes, I would love to run some extra laps. I was awarded the third-place medal, the only male out of three contestants. I read Alfred, Lord Tennyson's "The Charge of the Light Brigade." On the comments line, each of the judges had penciled, in large block letters, LOUD! I did not wear the medal to practice.

Because I was a star athlete (I feel confident saying this, my coach having died years ago and most of my teammates incarcerated) and because I volunteered for the Marines and Vietnam and because the civic leaders knew my folks had done their best, I was permitted to drive out of town rather than riding a rail, festooned in tar and feathers. Before my first book of poems was published, I warned my parents in plenty of time to put their house on the market.

August, 1977, the people of Abilene took me in. I explained I often wrote poems. They said, "Doesn't everyone?" I said my poems sometimes marched to the beat of a different drummer. They looked at one another, then said, "Okay." I asked how they felt about artistic fabrication. They understood we sometimes have to lie. In West Texas, a good story is almost always preferable to the truth. Here, poet is listed as a profession, and lying, if it's honest, is good.

West Texans don't have to work at being laconic or enigmatic. It comes with the open territory, with not needing to say much or bother explaining what we say. We know what matters: faith—how we need a lot of it, and love—how we mostly feel about each other and this land people who don't know better, refer to as God forsaken. Of course most Abilenians don't go around saying love out loud. That's the poet's job. And you know that the good poems, the ones that never quite get written, are always about love:

An old woman stands on the porch of a farmhouse as you jog by on your noontime run. She calls for help, and when you enter the house, you discover her husband an open-mouthed corpse on the couch in the living room cluttered with family photographs and figurines. She cannot help you locate the name and phone number of her son scribbled among the other numbers on the sheet of notebook paper tacked to the kitchen wall. When the middle-aged, youngest child drives up and steps softly into the room, he nods to you, then sits on the edge of the couch and pats his dad's cheek, smoothes his hair in place, and as if he were a priest granting absolution, closes his father's eyes.

Frustrated, rushed, you toss the saddle bags filled with textbooks, un-graded papers, and drafts of poems onto the back of your cruiser motorcycle and roar off down Ambler not thinking speed and a strong cross wind will lift the saddlebags into flight like some leather-winged, prehistoric bird hanging in the air a second before flopping onto the busiest street in North Abilene. And when you discover your loss, you are angry as you gear down and skid a U-turn, already wringing the throttle as you shift to second, to third, and hear the horn before you see the saddlebags extended from a window of the State School van filled with adult children. You turn again and follow the van to a supermarket parking lot where before you can climb from the bike, the door opens, and you are surrounded by smiles, short thick fingers touching you, one of the proud angels offering the saddlebags like a blessing.

The woman who comes at night and weekends to clean your office and empty the wastebasket is younger than you but missing most of her teeth and seems unable to lift her head. She knows you often work late and sometimes come in on Saturdays. The first time she used her pass key to unlock the door and discover you writing at the desk, she jumped and uttered a little cry. You laughed and apologized for frightening her. You said you were just leaving. Now, she knows your office better than you. When she dusts, she lifts one by one each photo of your family, placing each one back exactly. She has told you about her only son who will soon graduate from Texas Tech. He is tall and handsome like she remembers his father. One morning you find a hardback copy of your most recent book of poetry placed in the middle of your desk. She has also left a note saying she is moving to be closer to her son and would you mind autographing your book and leaving it for her to pick up when she dusts that evening.

Accepting the call to Abilene means you're among people who love a lot more than poetry.

Lawrence Clayton was a Hardin-Simmons University professor and dean and an author and historian specializing in western lore. He knew he was dying when he wrote this piece in 2000 for a publication he produced with other writers, called Christmas Pudding, *as a gift for their friends and families.*

MY LAST CHRISTMAS ????

LAWRENCE CLAYTON

At this time of year, our minds automatically turn to the first Christmas. This year, however, my mind is turned to the reality that this is one of my last Christmases, perhaps the very last. In October of 1999, I was diagnosed with Lou Gehrig's Disease, or ALS. My quality of life has deteriorated since that time to a very frustrating level of physical ineptness, especially with my hands. I will not try to list the multitude of small manipulations of everyday life that I can no longer do.

I feel fortunate that my disease does not require radical surgery or therapy, convalescence, trips to Houston for treatment, or other interruptive procedures. Several friends my age have cancer or heart problems, catastrophic disorders. My disease, in contrast, is a calm, gradual, disgusting, maddening encroachment on the quality of life for me and my family and friends. It is a surreal nightmare from which the only awakening is death.

What is one to do in this situation? I grappled with the ultimate reality and decided to do nothing different from what I have always done—enjoy my family, my work and my life—but to a greater degree of comfort in that knowledge. Like the mythic Sisyphus in Camus's discussion of absurdity, I find some comfort in knowing the rules, what to expect, and what not to expect, from life.

I have chosen as my model for living the rest of my life an example told to me by Keith Wells, a close friend and one of the few bona fide heroes I know. As a Marine attacking the Japanese fortress of Iwo Jima in World War II, Lt. Wells knew that chances were good he and many of his men would be killed in the coming battle. Wells made his decision not to despair but instead to do what he had been trained to do up to the time he could no longer do that. He remained true to the code of a warrior.

I have made the same decision. I am, in a sense, dead already. I will work and write as long as I am able and then accept the inevitability of death, a reality that has been here since I drew my first breath more than sixty years ago. I long assumed I would die in battle, as so many young men did in the wars that bracketed rather than interrupted my life. I remember several friends and a multitude of acquaintances who did not live this long.

I do not know when the end will come or what physical failings will accompany my last gasps on this earth. I just know for certain that the end will come. But I have known that all my life. Dying is part of living. Christ proved that centuries ago with the death of his physical body. With that knowledge, I can face this Christmas the same way I have all of those other wonderful Christmases --- with love, hope and joy.

And I am beginning to be curious about what waits for me on the other side.

[Lawrence Clayton died on December 31, 2000.]

THE OLD MESQUITES
WEATHER & NATURE

Joe W. Specht Collection

Prairie dog towns were numerous in and outside of Abilene in the early days.

The terrain and climate of West Central Texas have been defining influences on Abilene's history. Early observers arriving as the Texas & Pacific Railway pushed westward described the landscape where Abilene sprang up as "a bald prairie." Mesquite, ranging from a shrub to a tree, was ever-present, and while providing food, wood, and a sprinkling of shade, the plant's insatiable appetite for water is responsible for dried up creeks and shallow-flowing streams throughout the region.

The buffalo had already been killed off when Abilene was founded, but the black-tailed prairie dog (*Cynomys ludovicianus*) remained a ubiquitous inhabitant. Prairie dog towns often covered hundreds of miles. Even though the rodents were an important component of the ecological system, ranchers and farmers soon decided the "dogs" needed to be exterminated to prevent injuries to cattle and horses and destruction of crops. Like the buffalo, then, prairie dogs eventually disappeared from the scene. Today a smattering of their descendants resides at Redbud Park and the Abilene Zoo.

And, of course, there was the wind, always the wind. In July 1881, a sustained gust unroofed the courthouse in Buffalo Gap. Today, one only need look atop the Callahan Divide to see the whirling dividends spinning into county coffers.

But water—or the lack thereof—continues to be one of the forces shaping Abilene. Always cognizant of the need for a reliable water source, the city fathers supported the construction of Cameron Lake followed by Lytle Lake, Lake Abilene, Lake Kirby, and Lake Fort Phantom Hill, each time proclaiming the city's water needs had been solved. The building of the Fort Phantom reservoir proved to be especially fortuitous, although the bond election passed by only 150 votes. The lake became a reality in 1939, and the following year Abilene was awarded Camp Barkeley due to our abundant water supply.

Abilene's contrary creeks, all of which flow north, have also been a major influence, no more so than when overflowing their banks. Catclaw Creek has enjoyed special attention, with the moniker gracing book and song titles and even the name of a musical group.

For farmers and ranchers, the prairie dog was the scourge of West Texas, an animal to be exterminated. But few have been as original in their planning as W. Jeff Maltby, who schemed to not only kill but also to profit from the destruction of the little critters.

CAPTAIN JEFF'S PRAIRIE DOGS

K. O. LONG

The ability to attract or to grow its own colorful characters is one of the things that distinguishes Texas from the places where ordinary folks live.

W. Jeff Maltby was an adopted Texas son who arrived from Illinois around 1849 as a civilian employee of the Army. By the time of his death in 1908, Maltby had helped build Army posts in remote areas of Texas, fought against marauding Indians and had raised prize-winning vegetables such as a 103-pound squash. His adventures on the frontier with the Texas Rangers, as well as his accomplishments as a horticulturist, are recorded in *Captain Jeff*, a book written by a member of Company E of the Texas Rangers but credited to Maltby himself, who preferred to be known as "Captain Jeff."

In his later years, the visionary in Captain Jeff foresaw great things for the new city of Abilene, although it should be renamed Central City, in his opinion. His theories are reflected in newspaper extracts and letters included in his book.

In the midst of his optimism, Captain Jeff realized that West Texas would face tough economic times. He believed, however, that a solution was quite literally underfoot. Writing to the editor of the *West Texas Sentinel* in 1893, Captain Jeff proposed that Texas possessed a gold mine richer than any in California, and the state had only to turn a curse into a blessing in order to allow West Texas to blossom.

The curse was the dreaded prairie dog. Somewhere down the line, prairie dogs had greatly offended Captain Maltby. Killing an occasional prairie dog as the main ingredient in one of his "savory pot-pies" just wasn't sufficient. Captain Jeff's plan was simple enough. Texas would put a five-cent bounty on prairie dog "scalps" for a period of ten years. The captain estimated that there were fifty million prairie dogs in West Texas, and that it was possible to clear ten cents on each of the animals.

His ten-cent figure was based upon five cents for each pelt and the production of five cents worth of oil from each of the critters. The end product would be five million dollars in circulation in West Texas, which Captain Jeff believed would be used for purchase and settlement of land in the area. The resulting increase in tax values formed his Texas gold mine. It was his belief that four pelts would make a fine pair of kid gloves and that the oil would be suitable for sewing machines. In this manner, something good might be derived from the "worthless little kusses."

Captain Jeff even saw the hand of Providence at work, since all those miserable creatures must have been put in West Texas as a means by which settlers could obtain homes.

Alas, the prairie dog never became the economic windfall that Captain Jeff proposed. Had his plan been implemented though, it would have altered some of our perceptions about the Old West. Would prairie dog hunters have occupied the same place in society as buffalo hunters? Dog Paul, for example? Would we have old photographs of piles of prairie dog pelts stacked at the railhead awaiting shipment?

We'll never know. Of course, there is the possibility that Captain Jeff was pulling everyone's leg with his prairie dog plan, and that, too, would be in keeping with longstanding Texas traditions.

Water has always been a major topic of concern, conversation and civic attention in Abilene.

WATER, WATER, WATER

FROM NEWSPAPER ACCOUNTS

Prior to the sale of town lots on March 15, 1881, a newspaper announced: "Abilene has already established a graveyard! The town has a future. The surrounding country is rich. The only drawback is the want of water, which it is proposed to secure by sinking artesian wells."

On March 21, 1881, in further touting the benefits for establishing the town, an account noted, "There were three objections to the country around Abilene: No wood, no water, and the winds."

A few days later on an Abilene stopover, Jay Gould, the New York financier with controlling interest in the Texas & Pacific Railroad, painted the glories of the country in glowing colors, and a reporter covered the event.

"I am amazed," said the great Gould, "at the possibilities of this great country. Why, it is the finest country on earth. All you need to make it a paradise is a good supply of water."

From the back of the crowd, a cowboy spoke up. "You're dead right, Mr. Gould, all we need is water. But come to think of it, that's all hell needs, too."

When rain did fall, it could be a deluge as reported August 31, 1882. "On a Tuesday night the heaviest rainfall, probably, that had ever fallen in this section of the country did a lot of damage. On the headwaters of the Little Elm and Elm Creek, particularly, the rain was a regular waterspout for several hours. The water overflowed all the valleys. Fences, corrals, sheep, and in some instances, houses were almost swept away by the rushing waters. Out of one flock of sheep of 1,100, only about 300 were saved.

"Thousands of drowned prairie dogs were piled up along the tracks of the Texas and Pacific, near Abilene."

During the same period, the water available for personal consumption, often hauled from wells dug in the vicinity of Lytle Creek, created its own health risks as a citizen attested. "Yes, sir, there is considerable sickness here at present. Typhoid fever is prevailing, and it is clearly traceable to the abominable water we are compelled to use."

Although the severity of the drought of 1886 was legendary, this correspondent had yet to lose his sense of humor, as seen in an August 1886 update. "As the weather has been so dry here that the wells are empty and the fish in the creeks are carrying toad stools for parasols to keep the sun from burning their backs. Water is getting so scarce that the Baptist and Campbellites are beginning to favor baptism by sprinkling, and they have quit turning up their nose at the Presbyterians. Potato bugs are crossing the creeks like the Israelites crossed the Red Sea and for the same purpose—in search of water. A prominent prohibitionist has ordered a case of beer from Decatur, not necessarily as a beverage, but as evidence that he wants lather to shave with."

A letter from the Artesian Well Committee, headed by James H. Parramore and Henry Sayles, printed in the January 31, 1890, *Abilene Reporter* promised a solution to the city's water woes. "The sinking of an artesian well is of vital importance to the whole people of the Abilene country and more especially to the citizens of Abilene. It is believed that a sufficient quantity of artesian water, suitable for domestic purposes . . . would settle forever the most important question our city has to deal with, that is how to secure an ample supply of clear, wholesome water . . . ."

Six years later, the banner headline of the June 15, 1896, edition proclaimed "IT IS NOW LYTLE LAKE," as the rains descended and filled the reservoir. By 3 a.m. on that day, a river of water made it possible for the newspaper to report that "Abilene was now a city by a lake and the fire alarm will not again strike terror to the heart of the property owner and the householder. Close by our door lies spread out in the shape of a kite, a lake of pure, sparkling water fresh from the heaven. Abilene is happy today."

The lake that was supposed to solve the city's water problem "forever" proved to be inadequate. In 1919, Abilene citizens approved a bond project to create Lake Abilene on upper Elm Creek. When completed, an editorial in the August 10, 1922, newspaper boasted, "One of the main advantages of Lake Abilene, as we see it, is the bower of roses it is going to turn Abilene into. That also is a worthwhile accomplishment. But Lake Abilene does more than that. It also gives Abilene an inexhaustible supply of sparkling water, one of the first considerations in the location of industrial enterprises."

Lake Kirby, on Cedar Creek south of town, followed in 1927; yet, the water had barely had time to settle before *Abilene Reporter-News* editor Frank Grimes began touting the building of an even larger reservoir in the Elm Creek valley north of Abilene. In the March 17, 1929, edition, Grimes hyped further investment in water bonds: "Millions for water make Abilene growth possible. Looking to the future prepares now to get sufficient supply to take care of 210,000 persons."

Eight years later when Lake Fort Phantom Hill was about to become a reality, the *Abilene Reporter-News* reminded its readers. "Several times in its history Abilene has grown up to its water supply; it can go no further than that. But remember this: Every time it has increased its supply, Abilene has grown right up to it without exception. That was true several times in the town's early history. Always when we furnished the water the population increased. Always when a water famine threatened the population stood still or shrank."

Now into the twenty-first century, as Abilene prepares for the eventual construction of the Cedar Ridge Reservoir, which will cover more than 8,000 acres primarily in Shackelford County, Mayor Norm Archibald pointed out to constituents, "An adequate water supply is essential to West Texas. As each city plans for its future water supply, it makes sense that we look for ways to partner with other cities in West Texas to ensure our future and reduce cost of water resource development."

Probably the most famous poem to come out of Abilene was this one by editor Frank Grimes about the coming of spring. Elementary students memorized it and loyal Reporter-News *readers could recite it.*

THE OLD MESQUITES AIN'T OUT

FRANK GRIMES

We see some signs of returning spring—
The redbird's back and the fie'larks sing.
The ground's plowed up and the creeks run clear.
The onions sprout and the rosebud's near;
And yet they's a point worth thinkin' about—

We note that the old
mesquites ain't out!

The fancier trees are in full bloom.
The grass is green and the willows bloom.
The colts kick up and the calves bend down.
And spring's a-pear-ently come to town;
And yet they's a point worth thinkin' about—

We note that the old
mesquites ain't out!

Well, it may be spring for all we know—
There ain't no ice and there ain't no snow.
It looks like spring and it smells so, too—
The calendar says it's plenty true—
And still they's a point worth thinkin' about—

We note that the old
mesquites ain't out!

Elmer Kelton, who lived in San Angelo, often visited Abilene and was a favorite author of many local residents. Included below is the prologue to The Time It Never Rained, *Kelton's signature novel about the drought of the 1950s. Although it wasn't written about Abilene specifically, it certainly applied to all of West Texas.*

THE TIME IT NEVER RAINED

ELMER KELTON

It crept up out of Mexico, touching first along the brackish Pecos and spreading then in all directions, a cancerous blight burning a scar upon the land.

Just another dry spell, men said at first. Ranchers watched waterholes recede to brown puddles of mud that their livestock would not touch. They watched the rank weeds shrivel as the west wind relentlessly sought them out and smothered them with its hot breath. They watched the grass slowly lose its green, then curl and fire up like dying cornstalks.

Farmers watched their cotton make an early bloom in its stunted top, produce a few half-hearted bolls and then wither.

Men grumbled, but you learned to live with the dry spells if you stayed in West Texas; there were more dry spells than wet ones. No one expected another drought like that of '33. And the really big dries like 1918 came once a lifetime.

Why worry? they said. It would rain this fall. It always had.

But it didn't and many a boy would become a man before the land was green again.

*When Robert A. Fink first published this poem in 1987, he entitled it
"Drought: Sure Signs in Merkel, Texas." But the sentiments fit Abilene
just as well.*

DROUGHT:
SURE SIGNS IN ABILENE, TEXAS

ROBERT A. FINK

The Farmers' Life insurance agent
washed his company car three times this week,
parked it in the driveway overnight.
Come Monday and no thunder,
he'll wax the pickup.

My next door neighbor forgets to close
his back porch windows when he leaves for work,
and the retired couple up the street
started yesterday to paint their house.
They claim they're bored with last summer's color.

Ten miles west of here, Jimmie Ruth's father
shot a rattlesnake and hung it from
the top strand of his barbed wire fence.
He noticed small birds walking backwards.
An owl flew over the house at noon.

But I. M. Richards and Mr. Petre
down at Miller's Feed & Seed farmed here in '52.
I. M. shuffles the dominoes
and spits into a box of sand,

swears this ain't nothing:

"The sky's still blue.
Nobody's seen a buzzard in the street.
And Truman's rheumatiz is acting up.
Pull yourself a chair and play this round.
We'll tell you when it's time to call the preacher."

NOW THAT'S PRAYING FOR RAIN!

KATHARYN DUFF

Shortly after 3 p.m. it happened.

Rain!

Seventy-three consecutive rainless days, then a good shower—and immediately many began taking credit for the miraculous moisture.

At least a couple may be due recognition for bringing on the drought-breaker.

Dr. Ed Grosbeck, who heads up the academic affairs at Hardin-Simmons University, can lay some claim to the shower.

At Abilene Rotary Friday he listened as the fellows sang "Home on the Range." He heard that line ". . . and the sky is not cloudy . . ." and decided this had been true too long.

Dr. Grosbeck arose at 12:30 p.m. and announced to Rotarians he was scheduling immediately at H-SU an intercollegiate rodeo. That always brings rain. Exactly two and half hours later it began thundering.

Charles O. Davis of Rule may be due more credit.

About the seventy-second day without rain Davis decided, in all sincerity, that the time had come to start praying. He sent us a copy of a suggested prayer, one to be prayed earnestly. We read it, in that spirit, and right away the raindrops began to fall.

His supplication, quoted in full:

O Lord, in Thy Mercy grant us rain and by that we don't mean a shower.

We want to go out and watch the lightning rip across the southwestern sky in hot blue forks as the clouds roll in on us. We want to hurry home to close the house with the first fat drops, the size of marbles on a suddenly rising wind, chasing us and plunking on the car hood. We want to scramble all over the house, just as the first sheets descend, frantically slamming down the windows.

O Lord of Hosts, we want to look out of the windows and watch the regiments of close-packed raindrops march diagonally down. We want to hear the gurgle of the gutters under the eaves, and then the sputter of the downspout.

God of Israel, Isaac and Jacob, let it come down so hard, let the drops dance so high that the streets and sidewalks seem covered with a six-inch fog of spatter-drops. Then let it just keep up for a while, and then begin to slack off, and then turn right around and get a lot worse, swishing, pounding, spattering, pouring, drenching, the thunder coming—Crackity BAM!—and the lightning flashing so fast and furious you can't tell which flash goes with which peal of thunder so that the women will get scared and climb on top of the beds and scream at you not to get too close to that window.

Then, O Jealous God, repeat the whole act about three times, and in the middle of the second time we will climb up in the attic and put the wash pan under that tiny leak in the roof which usually we can't even notice in an ordinary rain.

And after a couple of hours kind of taper it down, O Lord, to a good steady rain—not a drizzle, but a businesslike one that keeps up until just about dawn and then spits a few drops occasionally during the morning from a gray sky.

Texas is indeed the Promised Land, O Lord, and if it gets a break it will flow with milk and honey.

But we can't live much longer on promises.

So in Thine own way and in Thine own time make up Thy mind, O Lord, and we will bow before Thy Judgment and praise Thine everlasting name.

Amen.

And again, amen.

One of the more effective—and humorously controversial—Abilene Clean and Proud campaigns involved getting the public to plant more crape myrtle trees in 1997. A suggestive billboard set off the fireworks, as Bill Whitaker reported in his column in the Abilene Reporter-News.

THE CRAPE MYRTLE SEX SCANDAL

BILL WHITAKER

If those charged with cleaning up Abilene agree on one thing, it's that sex sells. Especially when it involves plants.

A front-page story appeared in the *Abilene Reporter-News* about a campaign encouraging one and all to buy flowering crape myrtles to dress up Abilene. The story also concerned one or two people who took offense at the campaign's billboards. The billboards around town feature a shapely woman of high class. They read: "Myrtle's coming. Get your bed ready." Which, of course, those one or two people in our fair city of 116,000 took as needlessly suggesting sex or at least planting the notion in young minds.

Folks who don't know this city well might say it's typical of Abilene, with its Bible Belt mentality and puritanical values, but that's not exactly fair. In fact, the other 115,998 people in town simply laughed off the very idea of Abilene Clean & Proud billboards promoting rampant sex. What's more, some folks decided to show how ridiculous they think such criticisms are by going out and buying crape myrtles—something they might not have done had the billboards not drawn fire.

Donna Albus, head of Abilene Clean and Proud and a pivotal member of the campaign to drape Abilene in crape myrtles, discovered to her surprise that the scandal had gained headlines far beyond

Abilene. "Well, it made the front page of the Galveston paper," Donna told me. "Then I got a call from Betsy Howie, director of Keep Texas Beautiful. She'd gotten a fax of it from someone in Fort Worth."

"Donna, we may have to rescind your affiliation with us," Betsy said. "Any affiliation dealing in sex, we just have to rescind." Fortunately, the state director was joking, but it's been like that ever since the story surfaced, first in the hometown newspaper, then in papers across the state. Donna says the story has even been reported on Cable News Network.

Meanwhile, crape myrtle orders are coming in like crazy. Hardin-Simmons University ordered 225 crape myrtles, the golf course in Clyde ordered a hundred, and BFI, which runs the local landfill operation, purchased 250 and donated them to be planted in public places around Abilene. "We're just selling crape myrtles out the wazoo," Donna said.

So the bizarre publicity certainly hasn't hurt. In fact, Abilene and the surrounding area may be blooming crazy because of it.

Whether it cleared up the great alligator mystery of the 1950s or not, it made for a pretty good story.

ALLIGATOR ON THE LOOSE

MIKE ROARK

Jim Freeman wanted to clear his conscience, so more than fifty years later he came clean about his involvement in the great alligator mystery of the late 1950s.

Freeman lives in Southeast Texas, but back in the day his family lived on Marshall Street in Abilene. Freeman's friend Lowel "Porky" Mosley came to live with the Freemans in 1958, or maybe it was 1959. Mosley lived in Florida, and his parents were moving overseas. He didn't want to leave the country, so he came to Abilene to stay with his friend. When he made his trek from Florida to West Texas, Mosley brought along an eighteen-inch alligator.

"We called him Ally Gator," Freeman said. "We kept him in a harness clipped to the clothes line and would play with him in the backyard. One day we came home, and the harness was empty."

Freeman and Mosley were ready to search for their pet, but Freeman's mother would hear nothing of the sort. "Mother wouldn't allow us to look for Ally or even talk about him," Freeman explained. "She swore us to secrecy about it all." Freeman said his mother would never want to admit her son illegally possessed a reptile.

About a year later, an alligator showed up a couple blocks away in the cellar of a house. Freeman wanted to rush over and see his old pal, but again, his mother forbade it.

The alligator was given to the Abilene Zoo with a certain amount of fanfare, and many people wondered how an alligator came to be found in a neighborhood in Abilene, Freeman said.

"There was a story about it in the *Reporter-News*," Freeman said. "Mom cut it out, and I have it somewhere."

A couple of years ago, Freeman brought his granddaughters to Abilene to visit family and friends, and they ended up at the zoo. There in the gator pond, Freeman saw a big old alligator that appeared to have a gator tear in his eye.

"I wondered if that could be Ally," Freeman said. "I asked a volunteer how long that alligator had been at the zoo, and she told me for 'longer than the forty years I've worked here.'"

Zoo director Bill Gersonde said there are no records on animals from the old zoo. The newest alligator in the current zoo that was built in the mid-1960s was received in 1966. Alligators live to about fifty in the wild, according to the Smithsonian National Zoo website.

So, was that Ally Gator that Freeman saw in the zoo? "If I was a betting man, I'd say it was," he answered.

It appears that the mystery has finally been solved.

When a Reporter-News *reader sent in a question to Ask Doug about Abilene creeks flowing north, rather than south, Doug Williamson turned to Brent McClellan, the city's storm-water services administrator, for an answer.*

WHY ABILENE CREEKS FLOW NORTH

BRENT McCLELLAN

All six of Abilene's creeks empty into one creek—Elm Creek—which empties into Fort Phantom. These six creeks are Catclaw Creek, Cedar Creek, Elm Creek, Little Elm Creek, Lytle Creek, and Rainey Creek.

Little Elm Creek is the first creek to empty into Elm Creek just south of I-20 and west of Winters Freeway. Catclaw Creek is the next to convey water into Elm Creek, which occurs just north of I-20 and east of Highway 83/84. Finally, Cedar Creek drains into Elm Creek just before emptying into Fort Phantom. Lytle Creek and Rainey Creek convey their water into Cedar Creek further upstream.

Water flows north instead of south in Abilene due to the Callahan Divide, which is located south of Abilene. North of this divide the water is part of the greater Brazos River watershed and thus is flowing north to enter the Brazos River basin. To get to the Brazos River, the water flows through two gaps: Buffalo Gap (Elm Creek watershed) and Cedar Gap (Cedar Creek watershed).

The water that goes through Abilene, however, winds up in Lake Fort Phantom Hill due to a man-made dam that was created to provide water to citizens of Abilene. The water south of the Callahan

Divide is part of the greater Colorado River watershed and thus flows south to the Colorado River basin.

Water that falls in Buffalo Gap and Coronado's Camp make it to Fort Phantom, while water that falls in Tuscola flows to the Colorado River.

Sherilyn Hanks meditates on childhood summers spent playing on the banks of Catclaw Creek.

HAUNTING ECHOES

SHERILYN HANKS

Catclaw Creek lazily curls through the park and between quiet residential streets, making its own history. A pungent, musty area of haunting echoes and elusive animals, the creek mystically draws youngsters with a promise of adventure and memories of ages past.

Growing up in this civilized wilderness, I was one of the numerous sweaty, brown-skinned street urchins who lived in mud-stained clothes. No one ever told me that playing in the creek was dull and boring, so I always considered it a haven—an escape.

The rugged terrain of the creek bank housed hiding places for children and animals. Playing cowboys and Indians, hide-and-seek, and army were only a few of the many activities we enjoyed. Imaginations ran rampant as we remained from early morning to late evening in the region of the creek.

On the creek bank, smelling and looking as if they had been stored in wooden chests for a hundred years, scrawny, gray scrub bushes dotted the rugged terrain. Huge, spiny tumbleweeds were carelessly tossed about by the summer winds. Those which collided with the scrub bushes built a latticework windbreak which captured runaway scraps of paper and debris and made wonderful "hills" for ambushing Indians.

Our two concessions to reality were lunch, more often eaten in the creek than in the house, and the late afternoon visit of the ice cream truck. At the first tinkle of the bell, we would yell "time out" and run to get the money we kept by the front door. Much slurping and dripping indicated our enjoyment of the moment and gave us a brief respite in our day of frenzied activity.

Even more interesting than the games on the creek bank were the beckoning depths of the creek bed. Less than a foot of murky brown water crawled through the creek bed, licking at the tiny green plants hanging on the edge. Small stagnant pools carved by amateur explorers mirrored our iridescent, blue-green reflections and made wonderful wishing wells for our tiny pebbles.

While exploring the water's edge, we could usually hear the popping sounds of curious turtles whose snake-like heads often popped up from the slow moving water to observe us. After a cursory glance, the heads disappeared, leaving a bubble floating on top of the water. Small bugs of all sorts were constant companions. Unwelcomed snakes would at times be seen slithering in dirty brown water. More enjoyable "critters" were the crawdads.

Fishing for crawdads was a favorite pastime of the "creek crew." As we crouched on the water's edge, our eager eyes watched for little flurries in the water. Small beady eyes and flickering antennae would cautiously break the surface of the water. Only then did we plan our strategy. Watching the movement of the water, we could quickly grab the scaly crawdad by its thick neck, avoiding the dreaded, thrashing pinchers. On special occasions, after forty or fifty crawdads had been caught, the long awaited "crawdad tail fry" was planned. We, the neighborhood fishermen, combined our catches and began pinching the crawdad tails off. With a quick motion like the peeling of a banana, the scab-like shell was off. Gagging and retching, especially by the girls, accompanied the chore, the nauseating stench of creek water, mud-caked sweaty bodies, and mashed animal entrails permeating the entire creek bank area.

We would carefully take the crawdad tails to a kitchen and a mother—mine usually—and then sit in the yard to await our feast, the tempting fragrances making our mouths water. When the platter of fried tails arrived, there would be much licking of fingers and smacking of lips. That was a life of luxury for eager young adventurers.

After a day of frenzied activity, the entire area began to quieten, and the atmosphere of Catclaw Creek changed. Wistful goodnights were called up and down the streets as we trudged home, kicking the can one last time, tired but content. Tomorrow promised to be another day of searches for buried treasure and secret hideaways. The cooling breezes gently lulled the tired creek to sleep as dreams of tomorrow floated in the heads of the sleepy children.

*In 1995 Greg Young, a pharmacist with the knack for turning a phrase
and a voice to match, joined Catclaw Creek, and he volunteered to write
the group's theme song, which kicks off the band's 2003 self-released CD,
Catclaw Creek.*

CATCLAW CREEK

GREG YOUNG

When it's hot and dry in the summertime in good old Abilene
the bobcats on the Catclaw Creek carry a canteen.

> (Chorus)
> Oh the Catclaw Creek, she catches rain whenever the rain
>   comes down.
> We only get two feet a year, but on that day we drown,
>   son, on that day we drown.

I used to swim on Catclaw Creek when I was young and hip.
Sometimes I'd wear my cut-offs. Sometimes I'd skinny-dip.

The Catclaw Creek, she flooded back in '95.
It rained so hard, it rained so long, we prayed for hot and dry.

> (Chorus)
> Oh the Catclaw Creek, she catches rain whenever the rain
>   comes down.
> We only get two feet a year, but on that day we drown,
>   son, on that day we drown.

The Texas Parks and Wildlife tried to drain that Catclaw Creek.
They gave up after forty years 'cause the dust was just too deep.

I've heard it told one day it snowed on the Fourth of July.
By the middle of the day it melted away and the Catclaw Creek
was dry.

We've sung a lot about Catclaw Creek, but we haven't sung enough.
If you want to know more about Catclaw Creek, read the book by
Katharyn Duff.

> (Chorus)
> Oh the Catclaw Creek, she catches rain whenever the rain
> comes down.
> We only get two feet a year, but on that day we drown,
> son, on that day we drown.

REUNION OF CHAMPIONS
SPORTS & LEISURE

Independence Day race at Fair Park, 1925

Hardin-Simmons University Collection

Abilene has a rich sports tradition with a special emphasis, of course—this being West Texas—on high school football. But other sports, over the years, have also claimed their rightful place in sports and leisure lore.

We begin this section with the story of a high school football coach many Abilenians may not be familiar with, but who is revered in the older black community—Louis Kelley. Kelley starred at

Woodson High School at a time when the better-known crosstown Abilene High Eagles were winning three state championships, compiling a forty-nine-game winning streak, and being named Team of the Century in high school football. Yet Kelley went on to make quite a name for himself, on and off the field, in forty years as a high school coach.

Our section recalls champions then and now—in football, basketball, baseball and track—as well as tales about early day car racing, private club poker, minor league baseball, and a plane crash that the team lived to tell about. As with the other sections in this collection, many, many more stories could be told. But here are a dozen to enjoy.

LOUIS KELLEY EXCELLED ON, OFF THE FIELD

EDDIE SORIANO

Sports, like many other things in life, run deeper than what the average person sees on the playing field. What seems to be the great athleticism of one person is often a mask for the athleticism of many.

Take, for example, the case of the 1959 New Mexico State University football team. The team, led by future hall of fame coach Warren B. Woodson, went 8-3 and won the 1959 Sun Bowl in El Paso, Texas. [Woodson also coached at Hardin-Simmons 1941-42 and 1946-51; his 1942 and 1946 teams were undefeated.]

The team was led by its dominating backfield, including quarterback Charley Johnson, who was fifth in the nation in passing and was named the Sun Bowl MVP. The backfield also included the nation's leading rusher in Pervis Atkins and another great halfback in Bobby Gaiters, who rushed for a game-high 123 yards during the Sun Bowl.

Johnson, Atkins and Gaiters all went on to have careers in the NFL. However, at the end of that 1959 season, when it came time for the team to vote for most valuable player, none of these great athletes was chosen.

The player that the team felt was the most important part of their great season was the fourth part of that great backfield, full-back Louis Kelley, the man entrusted with creating holes for two of the best halfbacks in the nation to run through, the man who protected his future Pro Bowl quarterback from oncoming rushers, the man who did all this and more, and did it without even a single complaint.

"I felt honored," Kelley said. "I took pride in what I did. I knew those guys were the stars of the team and my job was to protect them as much as I could, but it was a great honor for them to thank me in that way."

Danny Villanueva, who was the kicker for that 1959 team, recalls that Kelley was a great high school running back in his own right coming out of Woodson High School in Abilene, Texas.

"Here's a guy who came to NM State with fame as a running back but was asked instead to become the blocker and protect the three stars of the team," Villanueva said, "and he did it without a word or complaint. He paved the way for Charley, Pervis and Bobby to go to the pros."

Clem Mancini was also part of that 1959 team and now lives in Lubbock, where Kelley now resides. "He was a good football player and a vital part of one of the best backfields they ever had at NM State," Mancini said. "He just wanted to make sure we won, he didn't care about himself. He just played hard."

Although ferocious on the field, Kelley was the polar opposite off the field. "On the field he was competitive, determined and passionate," Villanueva said, "and then he gets off the field and it's hugs, high fives and being a funny guy."

Browning Yelvington, who was Kelley's teammate and roommate during that season, remembers Kelley always staying positive. It was at times difficult for Kelley, an African-American, living in the time of civil rights distress, according to Yelvington, who is white.

Yelvington describes Kelley as always making friends and never judging people even when they judged him, even mistreated him. "On the field he was the hardest hitter," Yelvington said, "but he was never a loudmouth or show-off. He always was very conservative and made friends with everybody."

Kelley credits his parents for instilling good morals in him and pointing him in the right direction. He also said that his high school teachers and coaches were great examples for his future.

Kelley said, however, that his time at NM State was probably what propelled him to the great high school coaching career he had after college. He has fond memories of that 1959 team and his time at the university.

"NM State got me started," Kelley said. "How they treated me was just great, from the coaches to the players to the students, it was just a great atmosphere."

After his time at NM State, in which he became the first African-American athlete to graduate from the university, Kelley went on to become one of the all-time winningest coaches in Texas high school history. He coached for forty years in the Lubbock area, including twenty-six years at Estacado High School where he won two hundred games and seventeen district championships before his retirement in 2000.

Kelley said he tried to teach the lessons he learned during his playing days in school to his student-athletes. "Don't worry about the things you can't control," Kelley said he would tell his players, "just worry about the things you can control and that means working hard every day, getting your class work done and being a good person."

Kelley's high school coaching success often came with teams that were undersized compared to the other high school teams in the state, which exemplifies even more the impact Kelley had on the kids. "He got underperforming kids to play at a high level and that's why he is so revered in the Lubbock area," Villanueva said, "because they know what he did with kids that normally would not have achieved what they did under his direction."

Indeed, in Kelley's forty years of coaching high school football, he helped 135 of his players get full football scholarships to continue their education and twelve of his former players made it to the NFL.

Louis Kelley has a long list of accolades on his resume—the inaugural Abilene ISD (later Big Country) Athletic Hall of Fame for his high school play, the New Mexico State Athletic Hall of Fame for his college career, and the Texas High School Football Coaches Association Hall of Honor and the inaugural Lubbock Hall of Honor in 2011 for his high school coaching career. He was even voted the Lubbock All-City Coach of the Century in 1999 by the *Lubbock-Avalanche Journal*.

Louis Kelley, however, isn't about accolades. As he demonstrated during that great 1959 season at NM State, Louis Kelley is about the good of the people around him.

"When those guys landed on the front page of newspapers it gave me a lot of pride that I helped them achieve that," Kelley said. "It didn't matter to me if my name was never mentioned because I knew that I and the rest of the team contributed to their success."

One thing is for sure, whether opening up holes for his teammates to score touchdowns in southern New Mexico or mentoring his high school players so they can become better people in the plains of West Texas, Louis Kelley has always been the one clearing the way for greatness.

And in doing so, whether he recognizes it or not, he has become great himself. It is a greatness found in quiet leadership and commitment to his team's success. More than just football players, he molded young boys into good men. Therein is the key to the greatness of Louis Kelly's life.

Fair Park, or what is known today as Rose Park, was home to the West Texas Fair beginning in 1914 and the venue boasted a dirt automobile race track which hosted some of racing's biggest names in the 1920s and brought thousands to Abilene in order to watch the spectacle whizzing about the West Texas Speedway.

THE WEST TEXAS SPEEDWAY

JAY MOORE

For more than forty years, the moving force behind the West Texas Fair was a local gasoline distributor by the name of D. H. Jefferies, who volunteered countless hours to improving the fair. One idea implemented by Jefferies in 1919 in order to put the fair on firm financial footing was to capitalize on the newfangled spectacle of automobile racing. He pushed to change the fair's horse track to accommodate auto racing.

Jefferies understood that people would pay to come and see something as astonishing as a car whizzing dangerously around a track at speeds approaching a hundred miles per hour. So he saw to it that the old horse track's curves were banked and that extra grandstands were put up to handle the anticipated crowds. He dubbed the new-styled track the West Texas Speedway.

And the people did come, often suffering through a blizzard of blowing dust in order to watch racers from across the country fly around the dirt track—and even witnessing the occasional crash. In 1923, Dick Calhoun crashed his Ford and was thrown several yards through the air. After being loaded into an ambulance and rushed to the hospital, the sympathetic Abilene crowd took up a collection to help pay for Calhoun's medical treatment.

Auto races held during the fair proved so popular that soon Jefferies persuaded the Fair Association to hold races at other times of the year—and so began the tradition of annual July 4th races.

In the spring of 1926 Jefferies successfully enlisted a fairly unknown driver by the name of Frank Lockhart to commit to the Independence Day race. Then in May of that year Lockhart was vaulted out of obscurity when he won the fourteenth running of the Indianapolis 500. This big win prompted Lockhart to try to void his contract and skip his Abilene appearance, but Jefferies held the Indy winner to his pledge. And so, two months after his big win, the twenty-three-year old boy wonder from Southern California brought his racing Miller Special to Abilene to take on the likes of Harry Milburn in his Duesenberg, George Souders driving his Chevrolet, and Herbert Hass in his Hudson Super-Six.

It is difficult to appreciate the economic impact such races brought to Abilene. In 1926, with the population of Abilene at around 24,000, the July 4th race crowd that same year was estimated at 12,000. One young race fan from Lubbock commented he had never seen so many people from Lubbock, except in Lubbock. Hotels placed cots in any available space and still hundreds slept in their cars; more than 300 spent the night in the depot park.

Spectators filled the grandstands, circled the track, and stood in the infield to watch Frank Lockhart push his racing machine to first place and the $1,000 prize. He covered the thirty mile race in twenty-eight minutes and twenty-three seconds.

In the late 1920s and the 1930s, the track infield served as the home field for polo matches. Abilene had two polo teams as the sport found a temporary burst of popularity across the country. West Texas Utilities fielded one team and the other was known as the Abilene Polo and Saddle Club. The first contest was held in 1927 as the Abilene Club went up against a team from Dallas and defeated them 7 to 3.

Auto racing at Fair Park came to an end in the 1930s. As fewer and fewer people could afford the price of admission, the once popular auto races fell victim to the Great Depression. In the 1940s, the banked curves were graded flat once more and horse races were again held at the track as part of the West Texas Fair.

The grandstands are long gone as is the track itself. About the only reminder of the popular attraction is that stretch of South 9th Street—running in front of the National Guard Armory—that once paralleled the back stretch of the old West Texas Fair Speedway. Now, just an Abilene memory.

In a 2001 series on the 100 top minor league baseball teams of all time, the 1946 Abilene Blue Sox were ranked number ninety-four. The team, presided over by twenty-five-year-old sportswriter and future politician Howard Green, drew 100,000 fans in 1946 to its stadium at the present location of H-E-B grocery at Barrow and South 14th.

The most famous alumnus of that 1946 team was its power-hitting first baseman, Danny Ozark, who later became a major league manager. Thirty years later, Abilene Reporter-News *sports editor Bob Lapham reminisced with Ozark about that summer of '46.*

SUMMER OF '46 WITH THE ABILENE BLUE SOX

BOB LAPHAM

"It was a time to have fun, and we did. We had a great time that year, and I recall Abilene being a really nice place."

Danny Ozark, a native of Buffalo, New York, came out of the service with a super-powerful bat. He was signed by the Brooklyn system Branch Rickey put together and was sent to Abilene. With the Blue Sox, Ozark hit .325, 31 home runs and had 142 runs batted in.

Blue Sox followers remember that wide, Joe DiMaggio-style stance, and those rainbow homers he would send over the left-field fence. Ozark was slow of foot and that probably kept him from making the major leagues. He spent the next four seasons with the Fort Worth Cats.

I had to insert a personal reflection, one that went past my admiration of watching Ozark hit those homers and then make the rounds, pulling ones and fives through the mesh wire behind home plate from happy Abilene fans who watched their team sweep to the

West Texas-New Mexico League title, only to lose to Lubbock in the playoffs four games to one.

I didn't go into all the details with Ozark, but as I recalled them in my mind, it involved a bunch of buddies. I don't remember all [who played] on that parched South 14th Jefferson Junior High field, but they most likely included Tommy Estes, Jim Spradling (the first brush-back pitcher I ever knew; we were all eleven years old that summer), Macky Newton, Tommy Seale, Tommy Overman, Bob Fry, Bob Black, Bill Pierce and Frank Hunt.

I don't recall who it was that lazy summer morning—but fear it was myself—who decided that the greatest compliment we could pay a Blue Sox was to ask him to umpire our game that had an 8:30 a.m. start. Ozark shared a room with a super center fielder named Ed Krage, in a house just down South 14th. Hunt, I think it was, and I peddled our bikes there, got off, knocked on the door and looked straight up as a sleepy Danny Ozark (our hero!) scowled down at us. I still remember the less-than-diplomatic rejection we received.

Ozark, of course, didn't remember it. What, or whom, did he remember from the old Blue Sox?

"Ed, of course, and I remember Stubby (Hayden Greer, the manager), who was just a young guy like the rest of us. My best friends were Johnny Hall, Leo Thomas, (catcher) Kenny Quevreaux, (pitcher-outfielder) Ken Olson, I guess. I remember those are the ones I kept in touch with the longest down through the years. I still hear from Leo every now and then."

Thomas, the third baseman, made the majors briefly. So did pitcher Hall, who endeared himself to Abilene fans with his fireball delivery that every now and then would catch the hitter off stride when replaced by the famous Hall "blooper ball." "Johnny could've lasted longer (at Brooklyn in the early 1950s)," Ozark recalled. "But he ruined his arm shortly after that."

We spent the remainder of our conversation with my tossing out names and Ozark quickly remembering them with a laugh or an "um-hum," names like Lubbock Hubber manager Hack Miller, the original obscene gesture public figure who used to get thrown out of every other game in Abilene, and once refused to leave. I remember I was bat boy for the Hubbers that night and couldn't believe it when Miller responded to boos in response to his beefing at the ump by waving that solitary finger high in the air; and really couldn't believe it when Miller had to be dragged off kicking and screaming by two policemen.

Or Big Joe Bowman, who went on to set a minor league record seventy home runs playing for Clovis.

"That was a lot of fun, a whole lot of fun," Ozark said again of his Abilene days.

It was for me, too. Hustling out there to meet the bus or station wagon and scuffle with five or six other chums to be at the front of the line when the bat boy for the visitors was selected. If I missed there, I'd head for the scoreboard in left-center. Squatter's rights prevailed there; first one got to run the board.

If I missed there, there was always the chance of catching up with a foul ball to provide free admission. Or, in a pinch, sneaking under that low place in the fence under the right-side bleachers.

If I was bat boy, I got no pay. Just the broken bats, and if I was lucky a discarded ball or two. The scoreboard was also no pay. They were just ways to get to watch the Blue Sox, and heroes like Danny Ozark.

Like Danny, recalling the Summer of '46 was a fun trip for me, too.

[Danny Ozark managed the Philadelphia Phillies to three straight National League East Division championships in 1976-77-78. Ozark was also known

for his reputed malapropisms, including these: "Half this game is ninety percent mental." "It is beyond my apprehension." "Even Napoleon had his Watergate."]

*The Abilene Club opened when H. O. Wooten built the Wooten Hotel
in 1930, which included facilities for Abilene's first "gentlemen's club."
Former Mayor Elbert E. Hall reminisced about it in his book,* Page One.

POKER AT THE ABILENE CLUB

ELBERT E. HALL

The poker room action began every day at a little after noon and generally lasted until suppertime, when one of the regular winners, finding himself twenty dollars to the good, would stand up and announce that it was milking time or that his back was killing him or that he needed to go run his dog. Saturday nights the game might run until the lights were flashed by the patient steward.

One of the town's better insurance fellows served as banker for the game, exchanging chips for cash or checks, settling disputes and determining how much credit might be extended. It wasn't a big game except for the times when some high roller came to town looking for action and these didn't meet with too much success in competition with the hard-bottomed regulars. Oswald Jacoby, not a bad card player himself, went back to bridge after a couple of sessions of "Hold 'em" with the brothers.

Ben L. Cox was a regular at the game. Ben L., a local attorney with the looks and humor of Will Rogers, was the greatest storyteller ever and worth losing to just to be around, except that he almost never won.

In one of his races for a seat in the Texas Legislature, Ben L., who really was a very successful lawyer, had been accused by his opponent of being nothing but a broken-down poker player. Ben L. ignored the charges for most of the campaign but finally, in a speech from the bandstand on the Federal lawn (where the post office is now), he declared the accusation a base canard.

"I can give you the names," he told his audience, "of eight respected and competent poker players, any one of whom will testify that I am not a poker player, never have been and surely never will be." The matter thus settled, Ben L. went on to discuss the issues of the day and eventually to win his race.

It was Ben L., incidentally, who put a visiting player in his place one afternoon. In an effort to make a busted flush stand up, this gentleman shoved in all his chips and then, in violation of house rules, reached in his hip pocket, took out his wallet and tossed it in the pot.

"I'm betting whatever's there," he said.

Ben L. thought for a minute, reached down and untied his shoe, took it off and put it in the center of the table.

"Well," he said, "if we've gone to betting leather, I'm raising you one Florsheim."

THREE OLYMPIC GOLD MEDALS

GARNER ROBERTS

In 1956 Bobby Joe Morrow, a sprinter from San Benito, Texas, who had recently completed his sophomore season at Abilene Christian College, won three gold medals at the summer games of the XVI Olympiad in Melbourne, Australia.

"It's something an athlete works for all his life," Morrow remembered fifty years later. "Then he finally gets the opportunity, and the opportunity pays off. The American flag is hoisted on the flag pole, and the Star Spangled Banner plays. It's unbelievable the feeling you get, the tingle that you get up your spine. It's something an athlete will never forget as long as he lives."

Morrow's performance was the highlight of a record-breaking U.S. men's Olympic track and field team that certainly was one of the best in history. The U.S. men dominated the competition, winning fifteen of the twenty-four events and taking home a total of twen-ty-eight gold, silver and bronze medals. America's twelve succeeding teams have failed to reach those standards.

Morrow became the first man since the legendary Jesse Owens to sweep the three Olympic sprint gold medals, he appeared on the cover of *Life* magazine and on national television, he was named Sportsman of the Year by *Sports Illustrated*, and he received the Sullivan Award as amateur athlete of the year in the U.S.

Paul O'Neil, writing in *Sports Illustrated* of Morrow's award, said, "Athletic prowess was not the sole reason for Bobby Morrow's selection. His multiple victories, gratifying though they may have been to his countrymen, could hardly have qualified him for the honor if they had not also served to dramatize the spirit as well as the accomplishments of the Olympic movement. Bobby Morrow is an unusual young man, and none symbolized more eloquently than he the ideals of sportsmanship which the athletes of the U.S. Olympic team took with them to Australia."

The Games of 1956 in the southern hemisphere opened Thanksgiving Day, Thursday, November 22. After qualifying heats the next day, Morrow rode a bus to the stadium November 24, and two hours after winning his semifinal heat, he settled into the starting blocks for the Olympic 100-meter final.

"I tried not to get distracted, to mind my own business, put my blocks down and do what I came to do. I knew I had to get a good start. I was usually a slow starter and had to make up the difference. I think I came out about even, but I could see midway through the race I had to pick it up a little bit."

He did just that, winning before a standing-room-only crowd of more than 110,000 people at Melbourne's Cricket Grounds.

With his thirty-six-year-old coach Oliver Jackson supervising training sessions in Melbourne and watching races from the stadium seats, Morrow added gold medals for the 200 meters on November 27 and 400-meter relay on December 1. Morrow's eleven-race Olympic experience ended with a relay world record of 39.5 seconds with U.S. teammates Ira Murchison, Leamon King and Thane Baker.

Morrow won fourteen national sprint titles at AAU, NAIA and NCAA Division I national meets in the 100 and 200 in his four-year Abilene Christian career. He won eighty of his eighty-eight collegiate races and set seventeen world records.

''He had the most phenomenal career I guess that a sprinter has ever had,'' Jackson said. "Bobby was the easiest guy to coach you ever saw. He was the type of guy we needed here in our program. He was so dedicated to winning that he would pay the price. We told Bobby he could be the Olympic champion, but it's going to take a lot of work, but he was willing to do it. I never heard Bobby fuss or argue about the workouts.

''Bobby had poise and a fluid motion like nothing I've ever seen. He could run a 220 with a root beer float on his head and never spill a drop. I made an adjustment to his start when he was a freshman. After that, my only advice to him was to change his major to speech because he'd be destined to make a bunch of them.''

Chuck Moser compiled an incredible record of 78-7-2 in his seven years as head football coach at Abilene High in the 1950s, including three consecutive state championships and a forty-nine-game winning streak. The Moser teams were named Team of the Century in 2000 by the Dallas Morning News. *However, for Moser, it wasn't all about winning on the field.*

CHUCK MOSER'S ELIGIBILITY SLIPS

AL PICKETT

Chuck Moser's philosophy about the role of his football team in the school may surprise some.

"There is only one reason to have a good athletic program," he said, "and that's so you'll have a lot better school system. I got into my players and our athletic program that the best student in that class—maybe not the smartest—is the one who will set the example for listening and studying and passing those tests. If you do anything in that class that the teacher doesn't like, she will tell me and I will take care of it. The kids knew that. Our kids were smart, and they set good examples. In turn, the teachers loved us. We had some teachers who wanted to win worse than I did, if that's possible."

Moser's eligibility slips were as much a part of being an Eagle as going to practice itself. When Texas House Bill 72 passed in the mid-1980s, some observers considered the no-pass, no-play rule a revolutionary idea. It wasn't; Moser had his own form of no-pass, no-play fifty years ago. He required every player on his team to take an eligibility slip to each teacher each week. The teacher had to sign the slip, fill out the student athlete's grade, attendance record, and attitude. The teacher could also make comments on the eligibility slip, which the student athlete had to turn in to Moser each Monday. If a player wasn't passing three courses, he couldn't play the following Friday. That rule was set in stone and would later play a role in Abilene's winning streak.

Twyman Ash, an all-state end on the Eagles' 1954 state championship team, said the eligibility slips were taken seriously. "If there was any comment on it like you were talking too much in class, he made you run. There was an old horse-racing track around the field at Fair Park. It was five-eighths of a mile, and he sent you out there. It was like running on a plowed field. Those teachers loved that guy."

David Bourland, starting quarterback on the Eagles' 1955 state championship team, also learned the importance of the eligibility slips. "The only time I ever got in trouble was my senior year. My home room teacher, Mrs. Turner, wrote on the slip that I talked too much. Coach Moser called me in. He said there's a comment on your slip that you talk too much. He said, "That's just ten hundred-yard dashes after practice, but you can handle it." Bourland said Moser made it clear to him that it better not happen again—and it didn't.

Assistant coach Wally Bullington said Moser's version of no-pass, no-play had the support of teachers and parents. "The most important question on the eligibility slip was attitude. The teachers loved it. It spilled over to the whole school. They set the tone for attitude and discipline for the whole school. And you'd better not try to forge a signature.

"The parents supported him. He'd tell the parents in a meeting before the season started that he didn't know if their boys hung up their clothes at home but they better not have any equipment lying on the floor in the locker room. He was teaching them things for life.

"He had a curfew. He called enough to let them know he would call. He wanted kids to do well in school, behave, be a role model, and have a spiritual life. He taught a Sunday school class at St. Paul Methodist Church."

The players took the curfew seriously. Hollis Swafford, a starting end on Moser's 1953 and 1954 teams, said, "If you had a date on a weekend and you were running late, you felt like he was at the door waiting on you."

The Abilene High Eagles, state football champions in 1954 and 1955, looked to make it three in a row against the Corpus Christi Ray Texans on December 22, 1956, in Memorial Stadium in Austin. One veteran sportswriter said, "If Abilene can beat this rugged ball-control Ray team, I'll go along with Abilene as being the greatest in schoolboy history."

THREE IN A ROW

MICHAEL GRANT

About 25,000 were in the stadium for the 2 p.m. kickoff. Abilene won the toss, received the kickoff and returned it to the thirty-nine. The Abilene offense and Ray defense trotted onto the field. The Eagles formed their military huddle, facing the defense, interior linemen in front, ends and backs behind, the quarterback facing them. They looked at Gervis Galbraith, he looked at them. They had practiced the first play many times during the week. Now Galbraith called it and it was official. The game was under way.

Galbraith told them the snap count, repeated it. They clapped and broke the huddle and came up to the line. Sure enough, the Texans were in the umbrella [defense]. End Kenny Schmidt took off deep. The Eagles were going for the home run on the first play of the game. Schmidt was clear and Galbraith threw, but the pass fell short.

It was a shot worth taking, and it might have worked, but now the surprise was gone. The Eagles shifted into what they did so well. Glynn Gregory gained eight on second down and fullback Bill Sides ran for four more, into Texan territory, but then a Galbraith-Gregory pitchout misfired. Ray's Frank Eddleman recovered the fumble at the fifty-yard line.

The Texan offense came to the line breathing fire. In five plays they had gained the Eagle nineteen and looked like a team that could beat the Eagle defense. Then end Stuart Peake broke through and hit quarterback Arthur McCallum. The ball came loose and bounded all the way back to the forty-four before McCallum could fall on it.

Unperturbed, McCallum threw to end Sonny Davis at the Abilene twenty-one. He threw again to Davis, this time to the Eagle four. Abilene was very much a team in trouble.

McCallum kept on a quarterback sneak to the two. Sub halfback Bart Shirley rammed to the one. McCallum tried another sneak and was piled up at the one-foot line.

On fourth down, the two teams massed at the goal line, Abilene in its gap-eight defense. The center Christian snapped the ball, the lines charged, and suddenly the ball was in the air above the tumult, floating free, describing a lazy parabola toward the left end of the Texan line. It landed directly in front of Eagle linebacker Gerald Galbraith, who smothered it at the three as fans on both sides screamed.

The Eagle backs lined up in the end zone. Gregory improved things somewhat with a three-yard dive to the six. In the huddle, Gervis Galbraith looked at right tackle Boyd King, "I asked old Boyd if he could take that old boy out (tackle Walter Beck)," Galbraith said. "Sure, run that old four-play," King told him. It was the right halfback dive play straight ahead, with straight-ahead blocking and a quick count, a good strategy against a defense massed on the line of scrimmage. If a halfback could pop through . . .

Galbraith called it: "Four Straightaway, on Set, on Set." The Eagles in their gold jerseys, standing in their end zone, broke the huddle with a clap of hands, trotted to the line of scrimmage at the six, fell into the hands-on-knees "ready" stance, looked across the line at the looming Ray defenders. Boyd King and Hubert Jordan, the right guard, found their men and took their splits to get the best blocking angle.

"Down," Galbraith called, with the downward inflection. The team dropped into its three-point stance. "Set," Galbraith yelled, but without time for the rising, anticipatory inflection, because the Eagles had charged. Galbraith took the snap from Jim Rose, pivoted right, handed to Jimmy Carpenter going by, and going by so fast that Galbraith barely got the ball to him. Boyd King got position on Walter Beck, just like his coach had taught him, and knocked Beck outside. Jordan blocked Floyd Brown inside.

Carpenter, all 153 fleet pounds of him, hit the hole in a flash and burst into the clear on the other side. A Ray halfback came up. Carpenter spun to the outside, flaring slightly toward the right sideline, and in a couple of strides was in high gear. It was a footrace with the Ray safety that Carpenter won easily, ninety-four yards to the end zone. His teammates sprinted all the way down the field after him, and after Gregory's kick, Abilene led, 7-0.

Men who have played football, for the rest of their lives may refer to a particular kind of traumatic event as "a fourteen-point turnaround." A team is on the goal line, about to score, when something happens—an interception runback, or a fumble and a ninety-four-yard run. Not only has the team lost its seven points, the other team has scored seven, more or less in the same breath. It is a terrific "what if" shock, and it had happened to the Ray Texans.

[Abilene scored an insurance touchdown on the first possession of the second half, on a sixty-two-yard run by Carpenter, on the same play, Four-Straightaway, and won the championship 14-0—without completing a pass for the third straight game!]

Carlton Stowers was co-captain of the Abilene High track team that won the state championship in 1960. Stowers, author of more than forty books, reflected on his high school days after a reunion with his teammates fifty years later.

REUNION OF CHAMPIONS

CARLTON STOWERS

In the trappings of adulthood, it seems, we have become so eternally busy with thoughts of tomorrow—career ladders to climb, mortgage payments coming due, concern over the kids' college funds—that there is little time left to reflect on the past. We allow ourselves no place to retreat, even briefly, from the weary unrest of new wars, old politics and endless economic concerns; precious few opportunities to escape to gentler, simpler times when worries were few, the music sweet and young friends were forever.

As they say, nostalgia's not what it used to be.

Such were my thoughts recently as I drove toward Austin, Texas, there to join fellow old geezers who had been invited to participate in an evening ceremony that was to be held in the stadium where the annual Texas high school state track and field championships were being conducted. Celebrating its one hundredth year, the meet's officials had decided to honor the schools which had won the most titles during its history. My alma mater had won seven. A lifetime ago I had been fortunate enough to have been a small part of that. And as I drove, memories, a half century old, flooded back. As if by some gentle stroke of whimsy, I could hear the rockabilly sounds of Elvis again, remember the powerful pout of actor James Dean, the names of old girlfriends, favored teachers and coaches, and the thrill of being a part of a team made up of people who have, over so many years, remained important to me.

If you are among those certain that athletics are over-emphasized and nothing more than a distraction to academic pursuit, read no farther. It is my unwavering opinion that all those lessons learned in long afternoons of practice, then in the competitive arena, gave purpose and direction to our young lives. We learned of goal-setting and sportsmanship, winning and losing, and the rewards of contributing to a team effort. For many of us, those lessons provided the opportunity to continue our education at the college level. In my house, and in those of most of my teammates, the option was simple: No athletic scholarship, no college.

And so in time we went our separate ways—off to the University of Texas, SMU, Oklahoma, Rice, Texas Tech and hometown Abilene Christian, just to name a few—yet stayed in touch.

We are all old now, gray-haired and more slow-moving. Once carefree teenagers, we are grandfathers today, dutifully attending sports competitions of a new generation. Sadly, some of us are gone after grim battles far more serious than simply striving to win a gold medal. But for those who remain, invited to regroup and gather in front of a crowd of 20,000 and once again be called Abilene High School Eagles, it was a time-travel respite that for a moment made all the ills of the world disappear. For a brief snapshot of time we were kids again, reunited to joke, embrace unashamedly . . . and remember.

As best I recall none of those gathered had been the product of childhood privilege, all the sons of hard-working, nine-to-five parents who were supportive, loving and proud. And without exception they had grown into adult successes, becoming doctors, teachers, and lawyers, CEOs, artists and coaches.

And their journeys began back when, as kids, they did their best to run faster, jump higher and throw farther than the competition they faced on those charmed spring weekends. I can still see Dr.

Charles McCook, determinedly anchoring our mile relay to victory despite a leg pain that would later be diagnosed as a fractured fibula; insurance executive Larry Rhodes setting the state record in the 880-yard run and old buddy Gerald Cumby reigning as the state pole vault champion in a time when poles were stiff and didn't catapult their carriers to two-story heights. Bobby Johnson, the state's best high hurdler, is retired now, still married to his high school sweetheart. Andy Springer might today be a successful businessman, but I remember him best as our school record-holder in the long jump. And James Blackwood, son of the local fire marshal, has, at last count, coached no fewer than seventeen Olympians.

Their names will mean little to most. Their youthful achievements are forgotten save for us who were there as witnesses, now surpassed by swifter, stronger athletes who have followed. But to me they remain special. That's the purpose of memories.

And so we gathered, uncomfortably nodding to modest applause for bygone accomplishments, then quickly retreated into the stands, back into the real world, giving way to a new and excited group of young athletes who would record far better times and distances than those of the ancient '50s and '60s.

And as we did so, it occurred to me that an occasional sip of nostalgia has a sweet and refreshing taste. If nothing else, it serves to remind us of who we were and how it charted the course to who we would become.

Losing the game wasn't the main thing the McMurry football team would remember about a road trip in 1963. The Brotherhood of Indian Belly Landing Experts (B.I.B.L.E.) was forged from the experience.

MCMURRY FOOTBALL TEAM SURVIVES PLANE CRASH

ABILENE REPORTER-NEWS

McMurry College football players and coaches were high in praise of each other when they arrived in Abilene after a harrowing night in which their chartered DC-3 twin-engine craft had crash landed at Barksdale AFB near Shreveport, Louisiana.

[The plane was returning from Monroe to Abilene after McMurry had lost an 8-7 contest to Northeast State College in Monroe on the last play of the game.]

Because the plane's elevator controls were jammed, it was almost impossible for the pilot to get the tail section down. The three McMurry coaches volunteered to lie in the tail section to give the plane better balance and weight down that section.

One of the McMurry players, junior Joe Coulson from Fort Worth, said, "The coaches went to the back of the plane, where there were no seat belts, to weight down the tail section. They knew if the plane broke up what might happen to them. One of the boys wanted to take their place, but the coaches sent him back to his seat."

The coaches were head coach Grant Teaff and assistants Hershel Kimbrell, who is McMurry's head basketball coach, and Buddy Fornes. All are married and have families.

When the plane first landed at Barksdale AFB, it bounded "about ten feet in the air," Kimbrell said, slightly injuring Kimbrell and Teaff.

Teaff said perhaps the most dangerous part of the whole episode was the initial takeoff at Monroe. He said the pilot realized the elevator controls were locked as he attempted to pull the plane off the ground because he could gain no altitude. "But we were moving so fast by then that he couldn't do anything about it—he couldn't stop, so he had to try and get in the air," Teaff said. The plane finally cleared a fence at the far end of the runway by ten feet or less.

Even after the plane got off the ground, it could gain no altitude and tried two landings at Monroe's airport before the pilot decided to try a belly landing at Barksdale AFB because it had a long runway.

"We tried landing at Monroe twice at speeds between 120 and 150 miles an hour," Teaff said. "On the second attempt, we blew out a landing gear wheel and damaged our landing gear," and the pilot had to swerve the plane sideways to get it back into the air.

The trip from Monroe to Shreveport took about forty-five minutes. Teaff said the coaches and boys prayed twice, once during the flight to Shreveport and a prayer of thanksgiving after the plane had skidded to a halt at the airbase.

Teaff said when the belly landing was made at Barksdale that the plane bounced for 100 feet and then skidded 3,000 feet more on its belly. "After he set it down the right propeller flew off and part of the motor. If the left propeller had come off, it probably would have gone through the cabin." The coach said the plane was "red hot" after its long skid and Air Force personnel told them that had the plane skidded another 100 to 200 feet it would have exploded because of the heat it had generated plus the full load of gasoline aboard.

The Air Force personnel were due a great deal of credit for their alertness, Teaff said. "As soon as we finally stopped, they were all over that area, spraying it with foam and preventing a fire or explosion."

Teaff said he was extremely proud of his athletes. "They were remarkably calm and composed, but I'll tell you, when something like this happens you've got a lot of people who are awfully close together. The good Lord was certainly with us this morning."

Abilene's Cooper Cougars beat Galena Park North Shore and future major league pitcher Brian Bohanon 1-0 in the Class 5A state baseball semifinal game on June 16, 1987, with a play that will always be referred to in Cooper lore as "The Catch." The next day Cooper had a much easier time winning the championship game over San Antonio MacArthur 13-3, the first of two state baseball titles in a row for the Cougars under Coach Andy Malone.

THE CATCH

PHIL ASHBY

One swing and one catch.

The Cooper Cougars and Galena Park North Shore Mustangs played seven classic innings Tuesday night, but little will be remembered except for two incredible moments.

For once, the classic matchup lived up to its billing. It's a shame that the Class 5A semifinal game won't be dissected pitch by pitch, out by out by our memories. Cooper second baseman Chris Feris' outstanding play on a grounder in the hole will be overshadowed. Jason Satre's near-perfect pitching performance won't get its just reward. That's just the nature of this game and the species that play it.

But Robert McAdams' home run off Brian Bohanon and his improbable, heart-stopping catch in right field will be unforgettable. And what's so ironic about this hot, muggy night was McAdams himself. A senior who struggled through District 4-5A with a .220 average, McAdams perfectly played the role of the unlikely hero.

We've heard of Brian Bohanon and his unhittable pitching. We've read about David Tollison, Scotty Pugh and the rest of Cooper's dashing lineup. We've watched Satre make hitters look silly inning after inning. So what does McAdams do? Simply steal every bit of thunder that helped build this matchup as seven innings of white-knuckled drama.

McAdams, a leadoff hitter who in the playoffs has more than atoned for his disappointing district season, has barely gotten a sniff from the college recruiters. Oh, there have been the obligatory letters and phone calls but little has blossomed. He just shrugs it off and then goes out and plays the game better than most seventeen-year-olds.

His two catches against Duncanville in the quarterfinals were, at the time, being termed major league. But after watching him run down a solid hit in the gap and fully extend to rob North Shore of a trip to the state finals, the previous catches seem strictly minor in comparison.

"At first, I didn't think I could get to it," he said. "But it just stayed up there a little while and I reached out and grabbed it."

His description doesn't do justice to the catch, but nobody's could. Even Bohanon, who wasn't throwing around many compliments after losing only his second game of the season, had to take notice. "He made a tremendous catch—I thought for sure it was through," said the Texas Rangers' No. 1 draft choice. "I thought we would score some runs, but I guess our luck just ran out. You can't win without scoring runs."

And you can't win without people like Robert McAdams who, when you least expect it, reminds us all that this is a team game.

Of course, today's state championship game still must be played, but it was hard to walk away Tuesday night without feeling it won't compare to the 1-0 gem and the night McAdams stole the show.

On December 19, 2009, Abilene High played two-time defending champion Katy for the Class 5A Division 2 state championship in football.

IT'S OUR TIME

AL PICKETT and CHAD MITCHELL

An estimated crowd of 30,000 in the Alamodome in San Antonio and a statewide television audience prepared for the Saturday night showdown between Abilene High, the Team of the Century in the 1900s, and Katy, which had won three state championships in the current decade.

Abilene High was trying to claim its first state title in fifty-three years, while Katy was trying to join a select company of only Waco (1920s), Amarillo (1930s), Abilene High (1954-56) and Midland Lee (1998-2000) to win three consecutive state titles in the state's largest classification.

One could feel the electricity in the air as the two teams headed back to the locker room for the final words of instructions from their respective head coaches. In the Abilene High locker room, head coach Steve Warren addressed his team for the final time in the 2009 season:

"You know, there have been a lot of people all week long talking about everything under the sun related to the state championship," he began. "And now, all the smoke has cleared, everything is set. The table is set, it's quiet, and it's just us. What a special time. What a special time.

"This is something you are going to remember for the rest of your lives. Tonight, one game, tonight, you are going to remember it for the rest of your life. For you seniors, I wish I could come around and talk to every one of you for an hour, and just hang out, you know we have done that a bunch over the years. I want you to know that I am proud of you, from my heart, I am proud of you because of the way you have elevated our program, you have taken us to the next step.

"We have slowly but surely been getting to the door. We are at the door. And we're fixing to kick that sucker in. So be proud of what you have done, you put your mark on this place like no other. Just a bunch of hard-playing, getting-after-it son-of-a-guns every day in practice. It started last January—you know, in the weight room, everything we asked you to sacrifice, you have done it, in a special way. And because of that, we are here, right now, one game for forty-eight minutes, one time, for forty-eight minutes, to create something special.

"Get a hold of each other. All right, now look at me. Turn it in to a forty-eight-minute fight and when you are feeling a little bit tired and you feel like you don't have much fight left in you, lean on your brother today, lean on him like you never have before, because he has been there for you since January. When this was a goal, since you stepped into the program as a seventh-grader. Karsten, Drew Carroll, all of you seniors, Kyler, lean on your brother today because he will be there for you.

"Say it with me: IT'S OUR TIME! IT'S OUR TIME! IT'S OUR TIME! IT'S OUR TIME!"

As the Eagles left the locker room and came down the tunnel, ready to run through the inflated Eagle head and on to the Alamodome turf, the Abilene High players were chanting, "It's Our Time!"

Instead of running through the Eagle head, however, tight end Parker McCay, walking on crutches for the first time since breaking his leg in the bi-district game against Arlington Lamar, led his teammates on to the field. The Abilene High players, walking with their arms locked together, followed McCay through the Eagle head and on to the turf, still chanting, "It's Our Time!"

Indeed, it was the Eagles' time and two-time defending state champion Katy was not prepared for what was about to hit them.

[Abilene High went on to win the game, 28-17, the school's seventh state football championship.]

PEYTON LITTLE LEADS WYLIE ONE LAST TIME

DANIEL YOUNGBLOOD

Having already claimed a spot in any discussion pertaining to the greatest prep athletes the Big Country's ever produced, Peyton Little didn't need a big state finals performance or a second state basketball championship to solidify her high school legacy. But that didn't keep her from delivering both.

Playing her final game in a Wylie uniform in Austin, Little put the Lady Bulldogs on her back one last time, scoring thirty-three points in a 59-45 win over Celina. And in the process, she brought her extraordinary high school career to a truly fitting end.

A starter as a freshman in 2009 on a team full of upper class talent, Little's potential was obvious the second she stepped on the court. That first season, she averaged 10.7 points and helped the Lady Bulldogs to a regional quarterfinals appearance that, somewhat incredibly, would prove to be the low water mark for her career.

In the three seasons that followed, Little never averaged fewer than twenty points and never had a season end without a trip to the state tournament in Austin. And after having her sophomore year end with an emotional state finals loss to Texarkana Liberty-Eylau, she played her final two seasons without experiencing a playoff loss.

It's not just that she won that makes Little's accomplishments at Wylie so impressive, but also how she did it. With an uncanny ability to rise to occasions and come through in the clutch, she often saved her best performances for the absolute biggest stages.

Take, for instance, the 2011 state final, when she set a 3A state finals record with forty-three points in an eight-point win. Then, of course, there was the 2012 Region I-3A final when she scored forty-one points in a narrow victory over an extremely talented Kennedale team.

Few performances put this quality into clearer focus than the one she put forth in the 2012 state finals. With her team leading a strong Celina squad by one point at halftime, Little scored twenty-three second-half points to lift the Lady Bulldogs to a comfortable win. And she did so despite a two-of-twelve shooting start that might have shaken a lesser player's confidence.

"That first half was rough. I couldn't really make a shot," said Little, who made six of her final nine shots. "I came back in the locker room and I sat down and kind of thought for a second. I was in my own world and I was like, 'This is my last sixteen minutes of high school basketball, I'm not going to go out shooting the ball bad.' I just went out there in the second half and I was just like, 'Let it fly.' I was hitting a few shots and we were winning. It was awesome."

Her ability to overcome adversity and confidence to play through failure are two of many positive qualities Little possesses that made her such a dominant force, Wylie Coach Tri Danley said. Also noteworthy, he said, are her competitiveness and work ethic—the latter of which was sometimes overlooked because of the effortlessness of her game.

To those who watched her regularly, though, the commitment was obvious. Through both her play and leadership, she made those around her better and helped a Wylie program with a strong tradition reach greater heights.

"She's set a standard that is hard to match," Danley said. "There are very few players like Peyton. I've been coaching girls basketball for fifteen years, and to do what she does, there's not many. We're going to look back ten years from now, and I'll just thank God that I got to coach her and these players will be thankful that they got to play for her."

"Our economy and some would say even our character takes on a contrary dimension: high energy costs may not be well-received nationally but they're good for West Texas. On the other hand, just when the MX is poised to deliver our economic salvation—wouldn't you know it— peace breaks out. If it weren't for prison overcrowding, we'd be in for real trouble. This kind of tension has perhaps perpetuated what people around here often characterize as rugged self-reliance." —Paul Lack, "Beyond the Frontier Heritage," *Mesquite* 1991-92

PARTING TRIBUTE
PASS THE WORD

The Frontier Texas history museum opened in downtown Abilene in 2004.

We close on a lighter note, with a piece designed to recognize some of Abilene's distinctive characteristics while gently poking a little fun at ourselves in the process. We could conclude with something on the order of 100 Things We Like about Abilene, but maybe we'll save that for another day, or you can write it yourself.

Meanwhile, here are 52 (pretty much) True Facts about Abilene.

★

Tongue gently in cheek, Abilene author and businessman Glenn Dromgoole penned this tribute to his adopted hometown in 2006.

52 [PRETTY MUCH] TRUE FACTS ABOUT ABILENE

GLENN DROMGOOLE

A sense of community.

A sense of history.

A sense of humor.

Three requisites for living in a place like Abilene, where we've always just kind of made it up as we went along.

I am a native Texan and I have lived in Abilene more than twenty-five years. My intention here is to gently poke a little fun at my favorite city while working in some of the distinctive characteristics that make it what I consider to be the best kept secret in Texas.

Point with pride.

Have a laugh or two.

Pass the word.

Here are 52 (pretty much) True Facts about Abilene.

1. It doesn't take long to get to a great barbecue place—or anywhere else.
2. We don't have a rush hour, just a rush minute or two.
3. Someone said "Keep Abilene Boring" and we take that as a compliment.
4. There's not a church on every corner, just every other corner.
5. Quoting the Bible in Abilene is a contact sport.

6. Speaking of sports, we actually have forty-four college sports teams here.

7. You won't find a more enthusiastic mayor anywhere.

8. We have more cultural events than any other Texas city our size.

9. Our downtown and cultural district are often cited as examples to other cities.

10. A yellow traffic light means speed up and look both ways.

11. A green traffic light means wait until someone honks.

12. Animals come from all over the world just to live at our zoo.

13. College students come here from every state in the U.S. as well as dozens of other countries.

14. Dyess Air Force Base is home to the B-1, the C-130, and the Abilene economy.

15. When we say "Friendly Frontier," that's what we mean.

16. We have smiles and smiles of Texas.

17. Three words define the Spirit of Abilene: Generosity. Service. Optimism.

18. Abilene is the best kept secret in Texas. (Pass the word!)

19. We like trees so much we name streets for them.

20. We actually like mesquite trees and write poems about them.

21. Mesquite-grilled steaks are evidence that God has a purpose for everything—and a sense of humor.

22. When we stole the courthouse from Buffalo Gap, we should have taken the big oaks as well.

23. Don't be surprised if it snows at Easter and is hot at Christmas.

24. People watch the evening news mainly to see how wrong the weatherman will be.

25. The wind blows all the time, usually from the north and the south—at the same time.

26. We have so much wind (some might say hot air) that it has become a thriving industry.

27. When it rains, we all go outside to make sure.

28. If we get one-tenth of an inch of rain in the official gauge, streets will flood.

29. You really don't want to be in Abilene during a dust storm.

30. "Hail" and "oil" are two-syllable words here.

31. The sun shines here on the just and the unjust, and just about every day.

32. The most appropriate response to a spectacular Abilene sunrise or sunset is "Wow!"

33. The school lunch menu is big news on morning TV.

34. Abilene was founded by, and divided by, the railroad.

35. We host the world's largest barbecue, greatest pancake feast, numerous horse shows, and one huge book sale.

36. We have our own song and sing it every chance we get. (OK, so maybe it's not "the prettiest town I've ever seen." It rhymes.)

37. The stars at night are big and bright—inside the Paramount Theatre.

38. Abilenian Slim Willet wrote the mega-hit song "Don't Let the Stars Get in Your Eyes."

39. If you have to go to the hospital, dozens of churches will pray for you on Sunday—and Wednesday.

40. Our crime rate is very low, if you don't count jaywalking.

41. The Frontier Texas! history center puts an exclamation point on our western heritage.

42. Most of us don't wear boots or cowboy hats all that often, but jeans are appropriate attire for virtually any occasion.

43. If you don't drive a pickup, you must be a Yankee.

44. If your pickup doesn't have a gun in the gun rack, you must be a liberal.

45. If you're a liberal Yankee, you probably paid too much for your house when you moved here. Thank you!

46. When someone says there's nothing to do here, they must not include killing fire ants.

47. Wherever you go in town, you'll probably see someone you know—and can't remember their name.

48. We must be doing something right because butterflies keep coming back.

49. Geographically we're close to the center of the state, but we lean to the west.

50. It's not far to Somewhere Else in Texas—nor from Somewhere Else to here.

51. Abilene is a great place to visit—and to stay.

52. Every day, every week, Abilene grows on you.

CONTRIBUTORS

Roy Helen Ackers documents Abilene society in a weekly column for the *Abilene Reporter-News* under the pen name MizCheevus.

Wally Akin managed the Paramount and Majestic theaters and was perhaps Abilene's foremost showman. He died in 1987.

Phil Ashby graduated from Hardin-Simmons University and has worked as a newspaper reporter, teacher and public school administrator.

Patrick Bennett is Associate Professor Emeritus of English at McMurry University and the author of *Talking with Texas Writers* and *Rough and Rowdy Ways: The Life and Hard Times of Edward Anderson.*

Jack Boyd wrote about 250 weekly stories for the *Abilene Reporter-News* about the semi-fictional village of Cedar Gap. Three collections of the stories were published as books, and they spawned a full-blown musical, *Cedar Gap Homecoming.*

Mary Hampton Clack was an early Taylor County settler who arrived in 1879 and established a home along Lytle Creek where she recorded her recollections of early days before Abilene. She died in 1948.

Tommie Clack was born near Abilene in 1882 and was an authority on the early years of Taylor County. Miss Tommie spent her adult life teaching three generations of Abilenians, mainly at Abilene High School where she was head of the English department for 33 years. She died in 1989.

Lawrence Clayton was Dean of the College of Liberal Arts at Hardin-Simmons University and author of thirty books including *Clear Fork Cowboys, Watkins Reynolds Matthews,* and *Historic Ranches of Texas.* He died in 2000.

David Coffey is Professor of History at the University of Tennessee at Martin and the author of *John Bell Hood and the Struggle for Atlanta, Soldier Princess: The Life and Legend of Agnes Salm-Salm in North America*, and *Sheridan's Lieutenants*.

Maude E. Cole, grandmother of A. C. Greene, was librarian at Abilene's Carnegie Library from 1926 to 1946 and author of *Claybound* and *Wind Against Stone*. She died in 1961.

Katharyn Duff was the popular Page One columnist for the *Abilene Reporter-News* for many years and the author of two histories of Abilene—*Abilene on Catclaw Creek* and *Catclaw Country*. She died in 1995.

William E. Dyess grew up in Albany and served as an officer of the United States Army Air Forces during World War II. He was captured after the Battle of Bataan and endured the subsequent Bataan Death March. After a year in captivity, he escaped and returned to the U.S. where he chronicled his experiences. He died in a training crash in December 1943.

Robert A. Fink is W. D. and Hollis R. Bond Professor of English and Director of Creative Writing at Hardin-Simmons University and the author of *Twilight Innings* and six books of poetry.

Donald S. Frazier is Professor of History at McMurry University, President and Chief Executive Officer of the Grady McWhiney Research Foundation, and author of *Blood & Treasure, Fire in the Cane Field*, and *Thunder Across the Swamp*

Loretta Fulton, longtime writer and editor for the *Abilene Reporter-News*, is the author of *Virginia Connally, M.D.: Trailblazing Physician, Woman of Faith*.

Ruth Bradfield Gay founded Gay Travel Service in Abilene and was a bridesmaid to her friend Hadley Richardson in Richardson's marriage to writer Ernest Hemingway. She died in 1976.

Michael Grant, a graduate of Abilene High, is the author of *Warbirds: How They Played the Game*. He lives and writes in California.

Bob Green, historian and narrator for the Albany Fandangle for twenty-seven years, spent his entire life on his family's ranch near Albany. He died in 2009.

A. C. Greene, considered the dean of Abilene writers, started his writing career in Abilene before becoming an editor in Dallas. Among his books were *A Personal Country, 900 Miles on the Butterfield Trial,* and *The Santa Claus Bank Robbery.* He died in 2002.

Frank Grimes was editor of the *Abilene Reporter-News* from 1919-1960 and a finalist for the Pulitzer Prize. He died in 1960.

James Haley is the author of several books on Texas history, including the award-winning biography, *Sam Houston,* and *Passionate Nation: The Epic History of Texas.*

Elbert E. Hall, an eminent and popular native Abilenian, was in the insurance business and served as Abilene mayor from 1981 to 1984. He died in 1992.

James Hallmark is a pioneer Abilene television announcer, newscaster, and commercial pitchman and former director of public relations at the West Texas Rehabilitation Center and producer of the Rehab's annual telethon.

Sherilyn Hanks taught English at Cooper High School and is a native Abilenian who spent hours playing in Catclaw Creek along Park Street.

Ray Hollis started in the "wrecking business" in the late 1940s, and over the years, in addition to the Guitar Mansion, his demolition crews took down the Queen Theater, Abilene Municipal Auditorium, and Rose Field House. He died in 1996.

Linda Honea was a free-lance writer for *The Abilenian* when she interviewed Lawrence Welk in Abilene in 1974.

Greg Jaklewicz, content editor and columnist at the *Abilene Reporter-News,* covered the arts and entertainment scene for the newspaper for several years.

Archie Jefferies, whose radio singing career began in 1938, was a popular and familiar presence on KRBC during the late 1940s and early 1950s with his band, Fraley's Butane Boys, sponsored by Fraley's Butane Company. He died in 2005.

Elmer Kelton wrote more than forty novels, including *The Time It Never Rained* and *The Good Old Boys,* and was voted by his peers as the greatest Western author of all time. He died in 2009.

John H. Knox grew up in Abilene, attended McMurry College in the 1920s, and went on to publish poems and as well as dozens of pulp fiction stories. He died in 1983.

Paul D. Lack, a Fellow of the Texas State Historical Association and author of *The Texas Revolutionary Experience*, was Professor of History and Vice President for Academic Affairs at McMurry University from 1971 to 2002.

Bob Lapham covered sports and entertainment during his long writing and editing career with the *Abilene Reporter-News* and is the author of two novels, including *Meet Me at the River Buddy Holly,* based on his experiences as a young backup singer for Holly.

Max Leach was public relations director at Abilene Christian College from 1942 to 1948 and then Professor of Psychology until his retirement in 1974. He died in 1998.

Clinton Lear was a U.S. Army lieutenant stationed at Fort Phantom Hill where he served as the post's quartermaster. He died in 1854.

K. O. Long, Jr. is a lifelong Abilenian and graduate of McMurry College and has served as Dean of the School of Business at McMurry University since 2005.

Charlie Marler has taught journalism at Abilene Christian University for nearly forty years and has written extensively about Abilene editor Frank Grimes, including *Lone Star Christmas,* a collection of Grimes' Christmas editorials.

Gary McCaleb, mayor of Abilene from 1990 to 1999, is a longtime professor and administrator at Abilene Christian University and the author of two books focusing on community life.

Brent McClellan is Storm Services Administrator for the City of Abilene.

Gerald McDaniel was Professor of English at McMurry University from 1976 to 1993 and at North Central Texas College from 1993 until his death in 2001.

Jane McHan, who worked for the West Texas Rehabilitation Center while serving as field instructor and Social Work adjunct at Hardin Simmons-University, is the development director for KUCB, community radio/television in Unalaska, Alaska.

Chad Mitchell, an Abilene minister, was chaplain of the 2009 Abilene High state championship football team and co-author with Al Pickett of *Brother's Keeper*, a book about the team.

Don Morris, the seventh president of Abilene Christian University, and the first alumnus to rise to its presidency, served as president longer than any of the school's other leaders, from 1940-69. He died in 1974.

April Nixon, a former City Hall reporter for the *Abilene Reporter-News*, is Chief Financial Officer for the City of Arlington, Texas.

Naomi Shihab Nye of San Antonio, a poet with an international audience, is a member of the Board of Chancellors of the Academy of American Poets.

Robert F. Pace, former Professor of History at McMurry University and author of *Hall of Honor: College Men in the Old South*, is Associate Rector at St. Andrews Episcopal Church, Amarillo, Texas.

Robert Lee Paschal arrived in Abilene in 1892 to teach at Simmons College before returning to Fort Worth where he was named principal of Central High School in 1906, retiring in 1935. Central High is now named R. L. Paschal High School. He died in 1958.

Sam Pendergrast has been a teacher of Spanish, English, and journalism, Hollywood ghost writer, and author of numerous publications including *Zen Chili: The Real Terlingua and Other Boondoogles*.

Al Pickett is a sports broadcaster in Abilene and the author of several books about Abilene and Texas sports, including *Team of the Century* and *The Greatest Texas Sports Stories You've Never Heard.*

John Rice was stationed at Dyess Air Force Base in the 1960s.

Rupert N. Richardson attended Simmons College (Hardin-Simmons University) and rose to become the school's president serving from 1945 to 1953. Renowned as an eminent American historian, Dr. Richardson was one of the founders of the West Texas Historical Association and author of *Comanche Barrier of South Plains Settlement.* He died in 1988.

Mike Roark was a reporter for the *Abilene Reporter-News* before he was named editor of *The Courier* in Russellville, Ark.

Garner Roberts, longtime sports information director at Abilene Christian University, is a freelance writer in Abilene.

Eleanor Roosevelt chronicled her life as First Lady in a newspaper column titled, *My Day.* She died in 1962.

Geraldine Satterwhite was for many years a lifestyle writer at the *Abilene Reporter-News.* She died in 1995.

Ruth Ann Shirley, a McMurry University graduate and history teacher at Magnolia Junior High School, received the West Texas Historical Association's 2009 Student Essay Award for "Prisoners Among Prisoners: Conflicts at Camp Barkeley, Texas."

Robert W. Sledge is Distinguished Professor Emeritus of History at McMurry University, Historian-in-Residence for the Grady McWhiney Research Foundation, and author of the two volume *A People, A Place: The Story of Abilene.*

Eddie Soriano is a writer for New Mexico State University Media Relations while completing his degree in journalism and mass communications.

Mary Helen Specht, Assistant Professor of Creative Writing at St. Edwards University, was born and raised in Abilene, and her fiction and nonfiction has appeared in numerous journals and magazines.

William Stafford was an American poet and pacifist and was appointed the twentieth Poet Laureate Consultant in Poetry to the Library of Congress in 1970. He died in 1993.

John C. Stevens was a student leader at Abilene Christian University and went on to serve ACU for twelve years as President and for nine years as Chancellor. During World War II he served as a U.S. Army chaplain. He died in 2007.

Carlton Stowers, author of more than forty books, received the A. C. Greene Literary Award in 2007.

Bill Whitaker was front page columnist at the *Abilene Reporter-News* before moving to Waco to be an editor of the *Waco Tribune-Herald*.

Doug Williamson, editor of the *Abilene Reporter-News,* began his career as a teacher before taking a reporter position with the *Waco Tribune-Herald*. He returned to Abilene in 1985 and was named editor in 2012.

Jim Wilson is an Abilene poet and veterinarian who has published several collections of his verse.

Ed Wishcamper, who retired as editor of the *Abilene Reporter-News* in 1979, was the author of *From Tents to Computers,* covering the first century of the newspaper's history from 1881-1981. He died in 2001.

Greg Young, a professional pharmacist by day, is a performing songwriter who has recorded with Catclaw Creek, in addition to producing his own solo albums, which include *Itinerant Poet* and *Old Dogs*.

Daniel Youngblood covered Wylie High School sports for the *Abilene Reporter-News,* including the basketball state championship teams starring Peyton Little.

Larry Zelisko has been a writer, editor and columnist at the *Abilene Reporter-News* for more than thirty years.

CREDITS

All citations to *Abilene Reporter*, *Abilene Daily Reporter*, and *Abilene Reporter-News* are reprinted by permission of the newspaper.

Prologue: The Spirit of Abilene

"Village of My Heart" by A. C. Greene, from *A Personal Country*. Reprinted by permission of University of North Texas Press.

"Abilene's Special Secret" by Glenn Dromgoole, from *Abilene Reporter-News*, August 30, 1987.

"Train Whistle" by Jay Moore, from *Abilene Reporter-News*, March 15, 1998.

Buffalo Days: Before Abilene

"A Perfect Arrowhead" by Bob Green, from *Abilene Reporter-News*, July 10, 1992.

"Site of the Indian Fights of 1871, Abilene" by Naomi Shihab Nye, from *Texas in Poetry 2*. Reprinted by permission of the author.

"Letter from Fort Phantom Hill" by Clinton Lear, from *Mail Call from Fort Washita*.

"Fort Phantom Hill" by John H. Knox, from *A Christmas Pudding: Nine Poems by Abilene Writers of 50 Years Ago and Today*.

"The Butterfield Stage" by A. C. Greene, from *900 Miles on the Butterfield Trail*. Reprinted by permission of University of North Texas Press.

"Buffalo Days" by James Haley, from *Texas: An Album of History*. Reprinted by permission of the author.

"Paso por Aqui" by William Stafford, from *The Way It Is: New and Selected Poems,* © 1991, 1998 by William Stafford and the Estate of William Stafford. Reprinted with the permission of The Permissions Company, Inc., on behalf of Graywolf Press, Minneapolis, Minnesota, www.graywolfpress.org.

"Let Them Eat Cactus" by Mary Hampton Clack, from *Pioneer Days . . . Two Views*.

"Frontier Failures" by Robert F. Pace and Donald S. Frazier, from *Frontier Texas: History of a Borderland to 1880*. Reprinted by permission of State House Press.

Here Comes the Train: Early Years

"Here Comes the Train!" by Tommie Clack, from *Pioneer Days . . . Two Views.*

"Let the Sale Begin" by Frank Grimes, from *Abilene Reporter-News,* March 15, 1936.

"Early Ordinances on Morals and Decency" by City of Abilene, March 1887.

"Moving the County Seat" by Katharyn Duff, from *The Abilenian,* Winter 1973. Reprinted by permission of Abilene Chamber of Commerce.

"The San Jacinto Day Shootout" by Robert W. Sledge, from *A People, A Place: The Story of Abilene, Vol. 1.* Reprinted by permission of State House Press.

"Chinese Laundry" by Tommie Clack, from *Pioneer Days . . . Two Views.*

"Cock Fighting" by Tommie Clack, from *Pioneer Days . . . Two Views.*

"A Hanging in Abilene," from *Abilene Reporter,* November 20, 1891.

"Police Chief Clinton" by Larry Zelisko, from *Abilene Reporter-News,* December 28, 1999.

"The First Dry Hole" by Katharyn Duff, from *Abilene Reporter-News,* March 22, 1981.

"Bankhead Highway" by Joe W. Specht. Written for *Abilene Stories.*

"Lindbergh Refused the Throne," from *Abilene Daily Reporter,* September 27, 1927.

"When Amelia Earhart Crashed in Abilene" by Bill Whitaker, from *Abilene Reporter-News,* June 3, 1997.

"The First Lady Visits Abilene" by Eleanor Roosevelt, from "My Day," March 13, 1939. Reprinted by permission of Alice Roosevelt Ireland.

Camp Barkeley & Beyond: Military Town

"How Camp Barkeley Shaped Abilene" by Jay Moore, from *History in Plain Sight: Camp Barkeley.* Reprinted by permission of the author.

"The Barkley in Camp Barkeley" by Jay Moore, from *History in Plain Sight: Camp Barkeley.* Reprinted by permission of the author.

"Making Out at the Paramount" by Wally Akin, as told to Jamie O'Toole, from *Mr. Paramount: Wally, the Showman.*

"German Prisoners Escape" by Ruth Ann Shirley, from "Prisoners Among Prisoners: Conflicts at Camp Barkeley, Texas," *West Texas Historical Association Year Book* 2009. Reprinted by permission of the author.

'Bataan Death March" by William E. Dyess, from *The Dyess Story.*

"Thanka You Verra Much" by Sam Pendergrast, from *"THANKA YOU . . .": The Story of Charlie Blanks*. Reprinted by permission of the author.

"Abilene's First Woman Doctor" by Loretta Fulton, from *Virginia Connally, M.D.: Trailblazing Physician, Woman of Faith*. Reprinted by permission of the author.

"A Tremendous Bargain" by Frank Grimes, from *Abilene Reporter-News*, January 21, 1952.

"The Day the B-1B Came to Town" by Jared Fields, from *Abilene Reporter-News*, April 24, 2010.

"Abilene and Dyess" by Doug Williamson. Written for *Abilene Stories*.

Growing Pains: Coming of Age

"When TV Came to Abilene" by James Hallmark, from *The Day Television Came to Cedar Gap, Texas*. Reprinted by permission of the author.

"Dealing with Racism" by Jane McHan, from *They Remember: Recollections of Members of the Carver Community of Abilene, Texas*. Reprinted by permission of Hardin-Simmons University.

"Discrimination Policy Challenged—Letter to *The Optimist* from ACU Students," from *The Optimist*, March 1954. Reprinted by permission of Abilene Christian University.

"A Letter to the Superintendent" by John P. Rice, from Steve Gallaway, "A History of the Desegregation of the Public Schools in Abilene, Texas, During the Wells Administration, 1954-1970." PhD diss., Texas Tech University, 1994. Reprinted by permission of Steve Gallaway.

"Hispanic Student Boycott," from *Abilene Reporter-News*, November 9, 1987.

"Abilene Goes Wet" by David Coffey, from *Historic Abilene: An Illustrated History*. Reprinted by permission of the author.

"Jorge Solis: A Man of Firsts," from *Abilene Reporter-News*, November 9, 1987; August 26, 1990; November 9, 1991.

"Razing the Guitar Mansion" by Ray Hollis, as told to Sam Pendergrast, from *Wreckin' Texas*. Reprinted by permission of Sam Pendergrast.

"The Woman Who Saved Downtown" by Glenn Dromgoole. Written for *Abilene Stories*.

"However You Spell It," from *Abilene Reporter-News*, April 8, 1956.

"The Abilene Paradox" by Robert W. Sledge, from *A People, A Place: The Story of Abilene, Vol. 2*. Reprinted by permission of State House Press.

"Circlin' Mack's" by Jay Moore. Written for *Abilene Stories.*
"All-America Fun" by April Nixon, from *Abilene Reporter-News*, June 30, 1990.
"The Last Day of Harold's" by Greg Jaklewicz, from *Abilene Reporter-News*, July 31, 2011.

Setting the Tone: Church & School

"Parson's Gift" by Jay Moore. Written for *Abilene Stories.*
"The Original Tonight Show" by Jim Wilson, from *Taking a Peek: poetry cracking the door but afraid to open it.* Reprinted by permission of the author.
"Stop This Collection Now (and Other Church Stories)." Reprinted by permission of Hardin-Simmons University, Abilene Christian University, and Balcony Publishing.
"Recollections from Simmons College" by R. L. Paschal, from a letter to Rupert N. Richardson, November 6, 1940.
"A Tip of the Hat to ACU" by Don Morris and Max Leach, from *The ACU Century: One Hundred Years of Faith and Excellence.* Reprinted by permission of Abilene Christian University.
"The First Day at McMurry College" by Paul D. Lack, from *Pride of Our Western Prairies: McMurry College 1923-1988.* Reprinted by permission of McMurry University.
"Too Much Jazz and Not Enough Jesus" by Gerald McDaniel, from "Did the Jazz Age Come to Abilene?" Reprinted by permission of Abilene Public Library.
"Dam-it the Dog" by Rupert N. Richardson, from *Famous Are Thy Halls: Hardin-Simmons University.* Reprinted by permission of Hardin-Simmons University.
"The First High School Band" by Bill Whitaker, from *Abilene Reporter-News*, August 19, 1996.
"Howitzer on The Hill" by John C. Stevens, from *No Ordinary University: The History of a City Set on a Hill.* Reprinted by permission of Abilene Christian University.
"A Tipi Tradition" by Loretta Fulton, from *Abilene Reporter-News*, October 6, 2011.
"A Prayer for Abilene" by Glenn Dromgoole, from *The Women There Don't Treat You Mean: Abilene in Song.* Reprinted by permission of State House Press.

Prairie Renaissance: Arts & Culture

"A Better Place to Live" by Katharyn Duff, from *The Abilenian*, Spring 1974. Reprinted by permission of Abilene Chamber of Commerce.

"Prettiest Town I've Ever Seen" by Joe W. Specht, from *The Women There Don't Treat You Mean: Abilene in Song*. Reprinted by permission of State House Press.

"Piano Lessons" by Katharyn Duff, from *Abilene Reporter-News*, April 15, 1981.

"Old Musician" by Maude Cole, from *Clay-Bound*.

"Wedding of the Century" by Geraldine Satterwhite, from *Abilene Reporter-News*, April 19, 1981.

"When Lawrence Welk Lived in Abilene" by Linda Honea, from *The Abilenian*, Fall 1975. Reprinted by permission of Abilene Chamber of Commerce.

"Bob Wills and the Butane Boys" by Archie Jeffries with Bettye Pearce, from *A West Texas Life*. Reprinted by permission of Bettye Pearce.

"Leltie Faucett and MizCheevus" by Roy Helen Ackers. Written for *Abilene Stories*.

"Don't Let the Stars Get in Your Eyes" by Joe W. Specht, from "Don't Let the Stars Get in Your Eyes: Slim Willet's Idiosyncratic Chart-Topper Lives On," *Journal of Texas Music History*, 9 (2009). Reprinted by permission of the author.

"Fifth Row for Elvis" by Greg Jaklewicz, from *Abilene Reporter-News*, August 16, 1997.

"Prairie Renaissance" by Mary Helen Specht, from *The Texas Observer*, August 11, 2010. Reprinted by permission of the author.

"Done with Distinction" by Gary McCaleb, from *The Gift of Community*. Reprinted by permission of Abilene Christian University.

Open Minds: Literature & Letters

"The Prophet from Abilene" by Charlie Marler, from "The Prophet from Abilene," *West Texas Historical Association Year Book*, 48 (1972). Reprinted by permission of the author.

"Young Minds of Abilene" by Patrick Bennett, from *Rough and Rowdy Ways: The Life and Hard Times of Edward Anderson*. Reprinted by permission of the author.

"The Disappearance of Gertrude Beasley" by Mary Helen Specht, from *The Texas Observer*, May 17, 2011. Reprinted by permission of the author.

"From Pony to Publisher" by Ed Wishcamper, from *From Tents to Computers: 100 Years with the Abilene Reporter-News, 1881-1981*.

"Getting a Job Riding the Railroad" by A. C. Greene, from "Getting a Job Via the Abilene & Southern," *Journal of Texas Shortline Railroads*, 2 (May-July 1997). Reprinted by permission of Lester Haines.

"Thinking About Cows at Ten O'Clock in the Morning, Abilene" by Naomi Shihab Nye, from *Texas in Poetry 2*. Reprinted by permission of the author.

"What a Darlin' Ballpeen Hammer!" by Jack Boyd. Reprinted by permission of the author.

"Called to Poetry, Abilene" by Robert A. Fink, from *Twilight Innings: A West Texan on Grace and Survival*. Reprinted by permission of the author.

"My Last Christmas????" by Lawrence Clayton, from *A Christmas Pudding: Art, Essays, Songs & Poems 2000*.

The Old Mesquites: Weather & Nature

"Captain Jeff's Prairie Dogs" by K. O. Long, from *Abilene Reporter-News*, September 3, 1992.

"Water, Water, Water," from newspaper accounts.

"The Old Mesquites Ain't Out Yet" by Frank Grimes, from *Abilene Reporter-News*, March 28, 1939.

"The Time It Never Rained" by Elmer Kelton, first published in *The Time It Never Rained*. Reprinted by permission of TCU Press.

"Drought: Sure Signs in Abilene, Texas" by Robert A. Fink, first published as "Drought: Sure Signs in Merkel, Texas," from *Texas in Poetry 2*. Reprinted by permission of the author.

"Now *That's* Praying for Rain" by Katharyn Duff, from *Abilene Reporter-News*, August 17, 1970.

"The Crape Myrtle Sex Scandal" by Bill Whitaker, from *Abilene Reporter-News*, September 24, 1997.

"Alligator on the Loose" by Mike Roark, from *Abilene Reporter-News*, January 17, 2011.

"Why Abilene Creeks Flow North" by Brent McClellan, from *Abilene Reporter-News*, May 22, 2012.

"Haunting Echoes" by Sherilyn Hanks, from *Mesquite*, Winter/Spring 1992-93. Reprinted by permission of the author.

"Catclaw Creek" by Greg Young, from *Catclaw Creek*. Reprinted by permission of the author.

Reunion of Champions: Sports & Leisure

"Louis Kelley Excelled On, Off the Field" by Eddie Soriano, from New Mexico State University Media Relations, December 7, 2011. Reprinted by permission of New Mexico State University.

"The West Texas Speedway" by Jay Moore, from *History in Plain Sight: Fair Park*. Reprinted by permission of the author.

"Summer of '46 with the Abilene Blue Sox" by Bob Lapham, from *Abilene Reporter-News*, October 3, 1976.

"Poker at the Abilene Club" by Elbert E. Hall, from *Page One*. Reprinted by permission of Bill Minter.

"Three Olympic Gold Medals" by Garner Roberts, from *Abilene Reporter-News*, November 24, 2006.

"Chuck Moser's Eligibility Slips" by Al Pickett, from *Team of the Century: The Greatest High School Football Team in Texas*. Reprinted by permission of State House Press.

"Three in a Row" by Michael Grant, from *Warbirds: How They Played the Game*. Reprinted by permission of the author.

"Reunion of Champions" by Carlton Stowers, from *Dallas Morning News*, June 13, 2010. Reprinted by permission of the author.

"McMurry Football Team Survives Plane Crash," from *Abilene Reporter-News*, September 30, 1963.

"The Catch" by Phil Ashby, from *Abilene Reporter-News*, June 17, 1987.

"It's Our Time" by Al Pickett and Chad Mitchell, from *Brothers Keeper: The Story of the Abilene High State Championship*. Reprinted by permission of the authors.

"Peyton Little Leads Wylie One Last Time" by Daniel Youngblood, from *Abilene Reporter-News*, March 4, 2012.

Parting Tribute: Pass the Word

"52 (pretty much) True Facts About Abilene" by Glenn Dromgoole. Reprinted by permission of the author.

SUGGESTED READING

For an up-to-date, comprehensive history of Abilene, read Robert W. Sledge's two-volume *A People, A Place: The Story of Abilene* (2008, 2011). Katharyn Duff told the city's story through its first one hundred years or so in her books *Catclaw Country* (with Betty Kay Seibt, 1980) and *Abilene on Catclaw Creek* (1969).

Abilene's early days are covered in *Pioneer Days . . . Two Views*, recollections by Mary Hampton Clack and Tommie Clack (1979). Also see *The Parramore Sketches: Scenes and Stories of Early West Texas* by Dock Dilworth Parramore (1975).

Jack North wrote about early families in *Pioneers of the Abilene Area* (1978) and has published two books of historical photos: *Early Abilene* (2010) and *Lost Abilene* (2013). Juanita Zachry was a dedicated chronicler of Abilene and Taylor County history. Her books include *Abilene, The Key City* (1986) and *A History of Rural Taylor County* (1995).

Historians Tracy Shilcutt, David Coffey, and Donald S. Frazier teamed up to write *Historic Abilene: An Illustrated History* (2000). Norma McMahon Taylor wrote about what it was like to live in Abilene as a grade-schooler during World War II in her *Valley View Days: 1939-1945* (2011).

Books about the area before Abilene was founded include *Frontier Texas: History of a Borderland to 1880* by Robert F. Pace and Donald S. Frazier (2004); *A Texas Frontier: The Clear Fork Country and Fort Griffin, 1849-1887* by Ty Cashion (1996); and *Interwoven: A Pioneer Chronicle by* Sallie Reynolds Matthews (1936).

From Tents to Computers by Ed Wishcamper (1981) told the story of the *Abilene Reporter-News* from 1881-1981, and the newspaper itself published a comprehensive collection of articles about Abilene's first 100 years in its *Abilene Remembered: Our Centennial Treasury Book* (1981).

A. C. Greene's tribute to his hometown as "the village of my heart" anchored *A Personal Country* (1969), still considered one of the best books about this part of the state. He also included quite a few Abilene stories in his book, *Chance Encounters* (2002).

Interesting Abilene biographies include *Judge Legett of Abilene* (1977) and *Pioneer Women of Abilene* (1981) by Vernon Spence; *Millionaire Cowboy* by Betty Kay Seibt (1983); *Mr. Paramount* by Jamie O'Toole (1983); *The Story of Charlie Blanks* by Sam Pendergrast (1989); and *Virginia Connally, M.D.* by Loretta Fulton (2011). Former Mayor Elbert E. Hall's recollections about Abilene are included in the limited-edition book, *Page One* (1981).

The histories of Abilene's universities are related in *Famous Are Thy Halls* (Hardin-Simmons, 1964) by Rupert N. Richardson; *No Ordinary University: The Story of a City Set on a Hill* (Abilene Christian, 1998) by John C. Stevens; and *Pride of Our Western Prairies* (McMurry, 1989), edited by Fane Downs and Robert W. Sledge.

Two books about the African-American community are *The Black Community in Abilene* by Jewell Pritchett (1984) and *They Remember: Recollections of Members of the Carver Community in Abilene* by Susan C. Allen, Jane McHan and Lawrence Clayton (2000). The *Abilene Reporter-News* published a special twelve-page section on "Hispanics in Abilene" on November 9, 1987.

Several books have dealt with Abilene sports. Al Pickett covered the Chuck Moser years in *The Team of the Century* (2004), as did Michael Grant in his *Warbirds: How They Played the Game* (2004). Pickett paired up with Chad Mitchell on *Brother's Keeper: The Story of the 2009 Abilene High State Championship* (2010), and he included several Abilene stories in his collection of *The Greatest Texas Sports Stories You've Never Heard* (2007).

The Women There Don't Treat You Mean: Abilene in Song by Joe W. Specht (2006) chronicled the dozens of tunes that have mentioned Abilene over the years—mainly because Abilene rhymes with a lot of words.

Two books of Christmas stories pertaining to Abilene are A. C. Greene's *Christmas Memories* (1996) and *Lone Star Christmas: Seasonal Editorials of Frank Grimes* by Charles H. Marler (1989).

Gunfire on South Front by James David Fuller (1993) told the history of the Abilene police department from 1881 to 1993. Susan Navarro explored *Eagle City, an 1878 Colony on Lytle Creek* (1981). Al Pickett discussed the history of the Wylie area in *Wylie: Surviving and Thriving for 100 Years* (2002).

Additionally, a number of theses dealing with various aspects of Abilene history are available through the university libraries or the public library, quite a few local churches have published histories of their congregations, and numerous writers and poets have written books about, or influenced by, life in Abilene. In 2001, Shay W. and Patrick Bennett updated *Culture on the Catclaw,* a lengthy bibliography of books and plays by Abilene authors.

As for video documentation of Abilene's past, the Dian Graves Owen Foundation and the Abilene Preservation League helped bring to the public eye in recent years a series of DVDs called *History in Plain Sight*, written and narrated by Jay Moore.

INDEX

—————— **A** ——————

Abercrombie, John Joseph, 28

"Abilene" (the song), 196-200

Abilene and Southern Railway, 245-246

Abilene Blue Sox, 292-294

Abilene Christian University, 122-124, 151, 156, 171-172, 182-184, 245, 298, 299

Abilene Clean and Proud, 272

Abilene Club (Wooten Hotel), 296-297

Abilene Community Theater, 192, 194

Abilene Country Club, 131, 203

Abilene Courts, 68, 70

Abilene Cultural Affairs Council, 224, 225

Abilene High School, 127, 135, 147, 179-181, 222, 284, 301, 304-306, 307, 315-317

"Abilene Paradox," 144-145

Abilene Philharmonic Orchestra, 192, 194

Abilene Polo and Saddle Club, 290

Abilene Regional Airport, 70

"Abilene Trophy," 82

Abilene Zoo, 258, 275

Ackerman's Saloon, 46

Ackers, Roy Helen, 211-213

Adams, Billy, 38

Akin, Wally, 90-91

Albus, Donna, 272-273

Alexander Building, 48

Allen, John, 38

Allen, Reese, 67

Allen, Rufe, 38

Ally Gator, 274-275

Ambler, E. T., 22

Anderson, Edward, 234-235

Anderson, George S., 22, 244

Arcade Saloon, 46

Archibald, Norm, 264

Ash, Twyman, 302

Aten, Laura, 81

Aten, Woodrow, 81

Atkins, Chet, 198

Atkins, Pervis, 285

—————— **B** ——————

Babb, Oswald, 234

Bacon, C. W., 73

Bailey, John, 124

Baker, Alfo, 16

Baker, Thane, 299

Bankhead Highway, 68-71

Bankhead, John Hollis, 68, 69

Bankhead, Tallulah, 68

Barkley, David Bennes, 82, 88-89

Barkley, Josef Bennes, 88

Barksdale Air Force Base, 310, 311

Barnett, Lynn, 224

Barnhill, Bob, 124

Barret, A. B., 171

Barrett, Howard, 204

Bassetti, Robert, 64

Batjer, Ernest, 157

Beasley, Gertrude, 230, 238-242

Beck, Walter, 306

Bedichek, Wendell, 204

Beech-Nut Packing Company, 74, 75

Bennett, B. F., 69

Berry, J. T., 48

Berry, R. L., 16

Berry, W. T. & Company, 48

Betty Rose's Little Brisket, 152

Bible, R. A., 212

Big State Jamboree, 215

Black, Bob, 293
Blackwood, James, 309
Blanks, Charlie, 84, 98-100
Blanton, Dixie, 16
Bledsoe, Files, 234
Bohanon, Brian, 313, 314
Bourland, David, 302
Bowen, Walter, 59-60
Bowers, Annie, 61
Bowlus, Dub, 116
Bowman, Joe, 294
Boyd, Virginia: see Connally, Virginia Boyd
Brazos River, 276
Brennan, Walter, 199
Brewer, Kristin, 151
Bridwell, Tucker, 139
Brown, Floyd, 306
Brown, Josh Roy, 199
Brown, Lester, 10, 197-199
Bryan, W. J., 22
Bryant, Gloria, 129
Buffalo, 23-24, 30, 34-36, 37, 38, 258
Buffalo Gap, TX, 24, 39, 42, 47, 52-54, 63, 132, 258, 276, 277, 324
Buffalo Gap Cemetery, 37
Bullington, Wally, 302
Butterfield Overland Stage, 24, 31-33
Butterfield Trail, 9, 32-33
Bynum, Raymond T. "Prof," 179-181

——————— C ———————
Calhoun, Dick, 289
Callahan Divide, 52, 246, 258, 276-277
Cameron and Phillips Lumber, 48
Cameron Lake, 258
Cameron, William, 48
Camp Barkeley, 10, 21, 81-89, 92-93, 99, 101, 102, 118, 208, 243, 258
Camp Cooper, 32
Campbell, T. C., 21
Canon, Joe, 140, 141
Cantu, Antonia, 88-89
Capra, Hannah, 225-226

Carnegie Library, 193, 194, 229, 232, 234-237
Carpenter, Jimmy, 306
Catclaw Creek, 10, 70, 195, 258, 276, 278-280, 281-282
Catclaw Creek (band), 281
Cattle Exchange Saloon, 46
Cedar Creek, 48, 264, 276
Cedar Gap, 115, 248, 276
Cedar Ridge Reservoir, 264
Center for Contemporary Arts, 193, 223, 224-225
Central State Bank, 48
Chicken-on-the-Run, 146
Childers Classical Institute, 172
Choate, Raymond, 15
Christian, Tobe, 151
Christian, Harold, 151-153
Christian, Russell, 151
Citizens National Bank, 66, 84
Clack, John B., 38, 201
Clack, Mary, 22
Clack, Mollie, 45
Clack, Tommie, 11, 57-58, 59, 201
Clayton, Lawrence, 255-256
Clinton, John J., 64-65, 194
Cole, Maude E., 235-237
Collinson, Frank, 34
Colony Hill, 38
Colorado River, 277
Comanche, 23-24, 37
Como, Perry, 214, 216
Compton Building, 139
Congregation Mizpah, 85
Connally, Ed, 101
Connally, Virginia Boyd, 101-103
Cook, Elmo, 92
Cooke, Harold G., 104
Coombes, Charles, 174
Cooper High School, 108, 147, 179, 313
Cooper, O. T., 212
Cooper, Oscar Henry, 21
Corley, Dan B., 49
Coronado's Camp, 277

Coulson, Joe, 310
Cox, Ben L., 296-297
Crawford, M. B., 63
Crosby, W. C., 74
Cumby, Gerald, 309
Cunningham, J. V., 62-63
Cypress Building, 139

D

Dallas, W. O., 175
Dam-it, 177-178
Daniel, Frances Hill Cooper, 212
Daniel, J. Neil, 212
Danley, Tri, 319-320
Darnell, Jack, 185
Davis, Charles O., 269
Davis, Genna Connally, 103
Davis, Sonny, 305
Deatherage, Earl "Popcorn," 209, 210
Deaton, Judy, 224
Delaney, R. W., 76
Delk, Lenda, 212
Delk, Steve, 212
Delmonico Saloon, 46
Derryberry, L. E., 73
DeVaugh, Eddie, 76
Dian Graves Owen Foundation, 139
Dinosaur Bob, 10
Dixie Pig, 83, 85
Dodge Jones Foundation, 139-141
Donaldson, Smokey, 215
"Don't Let the Stars Get in Your
    Eyes," 214-217, 325
Douglass, Ross, 168
Drake Hotel, 225
Dromgoole, Glenn, 14, 18-19
Dudley, Dave, 36
Duff, Katharyn, 11, 14, 192, 232
Dyess Air Force Base, 10, 21, 33,
    81-82, 106-108, 109-110, 125, 243,
    324
Dyess Elementary School, 125-126
Dyess, William Edwin, 21, 82, 95-97
Dykes, Spike, 285

E

Eagle Colony, 41-42
Eagle Field (Fair Park), 86
Earhart, Amelia, 44, 74-77
Eastus, Mack, 76
Ehrie, Bill, 109, 110
Elks Hall, 17, 139
Ellis, Sonny, 124
Elliott, Patricia, 134
Elm Creek, 70, 262, 263, 264, 276
Estes, Tommy, 293
Evangelical Methodist Church, 137
Evans, Silliman, 156
Everman Park, 22

F

Fair Park, 283, 289-291, 302
Fair Park Auditorium, 215, 219
Fair Park Methodist Church, 86
Fannin Elementary School, 133
Faucett, Leltie, 203, 211-213
Ferguson, Miriam A. "Ma," 203
Feris, Chris, 313
Fink, Robert A., 251-254
First Baptist Church, 22, 62, 86, 160,
    164, 175, 204, 243
First Christian Church, 175
First Church of the Nazarene, 86
First Methodist Church, 155
First National Bank, 55
First Presbyterian Church, 45, 156
Fitzgerald, Larry, 116
Fletcher, Mack, 215
Flint & Knapp Furniture, 62
Flores, Reyes, 22
Fornes, Buddy, 310
Fort Griffin, 41
Fort Phantom Hill, 28-29, 30, 31-32
Fox, Frank P., 66
Francis, Chuck, 16
Fraley's Butane Boys, 192, 208-210
Franklin Junior High School, 127
Freeman, Jim, 274-275
Friley, Douglass, 169
Friley, W. C., 167-170

Frizzell, W. H., 61-63
Frohman, Philip, 21, 160-161
Frontier Texas!, 192, 321, 325
Fry, Bob, 293
Fry, David, 183
Fry, Douglas "Fessor," 182-184
Fry, Neil, 183
Fulwiler, W. J., 243

G

Gaiters, Bobby, 285
Galbraith, Gerald, 305
Galbraith, Gervis, 304-306
Gamon, Andres "Andy," 128-130
Garren, Pat, 219
Gay, Ruth, 165
George, W. A., 64
Gerhart, Willis P., 157-162
Gersonde, Bill, 275
Gibbs, W. E., 55
Gibson, Bob, 10, 196-200
Gilbert, C. E., 55
Gill, Larry, 140
Gorsuch, Nannie Louise Scott, 15
Gould, Jay, 261
Grace Hotel, 13, 46, 141
Grace Museum, 139, 141, 224, 225
Graham, Don, 240-241
Green, Howard, 292
Green, Meridian, 199
Green, R. D., 181
Greene, A. C., 10, 11, 13, 15-17, 202,
    230, 236, 245-246, 257
Greer, Hayden "Stubby," 293
Gregory, Glynn, 304-306
Grimes, Frank, 10, 13, 98, 160, 173,
    204, 229-230, 231-233, 264
Grosbeck, Edward G., 269
Gruver, Merle, 85
Guitar, Earl, 136, 205-207
Guitar, John, 111
Guitar, Laura, 111
Guitar Mansion, 10, 111, 135-138
Guion, David, 246

H

Haley, Jack, 61
Hall, Elbert E., 212, 296-297
Hall, George B., 111
Hall, Johnny, 293
Hall, Julia, 183
Hall, Mary Eldridge, 212
Hallmark, James, 113-117
Hamilton, Clint, 221-226
Hamilton, George IV, 196, 198
Haney, Mrs. Bea, 212
Hanks, Bernard, 203, 211, 243-244
Hanks, Eva May, 203, 211
Hanks, Sherilyn, 278-280
Hardin-Simmons University, 20, 21,
    114, 140, 142, 164, 167-170, 174,
    177-178, 180, 239, 255, 269, 273,
    285
Hardin-Simmons University Cowboy
    Band, 10, 78-79, 180, 204
Harkrider, Mrs. Rupert, 212
Harold's BBQ, 9, 151-153
Harrington, H. T., 170
Harrison, Ira, 178
Harvey, John, 144
Hass, Robert, 290
Hatler, M. Waldo, 89
Hayden, Thomas E., Jr., 73
Hearst, William Randolph, 242
Heavenly Rest Episcopal Church, 21,
    157-162
H-E-B Grocery, 292
Heitchew, Houston, 235
Hendrick Home for Children, 200
Hendrick Hospital, 85
Hendrick River Ranch, 200
Hilgenberg, Mrs. L. W., 212
Hilton Hotel, 16, 78, 205, 208
Hollis, Ray, 135-138
Holloway, Jesse A., 134
Holly, Freeman, 16
Holt, Harry, 117
Hornbaker, Larry, 124
Houston, Duwain, 152
Hughes, Fred Lee, 110

Hunch Oil & Gas Company, 66-67
Hunt, Frank, 293
Hunt, James Winfred, 173-174, 185

I

Impact, TX, 10, 131-132

J

Jackson, Oliver, 299, 300
Jacoby, Oswald, 296
Jamaica Inn, 146
James, Sonny, 199
Jefferies, Archie, 208-210
Jefferies, D. H., 289-290
Jefferson Junior High School, 293
Jenkens, Millard, 175
Johnson, Bobby, 309
Johnson, Charley, 285
Johnson, Clover, 20
Johnson, Lyndon B., 21
Jones, Morgan, Jr., 104
Jones, Ruth Legett, 139, 140, 142
Jordan, Hubert, 305-306
Joyce, William, 227

K

Kelley, Louis, 283-284, 285-288
Kelly, Frank, 169
Kelly, John, 114
Kemp, Henry, 93
Kemper, Guy, 16
Kerrville Folk Festival, 200
KHSU (600 AM), 114
Kimbrell, Hershel, 310
King, Boyd, 305-306
King, Leamon, 299
Kinsolving Field, 72
Kirby Park, 20
Knox, John H., 234-235
Knox, T. S., 165
Krage, Ed, 293
KRBC (1470 AM), 114, 210
KRBC-TV (Channel 9), 113-117
Kreidel, Walter, 124
Kyker, Rex, 183

L

Lack, Paul D., 14, 321
Lake Abilene, 258, 263
Lake Fort Phantom Hill, 258, 264, 276, 277
Lake Kirby, 258, 264
Langford, Charity, 83
Langford, Charles, 83
Lapham, Bob, 292-294
Lear, Clinton, 28
Lear, Mary, 28
Lee, Robert E., 30, 32
Legett, K. K., 22, 140, 142
Legett Mansion, 160
Lindbergh, Charles A., 44, 72-73
Linton Drug Company, 48
Little Elm Creek, 262, 276
Little, Peyton, 318-320
Lockhart, Frank, 290
Long, Ellis, 124
Loudermilk, John D., 196, 198-199
Lowery, Quincy, 168
Lytle Creek, 24, 41, 201, 262, 276
Lytle Lake, 41, 75, 258, 263

M

Mack, Bill, 217
Mack Eplen's Cafeteria, 146
Mack Eplen's Drivateria, 10, 146-148
Magnetic Quill, 55
Malone, Andy, 313
Maltby, W. Jeff "Captain Jeff," 259-260
Mancini, Clem, 286
Mann Junior High School, 121
Matthews, Julia Jones, 139-141, 212
Matthews, Sallie Reynolds, 23
McAdams, Robert, 313-314
McAlmon, Robert, 240
McAuliffe, Brandon, 152
McCall, Bill, 215, 217
McCallum, Arthur, 305
McCasland, Merle, 178
McCay, Parker, 316
McCook, Charles, 309

McDonald Dormitory (ACU), 183
McGee, Jinks, 65
McMahan, Mike, 110
McMahon, Howard, 21
McMurry University, 15, 20, 104, 134, 140, 156, 173-174, 181, 185-187, 238, 310
McMurtry, Larry, 238, 239, 240
Meek, Malcolm, 21
Mencken, H. L., 238
Merchant, Clabe, 53
Merchant, John, 60
Merkel, TX, 267
Mesquite trees, 257, 265
Michener, James, 227
Milburn, Harry, 290
Mildren, Jack, 10, 283
Miller, Darleen, 108
Miller, Hack, 294
Millican, Crystal, 151
Minter, George L., Jr., 212
Minter, Mabel Lockett, 212
Minter, Mary Pittman, 212
Minter, W. A., 45
Montgomery, Henry, 48
Moody, Dan, 203-204
Moody, Mildred Paxton, 72-73, 203-204
Moore, Jay, 14, 20-22, 146-148
Moore, Jimmie, 214
Moore, Omar, 217
Moore, Winston Lee: see Willet, Slim
Morrow, Bobby Joe, 298-300
Moser, Chuck, 21, 301-303
Mosley, Lowel "Porky," 274
Mulberry Canyon, 24
Murchison, Ira, 299

— N —
National Center for Children's Illustrated Literature, 192, 227-228
Newton, Macky, 293
Norton, Howard, 124

— O —
Oberwetter, Emil, 34-36
Old Abilene Town, 146
Oldham, DeMarcus, 75
Oliver, Jennifer, 152
Oller, Kenneth, 124
Olson, Ken, 293
Olympic Games (1956), 298-299
Optimist, The, 122-124, 182, 183
Overman, Tommy, 293
Ozark, Danny, 292-295

— P —
Palace Hotel, 46
Paramount Theatre, 22, 90-91
Parramore, James H., 164, 243, 263
Paschal, R. L., 167-170
Patterson, Isaac, 168
Paxton, George L., 66
Paxton, Mattie, 203
Paxton, Mildred: see Moody, Mildred Paxton
Peake, Stuart, 305
Pemberton, Ted, 124
Pennington, Billy, 16
Perkins, Dallas, 131
Perry, Jack, 16
Pershing Boulevard, 86
Pershing, John J., 89
Petroleum Club, 131
Phillips, Cameron, 48
Pickard, Julia Legett, 142-143
Pierce, Bill, 293
Pierce, Don, 215
Ponca Motel, 70
Prairie dogs, 22, 167-168, 257, 258, 260, 262
Presley, Elvis, 192, 218-220
Proctor, Earl, 16
Pruitt, Arnold, 16
Pugh, Scotty, 313

— Q —
Queen Theater, 84
Quevreaux, Kenny, 293